Work Smarter with Microsoft OneNote

An expert guide to setting up OneNote notebooks to become more organized, efficient, and productive

Connie Clark

BIRMINGHAM—MUMBAI

Work Smarter with Microsoft OneNote

Associate Group Product Manager: Alok Dhuri
Publishing Product Manager: Harshal Gundetty
Senior Editor: Nisha Cleetus
Content Development Editor: Rosal Colaco
Technical Editor: Pradeep Sahu
Copy Editor: Safis Editing
Project Coordinator: Manisha Singh
Proofreader: Safis Editing
Indexer: Hemangini Bari
Production Designer: Prashant Ghare
Marketing Coordinator: Deepak Kumar

First published: April 2022
Production reference: 1140422

Published by Packt Publishing Ltd.
Livery Place
35 Livery Street
Birmingham
B3 2PB, UK.

ISBN 978-1-80107-566-4

www.packt.com

To my amazing husband, Perry, and my beautiful daughters, Ashley and Jessica. Thank you for all your patience and support during my first writing journey. Love you so much!

– Connie Clark

Contributors

About the author

With over 30 years of experience in computer software training, **Connie Clark** has taught and consulted with over 20,000 students. She helps to empower others and make them more productive with technology so they can achieve results. She's gained a reputation of teaching with patience and friendliness. She lives with her husband of 31 years and her two daughters on an acreage in Alberta. She likes to dance, but not exercise, always wanting things to be more fun and genuine. Check out her Mission Computers YouTube channel or reach out anytime by visiting her website.

I want to thank the people who have been close to me and supported me, especially my family – Perry, Ashley, and Jessica; my friends – Sherry, Sharon, Tobi, and Lori; and my loyal customers and business friends.

About the reviewer

Darren Austin is a consumer product executive whose career has been focused on pioneering many of the innovations that form the backbone of consumer technology experiences today – including mobile apps, messaging, e-commerce, location-based services, and cloud services.

He has over two decades of experience in leading product teams at early-stage technology companies as well as at established technology brands including Amazon.com, Motorola, AOL, Expedia, and Microsoft. He spent over 6 years at Microsoft in a variety of executive and leadership roles focused on education and collaboration products. During his time at Microsoft, Darren led the OneNote product team from 2015 to 2016.

Table of Contents

3

Creating Notebooks, Sections, and Pages

4

Entering Information into Your Notebook

Section 2: Navigating, Searching, and Shortcuts within Notebooks

5

Best Practices for Creation and Easy Retrieval of Notes

6

Categorizing and Searching Notes

7

Organizing and Easily Working with Pages, Sections, and Notebooks

Section 3: Inserting Information and Links into Your Notebooks

8

Adding Shapes, Videos, Web Pages, and More to Your Notes

9

Inserting Links and Attachments into Your Notebooks

10

Outlook and OneNote Belong Together

Section 4: Integrating OneNote with Other Microsoft 365 Apps

11

Using OneNote Online with OneDrive, SharePoint, or Teams

12

Printing and Sharing with OneNote

Section 5: Making Lasting Changes with OneNote

13
Making OneNote a Habit

14
Customizing OneNote Settings

15
Real-Life Examples of OneNote Notebooks

Index

Other Books You May Enjoy

Preface

I couldn't function without OneNote. Years ago, in an attempt to become a better role model for my students, and as an advocate of a paperless office, I started my journey with this program. Microsoft introduced OneNote in 2002 so that we could capture notes easily and effectively. This organizational power and ease of notetaking are what I want to share with you in this book. OneNote is a brilliant application, bundled with other Microsoft products but often overlooked.

In this book, I will not only help you understand the importance of OneNote, but I will also take you through how to use the program, step by step. You will learn how to create a notebook, enter information, categorize and search your notes, organize your notebook pages and sections, add shapes, videos, web clippings, documents, and emails, and much more. You will even find out how OneNote works best with other Microsoft programs, such as Outlook, OneDrive, SharePoint, and Teams.

So that you can succeed in adopting OneNote and benefit from all the time savings it can give you, I will also share with you how to make OneNote a habit, real-life examples of possible notebooks, and best practices for working with OneNote.

Armed with all this, I am confident you will start the journey with me and become a OneNote fan and advocate.

Who this book is for

If you save notes on your phone, wear out more spiral notebooks than you can count, or are a Microsoft 365 user and need to keep track of information, then this book is for you. Beginner experience with OneNote is recommended to get the most out of this book.

What this book covers

Chapter 1, OneNote - How and Where to Use it?, shows you where OneNote notebooks can be stored and how they can be accessed from any device. You will discover how OneNote can be a great resource on smartphones as well as tablets and computers (PCs and Macs).

Chapter 2, Exploring Screen Layout and Toolbars, teaches you about the OneNote screen so that you can easily move around OneNote and take advantage of all the shortcuts. You will discover the toolbars that will help you make your OneNote notebook a powerful and exciting resource, whether on your computer or mobile device.

Chapter 3, Creating Notebooks, Sections, and Pages, teaches you how to create a notebook and then divide up that notebook into sections and pages. You will find out how to add or rename sections and pages and discover how this is possible from your computer or mobile device.

Chapter 4, Entering Information into Your Notebook, teaches you how to capture information in containers within OneNote, and how to work with those containers to your advantage. You will find out how to handwrite in your notebooks, not only from your computer but also from any mobile device or touchscreen. You will discover how to arrange your notes so they work and look good. You will learn how to highlight, use styles, and enhance your notebook pages with color or rule lines.

Chapter 5, Best Practices for Creation and Easy Retrieval of Notes, as to effectively take on a new application, it is best to give some thought to the best ways of applying that application to your everyday work, gives you ideas on how to build best practices for your notebooks and, as a result, create a better system for yourself (and others). We will also talk about how to move and copy information effectively in your OneNote notebooks.

Chapter 6, Categorizing and Searching Notes, teaches you how to set up a system of tags so that you can easily retrieve notes as well as have a visual display of notes that matches how you would capture information on paper. You will learn how to create checkboxes and add highlighting, stars, and question marks to your notes so that these notes become more meaningful and easier for you to read. All of this, as well as the search function and recent notes, will help you move through your notebooks quickly and easily.

Chapter 7, Organizing and Easily Working with Pages, Sections, and Notebooks, teaches you how to move, copy, rename, or delete any part of your notebook (sections or pages) or the notebook itself. You will find out how to access the same notebook on multiple devices and discover how to color code or sort your notebooks, sections, and pages.

Chapter 8, Adding Shapes, Videos, Web Pages, and More to Your Notes, teaches you the best ways to insert images, shapes, videos, audio files, tables, web pages, and formulas into your notebooks. You will find out how easy it is to do math on a notebook page. You will also learn how to use the highlighter pens and discover why you should take pictures from your smartphone or tablet while in your OneNote notebook. Finally, you will learn how to dictate to your notebook.

Chapter 9, Inserting Links and Attachments into Your Notebooks, teaches you how to create links within your notebooks so that you can move from one notebook, section, or page to another. You will learn how to create cross-references to your information from any notebook without having to retype or enter redundant information. You will also find out how to link or insert files into your notebooks. We will look at linking from OneDrive, SharePoint, and Teams.

Chapter 10, Outlook and OneNote Belong Together, teaches you how to send emails from Outlook to OneNote. You will discover how to create an email address for your OneNote and learn about sending a page from OneNote via email. You'll also find out about a connection between Outlook appointments and OneNote.

Chapter 11, Using OneNote Online with OneDrive, SharePoint, or Teams, teaches you how to work with notebooks that are saved in OneDrive, SharePoint, or Teams. You will learn how to share notebooks and how to create a notebook from within Teams or SharePoint.

Chapter 12, Printing and Sharing with OneNote, teaches you how to print or share successfully from OneNote. You will also discover how to print from any application into your OneNote notebooks. You will find out how to send or share information to OneNote from your smartphone or tablet. You will also learn more about sharing notebooks within Teams and SharePoint.

Chapter 13, Making OneNote a Habit, helps you develop the consistency and commitment you need to make OneNote a powerful tool for your everyday work and personal life. You will also learn about how to get others on board with OneNote so you can easily share ideas and notes with others through OneNote. You will discover what it takes to develop unconscious competence with OneNote.

Chapter 14, Customizing OneNote Settings, teaches you which settings are crucial to your success with OneNote, while other settings are "nice to haves." You will learn how to access and change your settings to suit your needs. You will discover extra options available to you on OneNote for your computer and OneNote for your smartphone or tablet. You will also find out about bonus options such as the Class Notebook and Sticky Notes.

Chapter 15, Real-Life Examples of OneNote Notebooks, lets you explore examples of OneNote notebooks complete with their sections and pages, for work and personal use. Take a look at some of these real-life examples and copy them or tweak them so that you can save time in your notebook building process. Get inspired and get going!

To get the most out of this book

You will need Microsoft OneNote to follow along with the steps outlined in this book. You can find OneNote as an application included in Windows 10; we recommend this version as the book covers examples with this version in mind. OneNote is also available as part of Microsoft 365, but that OneNote version will look slightly different from the screenshots shown in this book.

OneNote is also available as a web application and an app that can be loaded on mobile devices such as smartphones and tablets. OneNote works well on Mac computers as well and most of the examples in this book will work in a Mac environment.

Software/hardware covered in the book	Operating system requirements
OneNote for Windows 10	Windows 10 or greater
Apple iPhone or iPad	iOS 15 or greater
Android phone or Galaxy tablet	Version 10 or greater
OneNote for Mac	macOS
OneNote for the web	Any web browser

Chapter 1, OneNote - How and Where to Use it?, will walk you through how to set up OneNote on your computer, smartphone, or tablet.

If your Microsoft account is not allowing you to access shared notebooks, please seek the advice of an IT professional.

Any errata related to this book can be found at the following link: `https://github.com/PacktPublishing/Work-Smarter-with-Microsoft-OneNote`.

Download the color images

We also provide a PDF file that has color images of the screenshots and diagrams used in this book. You can download it here: `https://static.packt-cdn.com/downloads/9781801075664_ColorImages.pdf`.

Conventions used

There are a number of text conventions used throughout this book.

`Code in text`: Indicates code words in text, database table names, folder names, filenames, file extensions, pathnames, dummy URLs, user input, and Twitter handles. Here is an example: "Do a web search for the words `clip to OneNote`."

Bold: Indicates a new term, an important word, or words that you see onscreen. For instance, words in menus or dialog boxes appear in **bold**. Here is an example: "This **Programs** notebook is divided into sections with the name of each software program that I support."

> **Tip or Important Note**
> Appear like this.

Get in touch

Feedback from our readers is always welcome.

General feedback: If you have questions about any aspect of this book, email us at `customercare@packtpub.com` and mention the book title in the subject of your message.

Errata: Although we have taken every care to ensure the accuracy of our content, mistakes do happen. If you have found a mistake in this book, we would be grateful if you would report this to us. Please visit `www.packtpub.com/support/errata` and fill in the form.

Piracy: If you come across any illegal copies of our works in any form on the internet, we would be grateful if you would provide us with the location address or website name. Please contact us at `copyright@packt.com` with a link to the material.

If you are interested in becoming an author: If there is a topic that you have expertise in and you are interested in either writing or contributing to a book, please visit `authors.packtpub.com`.

Share Your Thoughts

Once you've read *Work Smarter with Microsoft OneNote*, we'd love to hear your thoughts! Scan the QR code below to go straight to the Amazon review page for this book and share your feedback.

https://packt.link/r/1-801-07566-2

Your review is important to us and the tech community and will help us make sure we're delivering excellent quality content.

Section 1: The Anatomy of OneNote

In this section, we'll learn about the OneNote screen and toolbars. You'll discover how to easily create a notebook with multiple sections and pages and find out how to add notes (typed or handwritten) and even customize your notebooks to suit your personal style.

We'll learn about the advantages of OneNote and find out about the different versions available to us and all the different devices that we can access OneNote from. We'll get comfortable with all the menus and features in OneNote so that you know what is possible.

We'll then learn how to create well-organized notebooks with the right number of sections and pages and identify all the different ways to add information to our notebook pages. We'll also see how we can handwrite in OneNote, as well as customizing the look of our pages and text.

This section comprises the following chapters:

1
OneNote - How and Where to Use it?

OneNote is a Microsoft program like no other. However, before you can *truly* get a feel for OneNote, it is important that we identify why it is worth investing in.

There is an ever-increasing amount of information coming at each of us every day in many forms. With this information overload comes practical drawbacks: *Where do we record this information? How do we remember what is important to us?* Jotting down notes is usually a good solution to these issues, and in this chapter, we'll cover exactly why.

Microsoft OneNote is an application that is perfect for notetaking and capturing information in one place. Some examples of its usage are presented here:

- **Projects and meetings**: You can use OneNote to capture everything that you need to run a project. Things such as your notes from meetings and emails can be stored side by side with drawings or images, document attachments, and links to pertinent files or websites; best of all, this information can be shared with everyone on that project.

- **Ideas**: As ideas pop into your head, capture them in OneNote. Organize these ideas and get working on them quicker because they will all be together and easier to retrieve.

- **Personal information**: Track any medical information for yourself or your family by taking pictures of prescriptions or writing down notes during doctors' visits. You can also include research done on the web as links in these notes. Recipes are another perfect example of ways to use a OneNote notebook. You can capture recipes easily by using the built-in camera feature and taking a picture of an existing recipe card or page in a book. You can also link to a website for your favorite recipe, jot down notes, or record a conversation about recipe ideas or ingredients.

In this chapter, we will discuss why we use OneNote, and how to get started with it. We start here so that you can set yourself up to take full advantage of the power and flexibility offered within this program. In particular, we will cover the following topics:

- Why use OneNote as your digital notebook?
- Differences between OneNote and OneNote for Windows 10
- Notebook storage options
- Accessing your notebooks from different devices
- OneNote web application

A goal for this chapter is to get OneNote installed on your computer as well as on your smartphone and tablet. This way, moving forward, you can follow along with the instructions in this book.

Why use OneNote as your digital notebook?

In this section, we will start by looking at why it's worth using OneNote as your digital notebook. Before we get into that, though, let's get a full understanding of what OneNote actually is.

OneNote is readily available to anyone. This application comes with **Microsoft 365** and **Windows 10**, and you can also download it for free from Microsoft's website. Whether we take notes for ourselves or for the purpose of sharing with others, OneNote is an amazing solution that is an integral part of Microsoft 365 and integrates seamlessly with **Microsoft Outlook** and **Microsoft Teams**. Instead of using Outlook to send information about a project, use OneNote to capture all updates and references on a project shared with others. This is just one example of OneNote's ability to provide great solutions.

Aside from OneNote, our other methods of notetaking include old-fashioned pen and paper, the note-taking applications found on our phones (such as Apple Notes), and competing products such as Evernote. The downside of using these other note apps is the fact that they may not be available to you when you need them, or they may not be as integrated as OneNote can be with your current work.

In this section, we will focus on why OneNote may just be the best notes solution for you.

Advantages of choosing OneNote

Without further ado, let's look at the advantages of OneNote, assessing and comparing alternative options along the way, as follows:

- **Searchability**: *Find anything fast in OneNote* is my motto. In OneNote, we can quickly search for a word or phrase, or even a special tag such as *important* or *question*. In this case, if you tag a number of notes as *important* or *question*, then you can find all those tagged notes with ease in the future.

  The Evernote search feature works much the same as OneNote in terms of searching for words, phrases, or tags, showing the clear benefits of opting for digital notetaking applications such as these. Searchability is one of the big roadblocks we face with pen-and-paper notetaking: searching through your notes that were taken a while ago can be a time-consuming and laborious task. Furthermore, while the Apple Notes app does let you search for words, you cannot search for *important* notes or any other special category of notes.

- **Organization**: Being organized is what OneNote is all about. You have many ways to organize your notes so that they are easy to see and retrieve. Not only can you easily retrieve notes by the title or page name, but you also have sections that help you organize similar note pages together. You also have the search feature, as mentioned in the previous point, that can help you to find almost anything.

  In contrast to this, most other notes apps do not provide organizational options—it is up to you to make your note heading as specific as possible so that you can easily find it again in the list or gallery view. In Evernote, there is also a lack of organization by sections and pages; each notebook in Evernote has pages only, with no ability to divide notebooks by sections.

  Going back to our physical notebooks, we simply jot down everything on the next fresh page of the notebook, with very little ability to revisit those notes quickly to organize them by category. This method of notetaking, which is sequential regardless of the topic, does not help us when we are looking for all the examples that meet the same criteria or all the information on one topic.

- **Cross-platform**: You can install OneNote on any computer, phone, or tablet device. From all these devices, you can access the same notes; so, you can finish typing a note on your computer and then view it on your phone while you are away from the office. You can access OneNote from unlimited locations. Furthermore, OneNote can be synced locally with any of your devices so that if you have no internet access, you can still access your notes.

    While the Notes app is very accessible from your iPhone, it does not provide a local synced copy for your computer. The Notes app on the iPhone will sync through your iCloud settings and give you access via your computer's web browser. Furthermore, Evernote will let you access notes from multiple devices but with the free version, you are limited to syncing only two locations. While your traditional notebook is portable, you will only have access to your most recent notes (unless you want to cart all of your full notebooks around!). You also risk the practicalities of leaving your notebook at home or even losing it altogether.

- **Keeping everything together**: Using OneNote as your digital notebook will let you keep everything together. Not only will you have access to all notes you have written, but you can also have images, embedded videos, emails, documents, weblinks, web clippings, diagrams, and much more.

    Furthermore, all this information will be available to others if you share your notebook with them; for instance, you may want to share notebooks with your team when working on projects or committees together. Sharing for personal use could be handy when planning a trip with friends or when coordinating a big event such as a wedding or anniversary party. Some other things to consider are noted here:

  - In your Apple Notes app, you can insert pictures, documents, and drawings, but unless you are on your phone or iPad, you cannot access this information and the sharing of notes is limited. Evernote keeps all your notes together but unless you have a paid version, you will not have everything on all your devices (keep in mind that you can only have two device locations with the free Evernote app). In addition to this, integration with Microsoft products is not available. For instance, the Teams integration is not an option unless you pay for **Evernote Professional**.

  - A paper notebook can be full of character and overflowing with loose papers, ear-marked pages, highlights, and many other significant markers. However, this method can get messy and not really be the source of *everything* (as we may be missing the meeting agenda or other supporting documents that we still have to refer to on our digital devices).

To sum up, using OneNote as your notebook gives you the benefits of organization, searchability, and access to your notes and media anywhere, anytime. Because your OneNote notebook is digital, you can quickly access it on any device, and everything is together.

If you need to capture information for work or personal purposes, OneNote is your answer. There are different versions of OneNote, so let's explore that next.

Differences between OneNote and OneNote for Windows 10

OneNote has been available since 2003 and, as with any other software, it has been updated often.

At the time of writing this book, there are two versions of OneNote available, and they could both be present on your computer. This is a big confusion point for most people because someone in the office can open one version while others open the other version, and they will look slightly different. Microsoft was going to get rid of OneNote (2016) but because of all the comments from users, they decided to keep it. There are plans in the works for Microsoft to merge these two versions very soon. This book focuses on the newest version of OneNote, which is *OneNote for Windows 10*. In this section, we will compare the different versions of OneNote and how they differ from each other. Here are the current possibilities for the different versions:

- **OneNote for Windows 10**: This comes pre-installed with Microsoft Windows 10.

  > **Important Note**
  > In **Windows 11**, OneNote will not come pre-installed, but you can still download OneNote from the **Microsoft Store**.

- **OneNote (formerly known as OneNote 2016)**: This comes with **Office 2019**, **Office 2021**, and **Microsoft 365**. We will refer to this version of OneNote as the OneNote app. If you have Windows 10 and Microsoft 365, it is possible that you have both versions of OneNote on your computer.

- **OneNote for Mac**: This comes with Office 2019, Office 2021, and Microsoft 365 or can be downloaded from the **Mac App Store**.

- **OneNote for the web**: This will be available to you if you store your notebooks in the cloud. This version of OneNote is accessible anytime, from any computer or device. All you need to do is visit www.onenote.com and sign in to your Microsoft account.

In this section, we will look at the unique characteristics of two of the versions that could be on your Windows-based computer: OneNote for Windows 10 and OneNote (from Office 2019, Office 2021, or Microsoft 365). OneNote for the web is covered later in this chapter, while OneNote for Mac looks and works almost the same as OneNote for Windows 10.

OneNote for Windows 10 version

Here are some quick details about the Windows 10 version of OneNote. This may help you to identify which OneNote version you're using:

- Notebooks must be stored in the cloud, on either **OneDrive** or **SharePoint**. This means you can access these notebooks on any device from anywhere. You can also access them offline, as there will be a cached copy of the notebook on your device.

- Notebooks cannot be stored on a local computer's hard drive.

- OneNote for Windows 10 does not work with earlier versions of Windows, which must be why they put *Windows 10* in the name.

- There is no **File** menu.

- Sections are visible on the left side of the notes pages.

When people first use OneNote, they do not take note of where they started from: *Was it the Windows 10 menu or the Office suite icons?* I notice this happens often with my students when I am teaching how to use OneNote. Left-side tabs for sections means you are using OneNote for Windows 10, as seen in the following screenshot:

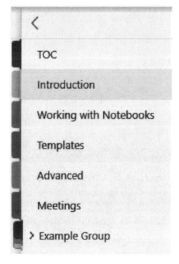

Figure 1.1 – Sections appear vertically on the left side of a notebook in OneNote for Windows

The location of the **sections** tabs is the easiest visual clue as to which OneNote version you are using.

OneNote version

When referring to OneNote, we are referring to the OneNote version that is part of Office 2019 or Microsoft 365. Here are some quick details about this version of the OneNote tool:

- Notebooks can be stored on your hard drive, on the company server, or in the cloud (on either OneDrive or SharePoint).

- OneNote will work with Windows 8 and above.

- A **File** menu is available at the top left of the screen.

- Sections are visible at the top of note pages, like so:

Figure 1.2 – Sections across the top of a notebook in OneNote

Although there are some differences between these versions of OneNote, the majority of the features will work the same to provide amazing notebooks.

Where and how you store your notebook(s) is the next important step in creating accessible and shareable notebooks. Let's look at our storage options next.

Exploring notebook storage options

Each time you create a new notebook (you will learn how to do this in *Chapter 3*, *Creating Notebooks, Sections, and Pages*), you create a new notebook file, so you can decide each time where you want this notebook to be stored. All your notebooks can be stored in the same location and using the same account name and password.

For instance, if you only use OneNote at work, then you can log in to that notebook automatically with the Microsoft account that is already attached to your work computer. Furthermore, if you always share your notebooks, you could have Microsoft Teams as your location, then each shared notebook can be shared with the appropriate team. *So, where can you store your OneNote notebook?* This file type is very different from a **Word** or **Excel** file, for example. This file type will house *all* of your sections and pages in one notebook.

Each notebook you create is actually a separate file. There is no **Save as** button. Where you store this file and which account you attach to it is important, because you want to know how to access it again. The storage of your notebook will also affect your ability to share the notebook.

Let's look at your location and account choices so that you understand how this works. With notebook storage, we need to consider the following:

- Location of the notebook file
- The account associated with the notebook file

In this section, we'll focus on these. To understand notebook storage better, we will explain the locations available and how accounts work.

Location of your notebook

While the OneNote app on Windows lets you store notebooks on local hard drives and on network shares, it is preferable to store them in the cloud so that you can access them from anywhere and from any device. OneNote for Windows 10 can only be stored on Microsoft OneDrive or Microsoft SharePoint.

If you are using Microsoft Teams, then you will be able to create notebooks, and these storage locations will be picked based on where you are in Microsoft Teams.

How does Microsoft Teams pick your notebook location?

If you create a notebook while you are in Microsoft Teams, there are two possible scenarios for where that new notebook will reside, as outlined here:

- If you are in the **Channel** area of Microsoft Teams when creating a notebook, then that notebook is stored on the SharePoint site that is associated with that team.
- If you are in the **Chat** area of Microsoft Teams when creating a notebook, then that notebook is stored on OneDrive (the OneDrive belonging to the person that created that notebook in the chat). The following table tells us about the location of OneNote notebooks within Microsoft Teams:

Microsoft Teams	Location of the notebook stored
Channel notebook	SharePoint
Chat notebook	OneDrive

Table 1.1 – Location of OneNote notebooks within Microsoft Teams

How you store your notebook depends on which version of OneNote you are using. Let's compare what's available for locations when we use OneNote for Windows versus OneNote.

Comparing the location for OneNote for Windows 10 with OneNote

You cannot save a notebook created in OneNote for Windows 10 on your hard drive, while OneNote (which comes with Office 2019 and Microsoft 365) can be stored on your local hard drive, on your company server drive, or on Microsoft OneDrive or Microsoft SharePoint.

Refer to the following table for location options:

Version	Hard drive of computer (personal computer or file server)	OneDrive	SharePoint
OneNote for Windows 10	No	Yes	Yes
OneNote	Yes	Yes	Yes

Table 1.2 – Location of notebooks, comparing OneNote for Windows 10 with OneNote

Where you choose to store your notebook will affect whether or not you can share that notebook. Let's compare the OneNote versions and see which sharing options are available.

Sharing notebooks

Although you have lots of choices for the location of your notebook, sharing your notebook is not supported in all these locations. You will not be able to share a notebook that is located on your local hard drive. If you store a notebook on your company file server, the sharing of that notebook will inherit any rules of access that the file server location has, and sharing would have to take place in the office or through a **virtual private network** (**VPN**) (if outside the office).

Refer to the following table for sharing options:

Version	Hard drive of computer	OneDrive	SharePoint
OneNote for Windows 10	N/A	Yes	Yes
OneNote	Via file server while in office	Yes	Yes
	Via VPN if outside the office		
OneNote web client	N/A	Yes	Yes
OneNote for Mac	N/A	Yes	Yes
OneNote for iPhone or Android	N/A	Yes	Yes
OneNote for iPad or Samsung Galaxy	N/A	Yes	Yes

Table 1.3 – Options for sharing OneNote notebooks based on the version of OneNote

The next consideration for your notebook storage is how much storage you have available with each option.

How much storage?

The amount of physical storage available to you for your notebooks is based on the storage available in the location your notebook is saved. OneNote itself has no storage limits.

Unless there are specific OneNote features that you need that are only available in the traditional OneNote app, we recommend using one of OneNote's modern apps (OneNote for Windows 10, OneNote for iPhone/iPad, or OneNote for Android) and using OneNote with the main account on your device (that is, a Microsoft account or a work/school account). This will ensure that all your notes are saved to the cloud and accessible on all your devices and will also ensure that you have full sharing capabilities.

Account associated with the notebook

When creating a notebook in OneNote, you will be prompted to log in to your Microsoft account. You may have a Microsoft account with your work email. If this account was set up with Microsoft 365 for Business, then this account is referred to as a **work or school account**. A Microsoft account is free for anyone, so it is possible that you have a personal Microsoft account as well. This personal Microsoft account could use any email address as the username.

With OneNote for Windows 10, you are always signed in to your Microsoft account. This account is set up under **Accounts** in your **Settings** area via the Windows **Start** menu: once on the **Accounts** screen, choose **Your info** to view the account you are signed in to. Note in the following screenshot, on the right-hand side of the screen, under **CONNIE**, the blurred line is where your Microsoft email account would show. You can link other accounts by choosing **Email & accounts** on the left:

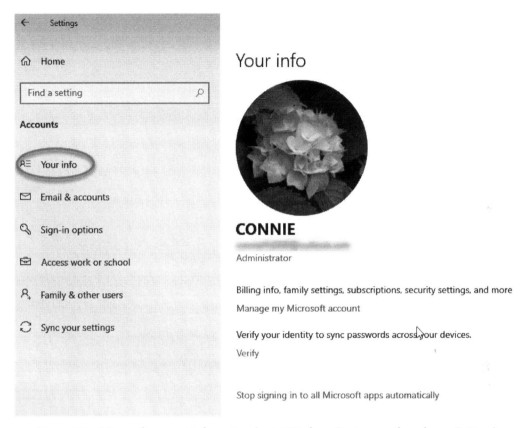

Figure 1.3 – Microsoft account information (go to Windows Start menu, then choose Settings)

If you have a work or school account, it will show under the **Access work or school** option, as illustrated in the following screenshot:

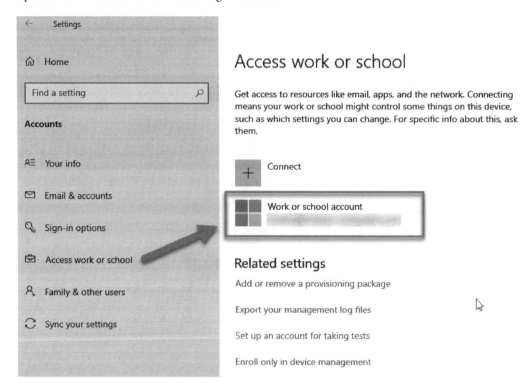

Figure 1.4 – Microsoft account: Work or school account option

When creating new notebooks in OneNote, the account used will be the main account on your computer. If you have a work or school account, then that account should be the main one.

If you have already created a notebook using one of your accounts, you can access that notebook and specify the account you used.

If you are signing in to a computer at work, you may be restricted to a certain Microsoft account, as set up by your Microsoft administrator (or **information technology** (**IT**) professional).

In addition to using OneNote for work (or wherever that main account is), you may want to access your notebook(s) on your phone, a tablet, iPad, or another computer. Let's find out how easy this is to do.

Accessing your notebooks from different devices

One of the best things about OneNote is the fact that you can access it from any device you own. All it takes is for you to log in to the appropriate Microsoft account on that device and then start opening notebooks.

In this section, we will discover which other devices we can have our OneNote notebooks on. We will also learn how to set up OneNote on these other devices so that we can view and access our notebook(s).

Opening OneNote from a different device/computer

Let's say you use OneNote on your desktop computer at work; you may also want to access this same notebook on your laptop, your phone, your iPad, or another computer (that doesn't belong to you). Let's look at all these options now.

Accessing your notebook from a different Windows device

If you are using OneNote for Windows 10 at work, then to access OneNote for Windows 10 on a different computer, it's easier if that computer has Windows 10 as well. However, if you don't have Windows 10 on that other computer, don't worry. You can still access that notebook using either OneNote for the web or the OneNote app.

To open an existing notebook on another computer, you need to take the following steps:

1. Go to the Windows **Start** menu and open **OneNote**. If you do not see **OneNote** immediately, go down the **Menu** list, where it should be listed alphabetically. If you do not have OneNote for Windows 10 on your computer for some reason, go to the Microsoft Store and download this program. If your computer does not have Windows 10, you will have to download OneNote (for Office 365 or Office 2019).

2. Once you open **OneNote**, you will see your Microsoft account email if you are using other Microsoft 365 applications or Windows 10. If the account is not correct for some reason, then go to the Windows **Settings** menu and choose **Accounts** to include the correct information. Then, proceed as follows:

   I. Inside the OneNote application, you will need to open up the notebooks that you want to work on. Under the **Notebooks** column on the left, choose **More Notebooks** (at the bottom). If there is no separate column for notebooks showing, you'll notice an icon of a stack of books on the left-hand side, as shown in the following screenshot. This will show or hide your notebooks area. Press on the books icon to show your notebooks and press again to hide them:

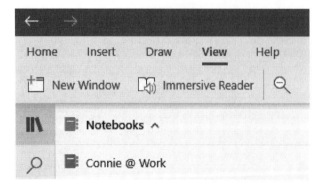

Figure 1.5 – OneNote screen with notebook show/hide icon

3. Provided the **Notebooks** area is visible, you can choose to open pre-existing notebooks with **More Notebooks** (at the bottom of the page), or you can add a new notebook by choosing **Add Notebook** at the bottom of the notebooks area.

Now, let's look at how to access OneNote from your Mac computer.

Accessing OneNote from a Mac computer

Accessing OneNote from your Mac computer follows most of the same steps as outlined in the previous section for Windows computers. The notebooks area looks and works the same as shown in *Figure 1.5*.

The difference is that there is no **More Notebooks** option; you can simply choose **Add Notebook** to add in another notebook that you created on another device.

Another option on the Mac is that you can use the **File** menu at the top of your screen and from this menu, you will see the **Open Notebook** option.

Now, let's look at how to access OneNote from your smartphone.

Accessing OneNote from your smartphone

You will need to download OneNote onto your smartphone and then open or create a notebook, as follows:

1. Search for `Microsoft OneNote` on the **App Store** of your iPhone, or the **Play Store** of your Android phone. Download the app.

2. Go through all the prompts to get the app started, as follows:

    I. Press the **Get started** button.

    II. Choose **OK** for the privacy options.

    III. Choose **Get started** to start your first notebook, as illustrated in the following screenshot:

Your Life, Organized

Capture, Organize, Collaborate.
Welcome to your digital notebook.

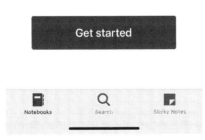

Figure 1.6 – OneNote download prompt when installing on iPhone

3. To start your first notebook, you must sign in to a Microsoft account, as follows:

    I.   At the top-left corner of the **App** screen, press the circular icon. The Android app opens directly to a **Sign in** screen titled **Welcome to OneNote**. You will then find a **Sign in** field and button at the bottom of the page.

    II. Choose **Sign in**.

    III. Type in your Microsoft sign-in email and password or create a new one.

4. Once signed in, you can create a new notebook using the plus sign (+) at the top right of the screen, or you can open existing notebooks by selecting **More Notebooks**, as illustrated in the following screenshot:

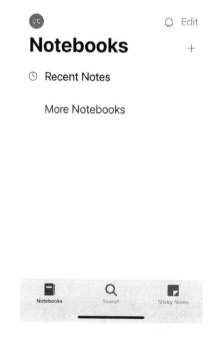

Figure 1.7 – OneNote initial notebooks screen

The instructions for downloading OneNote onto your iPad are almost the same, but there is one little difference that happens when opening up your notebooks. Let's look at that next.

Accessing OneNote from an iPad or a Galaxy tablet

You will need to download OneNote onto your iPad following the same instructions as detailed for a smartphone.

When it comes to opening up notebooks on your iPad, choose **More Notebooks** at the bottom of the first leftmost column. Select a notebook from the list that you wish to have open on your iPad.

On a Galaxy tablet, the **More Notebooks** option is shown closer to the top of the first leftmost column in OneNote.

In addition to using OneNote as an application on our computers, phones, or tablets, we can access OneNote via the OneNote web application. Let's look at how to do that next.

OneNote web application

The best thing about the web app for OneNote is that you don't even have to be on your own computer; any computer or device will give you access to your notebook(s).

This is assuming you have a web connection and that you are using OneDrive or SharePoint as the location for your notebooks. Here is how to use the OneNote web application:

1. Go to the login page for Microsoft at `www.office.com`.

2. Log in to your Microsoft account using the appropriate email and password. Do not save this login information to a device that does not belong to you.

3. Go to the waffle menu at the top left of the Microsoft window, as shown in the following screenshot:

Figure 1.8 – Waffle menu for Microsoft 365 on the web

Alternatively, you can select the OneNote icon from the column of icons displayed on the left of the screen.

4. Choose **OneNote**.

5. Click on **My notebooks** to see all notebooks you have created using the current Microsoft login, as illustrated in the following screenshot:

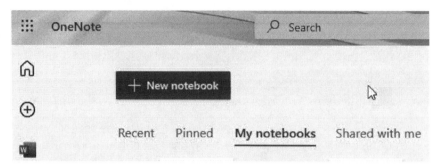

Figure 1.9 – New notebook button in the OneNote web app

6. To open one of the notebooks, click on the notebook name.

7. Click on the + **New notebook** button to add a new notebook.

8. If this is not your personal computer, then once you have completed working on your notebook on this computer or device, you should sign out of your Microsoft account by clicking on your icon at the top right and selecting **Sign out**. If you are working on your own computer, then do not sign out.

Summary

In this chapter, you learned some examples of where OneNote can help you stay organized, such as with projects, in meetings, when capturing your ideas, and even with helping to track information in your personal life. You also saw the advantages of OneNote with regards to searching, organizing, and accessibility, and how it compares to other notetaking methods. The differences between the OneNote versions were covered to help you to identify which OneNote version you have on your computer. Furthermore, information detailing the best place to store your notebook was presented so that you can understand your options for sharing and how OneNote integrates with other Microsoft products such as Teams, SharePoint, and OneDrive.

You also learned how to install OneNote on other devices so that you can open any notebook(s) from anywhere you choose. Last but not least, you were introduced to the OneNote web application so that you can open your notebook(s) anytime, anywhere.

Take the time now, before moving on to the next chapter, to get OneNote installed on your computer as well as on your smartphone and tablet. Then, you can easily follow along with the instructions in this book moving forward.

In this chapter, you discovered that the first installation of OneNote created a default notebook. In *Chapter 3, Creating Notebooks, Sections, and Pages*, we will go into detail on creating more notebooks and why that will be of benefit to you.

All of this sets the foundation for the rest of this book, starting with the next chapter, where we will explore more about using OneNote by identifying the parts of the screen, toolbars, and menus. We will look at all these different areas of OneNote as they appear on the computer, the smartphone, and the iPad.

2
Exploring Screen Layout and Toolbars

Now it's time for the big questions: *what can OneNote do? How do I use it?* When you learn the screen layout of OneNote and understand what is included in the ribbon (toolbars), then you can find out what OneNote can do. What's available to you on the screen and in the ribbon will give you countless ideas on how to use OneNote.

When you take the time to learn all about the OneNote layout and ribbons, you will increase your efficiency in the program and become more excited about what OneNote has to offer you!

In this chapter, you will learn the following:

- Understanding the layout of the OneNote screen on a computer
- Understanding OneNote toolbars on a computer
- Exploring OneNote's right-click menus
- Understanding the layout of the OneNote screen on mobile devices
- Understanding the layout of the OneNote screen on an iPad or Galaxy tablet

Starting with the parts of the OneNote screen, let's look at the layout of OneNote first.

Understanding the layout of the OneNote screen on a computer

Now that you have OneNote installed, let's learn about the parts of the screen so that you can navigate easily and take advantage of all the shortcuts provided.

Within the OneNote screen, we can change to a fullscreen view, access the settings, perform a quick search, and much more. The main components of the screen, as identified with numbers, are as follows:

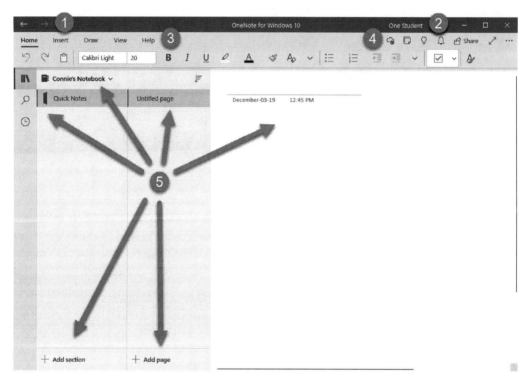

Figure 2.1 – The main screen of OneNote for Windows 10

Let's quickly take a look at each component:

1. **Back and forward buttons**: If you want to go back to the last notebook page you were viewing, use the back button. To go forward to the page after that one, use the forward button.

2. **Account name**: In *Figure 2.1*, the account name is **One Student**. This is the name attached to the Microsoft account that you are using for OneNote. Normally, this will show a person's name; for our example, here I am logged into a student account.

3. **Menu and ribbons**: The preceding diagram shows the **Home** menu and **Home** ribbon. Click on a different menu name to access a different ribbon. We will describe each of these ribbons later in the *Understanding OneNote toolbars on a computer section.*

4. **Icon bar on the right**: At the top right of the OneNote screen, there are many options for your notebook, including **Share** and settings:

Figure 2.2 – Icons at the top right of the OneNote screen

The icons shown at the top right (from left to right in *Figure 2.2*) are as follows:

- **Page sync status**: The cloud with a checkmark icon indicates that you are online and syncing your notebook. You could be syncing your notebook with either SharePoint or OneDrive, depending on where you are saving this notebook.

- **Open feed**: The icon that looks like two sticky notes will let you start an open feed so that you can see all the notes added (into any page, any section, and any notebook), with the most current note showing on the top. This feature could be handy if you are sharing a notebook with others (through **SharePoint** or **Teams**). Then, you can see their updates in real time.

- **Lightbulb**: *Tell me what you want to do* is the prompt that you will see when you click on this icon. This is your help function that lets you type in words or phrases related to your problem, and you can get guidance on carrying out that request.

- **Notifications**: The bell icon will show a number if there are changes made to a notebook on another device or by another person who is sharing that notebook.

- **Share**: The **Share** icon will let you share that page as a link or a copy. The link option is available if that notebook is already shared with others. Sending the link in an email would be a way for you to directly notify participants of a page that needs their attention. If you want to send a page to someone that is not currently sharing the notebook, then you can send a copy of that notebook page.

- **Enter fullscreen mode**: The double-arrow icon will let you access the full screen to view and edit the current page of your current notebook.

> **Important Note**
> To exit fullscreen mode and see your notebook pages and sections again, you will need to click on the four arrows at the top right of the full screen.

- **Three dots**: The three-dots menu icon will give you the option of printing and changing your settings.

5. **Notebook area**: The notebook area is where the notebooks, sections, and pages will be shown as well as the notes you are currently creating or editing. You can add more sections and pages from the + **Add page** and + **Add section** buttons at the bottom of the page. Search and other shortcuts for notebooks are also shown here.

The OneNote notebook area has a lot to offer. Let's check out the parts of this screen area:

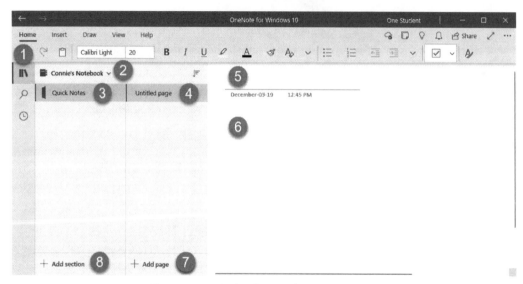

Figure 2.3 – Notebook area of OneNote screen

The different components of the OneNote notebook area are as follows:

1. **Hide navigation**: *Books on a bookshelf* is what I like to call this icon. When you click on this button, it will hide the sections and pages list (along with the notebook name) or it will make that information visible again. The hide navigation button is a toggle button; click it once to do something, and if you click it again, it will *undo* that action or go back to the way it was previously. Other buttons on this side toolbar include the following:

- The search button is listed below this hide navigation button. Use the search button to search for words, phrases, or tags.

- The clock button below search is a fast way to access recent notes.

2. **Notebook name**: The current notebook name shows at the top and if you click on the arrow to the right of that name, you can access other notebooks. In *Figure 2.3*, the notebook name is *Connie*, which is why it shows **Connie's Notebook**. This is a default notebook for the user that installs OneNote for the first time.

3. **Section name**: The sections of your notebook will be shown in this column. In *Figure 2.3*, the section name is **Quick Notes**.

4. **Page name**: The pages of your current section, of your current notebook, will be shown in this column. In *Figure 2.3*, the page name shows as **Untitled** because the page is empty and the name has not been created.

5. **Page title**: The page title is the same as the page name. When you type a title for this page (typing above the line shown in *Figure 2.3*), then the page name will change accordingly.

6. **Page content**: The notebook page is full of possibilities; this is where you start typing your notes or adding in all kinds of information (as you will learn in this book).

As you can see, there is a lot to do in OneNote. The layout of the screen should help you start in the right direction. Now let's move on to the toolbars and see what features are available in OneNote.

Understanding OneNote toolbars on a computer

To benefit from the true potential of any application, it is imperative that we access the toolbars. OneNote has a variety of toolbars that will make your notes more meaningful, interesting, and relevant to you. Let's review all the toolbars available and find out how they can enhance your OneNote experience.

The Home toolbar

The first toolbar you will see in OneNote for Windows 10 is the **Home** toolbar:

Figure 2.4 – The Home toolbar in OneNote

The **Home** toolbar is the toolbar you will use most often. I like to think of it as *Home is where you are most comfortable*, so always start there and return there. The **Home** toolbar typically has the most used features available on it. The **Home** toolbar in OneNote is similar to the **Home** toolbar you would see in other Microsoft products, such as **Word**.

To understand what is available to us on the toolbar, I have divided it into sections and will explain them individually. Here is a screenshot of our first section, starting with an undo icon:

Figure 2.5 – The Home toolbar undo and copy-paste section

In the first section of the **Home** toolbar, as shown in *Figure 2.5*, we have the following options:

- **Undo**: Use undo to undo what you did last.

- **Redo**: Use redo to reverse the result of an undo.

> **Important Note**
> Undo and Redo are available in other ribbons as well. Please note that they behave the same in each area.

- **Clipboard**: The clipboard will give you the choice of cut, copy, or paste.

Let's move on to the next section of the **Home** toolbar to see what we can do next:

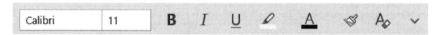

Figure 2.6 – The Home toolbar – font section

Personalize your notes and make them look better with the font section of the **Home** toolbar. Here is a description of each of the buttons, as shown in *Figure 2.6* (from left to right):

- **Font style and font size**: In *Figure 2.6*, the font style is **Calibri** and the font size is **11**.

- **Bold, italics, and underline buttons**: Just like in any other program, these buttons come in handy when you want to bold, italicize, or underline your text.

- **Highlight**: This is just like your highlighter pen, letting you highlight any text you select.

- **Font color**: In *Figure 2.6*, the font color is black, as shown by the dark black line under the letter *A*. When you click on this font color button, you can quickly change the font color by selecting one from the arrow that appears to the right.

- **Format painter**: The paintbrush is a great way to copy a format from somewhere else in your notebook and then apply that same format to a new area.

- **Clear all formatting**: If you do not like the font, color, size, or formatting of your existing text, you can simply select that text and click on the clear all formatting button.

- **Down arrow**: The down arrow button beside the clear all formatting button has some extra formatting choices for you, which include **subscript**, **superscript**, and **strikethrough**.

There are a lot of fonts to choose from and most of these may be familiar to you because of your experience with other Microsoft programs. Remember to choose your font choice first so that the new text looks the way you prefer. If you have existing text, simply select the text and then click the appropriate font button(s).

Now that we have font functions covered, let's move on to the next section, for alignment; it is always easier to read text when it is lined up nicely or separated with bullets or numbers:

Figure 2.7 – The Home toolbar – the alignment section

This part of the **Home** toolbar gives you all sorts of alignment options, which include the following (from left to right):

1. **Bullets**: Create a list with bullets.

2. **Numbering**: Create a numbered list.

3. **Decrease indent**: Move left with your indent, so that the text indents less. Use this if you hit the indent (right) key too many times or change your mind about an indent. This option is grayed out if there is no indent present with the text.

4. **Increase indent**: Move the text away from the left margin, that is, indent the text to the right.

5. **Down arrow**: Click on the downward arrow to see the paragraph alignment options, including **align left**, **align center**, and **align right**.

Different ways to position your text are easily accomplished with the assortment of alignment buttons provided on this section of the **Home** ribbon. Remember that just like the font buttons, you will have to select your text first when working with existing text.

We are almost at the end of the **Home** toolbar, so let's look at the last section now:

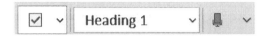

Figure 2.8 – The Home toolbar – the last section on the right

This last section of the **Home** toolbar provides some very unique features. These features can be a tremendous advantage to you in the speed and ease of recording and reviewing your notes. Again, let's look at each feature (from left to right):

1. **To-do/tag button**: This to-do button represents one of many **tags** available to you in OneNote. If you click directly on the to-do button (on the box with the checkmark inside), then you will see an empty box appear in your notebook. The arrow beside the to-do button will let you see a long list of tags available to you. We will be covering how to use tags in *Chapter 6, Categorizing and Searching Notes*.

2. **Heading 1/style button**: Use the **Heading 1** button to create an instant heading. This heading will include a larger font size, a different font color, and possibly a different font style. So, by clicking on one button for **Heading 1**, you have saved yourself the need to click on three separate font-type buttons. The arrow beside the **Heading 1** option will let you choose from a long list of other styles.

3. **Microphone/dictate**: Provided you have a microphone on your computer, you can use this button to dictate into OneNote. Simply click on an empty space of your notebook page, click on the dictate button, start talking, and watch the typing happen for you automatically. It's almost like magic! The arrow beside the dictate button will let you choose the dictation language.

Now that we understand what the **Home** toolbar can provide for us, let's check out the **Insert** toolbar next.

The Insert toolbar

The second menu option and toolbar you will see in OneNote for Windows 10 is the **Insert** toolbar. As the name of this toolbar indicates, this is where you go to find out what you can insert into your notebook pages. It is amazing how much we can add to our notebooks. This **Insert** toolbar shows how a digital notebook can offer more than any paper notebook you may carry around.

When you click on the **Insert** menu in OneNote, you will see the following toolbar:

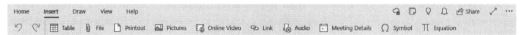

Figure 2.9 – The Insert toolbar

The buttons on the **Insert** menu, from left to right, include the following:

1. **Table**: The **Table** button in OneNote works just like the **Table** button in Word. Click and choose how many columns and rows you want for your table, then it will appear in your notebook. We will cover more on this topic in *Chapter 8, Adding Shapes, Videos, Web Pages, and More to Your Notes*.

2. **File**: Attach any file to your notebook page. When you click this button, you will be prompted with options as to how that file will be attached. This topic will be covered in *Chapter 9, Inserting Links and Attachments into Your Notebooks*.

3. **Printout**: Print the pages of your file onto your notebook page. When inserting the printout onto your page, OneNote shows that it is converting the file to a PDF. This printout of the file is not something you can edit; it is a static image on your page. This topic will also be covered in *Chapter 9, Inserting Links and Attachments into Your Notebooks*.

4. **Pictures**: Insert pictures onto your notebook page. When you click on this button, you have the option of inserting pictures from a few sources:

   - **File**: Insert a picture from the files on your computer. If you choose this option, you can browse your computer to find the file (that is, the picture) you wish to insert.

   - **Camera**: If your computer has a built-in camera, you can take a picture and OneNote will show that picture instantly on your notebook page.

   - **Online**: Find a picture online. If you choose this option, you are given a search box that references pictures on `Bing.com`. Type in a word you are searching for and then click on the picture you want to insert.

5. **Online Video**: Insert a link and thumbnail of an online video onto your notebook page. When you click on the **Online Video** button, you will be prompted for the URL of the video. Copy and paste a URL into this box, then you will see the video thumbnail appear on your page. This is a link to the original video, so it will not take up much space in your notebook.

6. **Link**: Insert any link into your notebook page. This link can be from a website or a file on SharePoint or OneDrive. In addition to providing the link address, you can specify the text to display so that it is easier to read:

   A. **Example address for link**: `https://www.microsoft.com/en-ca/microsoft-365/products-apps-services`.

   B. **Example of text to display: Microsoft 365 products**

7. **Audio**: Record audio and insert it into your notebook page (your computer would need a microphone for this feature to work).

8. **Meeting Details**: OneNote is integrated with Outlook for this feature. Insert the meeting details from an appointment in Outlook into your notebook page. You may be prompted to sign into your Microsoft account to start this process.

9. **Symbol**: Insert a symbol based on the choices available from the list provided.

10. **Equation**: Insert equations into your notebook page using the equation tools provided.

11. **Math**: You can either type the equation in or handwrite it (on an appropriate device – smartphone or tablet) and when you click the **Math** button, that equation will be solved.

12. **Stickers**: Choosing from many designs of stickers, you can insert a sticker onto your notebook page. This is a great feature for a learning environment where stickers are seen as rewards for a job well done.

13. **Researcher**: Instead of going to Google, use the **Researcher** button. It will prompt you for a word or phrase to research and then list all the relevant topics. At the top right of any of the topics found, there is a plus sign (+); use the plus sign to add the article to your notebook page.

> Tip
>
> If there is a down arrow at the end of your toolbar, click that arrow to see more toolbar options. Some screens are not wide enough to show all the buttons on the toolbar.

The **Insert** toolbar helps you add so much information to your notebooks. Now we need to move to the **Draw** toolbar to see how you can add drawings to your notebook pages.

The Draw toolbar

The third menu option and toolbar you will see in OneNote for Windows 10 is the **Draw** toolbar. This is where the fun begins. You get many colored pens to choose from and even an eraser, to get you out of trouble.

When you click on the **Draw** menu in OneNote, you will see the following toolbar:

Figure 2.10 – The Draw toolbar

The buttons on the **Draw** menu, from left to right, include the following:

1. **Select or type**: Select objects or type text with the toolbar icon that has an arrow, the letter *A*, and an I-beam cursor. Use this button to return to typing after you start using the drawing pens. When you are not drawing with pens or shapes, this is the default mode that you want to be in.

2. **Lasso select**: Use lasso select to draw a lasso around any drawings made with the pens; this lasso will select that drawing. While the drawing is selected, you can move it around or copy/paste it somewhere else. The **Ink to Text** button is *grayed out* and is only visible *after* lasso select has been clicked on.

3. **Insert or remove extra space**: If there is too much space on your notebook page, you can use this to remove that extra space. Similarly, if there is not enough space separating information on your notebook page, you can insert more extra space with this button. More on this topic in *Chapter 4, Entering Information into Your Notebook*.

4. **Eraser**: Use the eraser to erase any text that was drawn with the pens or any shapes that were drawn on your notebook page.

5. **Colored pens, pencil, and highlighter**: There are many colored pens to choose from in the **Draw** toolbar. You can also change the type of pen, the color, and the thickness.

6. **Draw with mouse or touch**: This button allows the user to freehand draw on the OneNote canvas.

7. **Shapes**: Choose from lines, basic shapes, and graphs to draw.

8. **Ink to Shape**: When you click on **Ink to Shape**, if you draw a basic shape with the pens, that shape will fix itself to be perfect. For example, if you draw a box that has wobbly-looking sides, **Ink to Shape** will turn it into a perfectly shaped box.

9. **Ink to Text**: If you use the pens to handwrite or print your text, then **Ink to Text** will help you convert this into typed text. You must use lasso select on your text before you click on the **Ink to Text** button.

The **Draw** ribbon helps make this digital notebook more like its paper notebook counterpart – you can doodle in this notebook! Let's move on to the next toolbar in line, the **View** toolbar.

The View toolbar

The fourth menu option and toolbar you will see in OneNote for Windows 10 is the **View** toolbar. With this toolbar, you can control how you view your notes and notebook layout.

When you click on the **View** menu in OneNote, you will see the following toolbar:

Figure 2.11 – The View toolbar

The buttons on the **View** menu, from left to right, include the following:

1. **New Window**: Open a new window for your OneNote notebook. You can move this new window to another screen. This will allow you to have two notebook pages or sections open on different screens.

2. **Immersive Reader**: When you click on **Immersive Reader** and then the **Play** button, the computer will read out what you have typed.

3. **Zoom out and in**: Use the magnifying glass icons to zoom in and out.

4. **100%**: This will restore your screen to 100% view, handy if you zoomed in or out.

5. **Page width**: When you click on the page width button, it will zoom to the full width of your content on the notebook page.

6. **Page Color**: Choose from different colors for the background of your notebook page.

7. **Rule Lines**: The **Rule Lines** feature is great to help you stay in the lines when drawing, but it is also a great background for any text page. Choose from different rule line options as well as grid lines. You also have the choice to select whether you want to always create pages with **Rule Lines**.

8. **Deleted Notes**: Click on this button to view any note pages or sections that you have deleted. These pages can be restored with a right-click or you can choose to delete them permanently. All items will be permanently deleted after 60 days. From the **Deleted Notes** button, you can choose either of the following:

   - **Empty Deleted Notes**: We use this so that all the deleted notes are permanently deleted.

- **Disable History for This Notebook**: If this is done, then deleted notes will not show for that notebook, and deleted notes cannot be restored. This will also prevent OneNote from keeping snapshots of your pages as versions – what you see is what you get and is up to date.

9. **Translate**: You can translate a section of your page or the entire page. Choose what language you are translating from and to. When you use this feature, you can replace text from one language with text in another language.

10. **Check Accessibility**: When you click on **Check Accessibility**, you will get tips on the right side of the screen as to what you can correct in your notebook so that it is more accessible to more people. For instance, if you use images, the accessibility checker will check to see whether you have used a description and alt-text on your image. Using descriptions and alt-text on images enables screen readers to describe your image for people who are blind or have poor vision.

11. **Replay**: The **Replay** button lets you replay your notebook page as if you were typing it in real time. For instance, if you type two lines of text and then use the **Draw** toolbar to circle the first line of text, and then you highlight the second line of text, **Replay** will show this happening on the screen again, in the order you did it. It's like a movie replay of everything you did on that notebook page. This can be great for presentations or teaching. In *Figure 2.11*, **Replay** does not show on the toolbar until you click on the arrow at the far-right end of the **View** toolbar.

12. **Hide Authors**: The **Hide Authors** feature is useful in shared notebooks. As different people contribute to the information on a page of the notebook, you will see their initials beside their addition or edit. If you do not want to see people's initials on a page, then click on the **Hide Authors** toggle button (this can be clicked on, and then later clicked off). In *Figure 2.11*, **Hide Authors** does not show on the toolbar until you click on the arrow at the far-right end of the **View** toolbar.

The **View** toolbar helps you to see what you want to see in your notebooks. Be sure to try out the options presented here.

Now for a toolbar that every program leaves for the end, just in case you need it: let's look at the **Help** toolbar and understand how we ask for help while using OneNote.

The Help toolbar

The last menu option and toolbar you will see in OneNote for Windows 10 is the **Help** toolbar. Finding out answers to questions while you are using the program is a perfect reason to check out the **Help** toolbar.

When you click on the **Help** menu in OneNote, you will see the following toolbar:

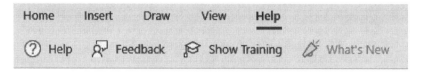

Figure 2.12 – The Help toolbar

The buttons on the **Help** menu, from left to right, include the following:

1. **Help**: Allows you to search for any topic.
2. **Feedback**: To provide feedback on OneNote and Microsoft, click on the **Feedback** button and you will be prompted to answer some questions.
3. **Show Training**: The **Show Training** button will list short training videos and additional help resources that you can access from Microsoft.
4. **What's New**: Find out what's new in OneNote when you click on this button.

OneNote for the Mac and the OneNote web version have the same toolbars listed in this section. There are some differences (between the Mac and web versions) on each toolbar, but for the most part you have the functionality you need. OneNote for the web has an additional menu/toolbar for **File**. From this **File** menu, you can print and share pages.

In addition to the OneNote ribbon bar/toolbar, you have extra options available from the Apple menu bar at the top of your screen. Over 50 buttons on the 5 toolbars have been mentioned in this chapter. There is a lot you can do to make OneNote a powerful resource. Compared to all this, the old paper and pen method of yesterday doesn't hold up.

But toolbars are not the only way to access features in OneNote. You can right-click in OneNote and get the relevant options based on where you clicked. Let's look at the power of the right-click menus in OneNote next.

Exploring OneNote's right-click menus

If you use a mouse, then you have probably done a right-click. This menu is special because it only pertains to the area that you right-clicked in. If you right-click somewhere else, you could see a different menu. Let's explore right-clicking in OneNote and see where it takes us.

Right-clicking a notebook name

When you right-click on a notebook name, you will see the following menu:

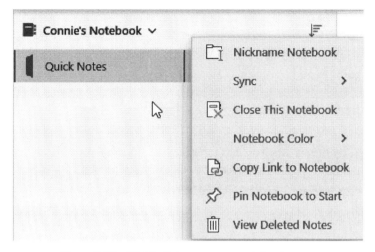

Figure 2.13 – Right-click menu on a notebook name

Let's look at each of these in detail:

- **Nickname Notebook**: You can create an alternate name for the notebook you have listed. This alternate name will not affect the original name of the notebook and will not be shown to anyone else that is sharing the notebook; only you will see the nickname. If you are sharing a notebook with others, be careful not to change the name too much, so that when they mention the original name you still know what notebook they are referring to.

- **Sync**: To sync all changes to a notebook, choose **Sync This Notebook** from the menu. If you have updated a number of notes, in different notebooks, and you want to access them immediately on another device, it is a good idea to use **Sync All Notebooks**.

> Important Note
> **Sync** is an automatic feature so you may not need to use this manual approach to sync very often (if ever).

- **Close This Notebook**: If you do not want to see a notebook in your list of notebooks available, you can click **Close This Notebook**. Closing a notebook does not delete or move it. If you close a notebook on your computer, that does not make it closed on your phone or any other device. A closed notebook can be reopened with the **More Notebooks** option in the notebooks area.

> **Tip**
>
> You normally do not close notebooks in OneNote unless you do not want to use it at all on a particular device. OneNote automatically syncs the notes in the background, so it is preferable to not close notebooks you intend to use again.

- **Notebook Color**: To make your notebooks stand out from each other, you can assign a color to each notebook. There are 16 colors available to you. This color applies to the notebook icon beside the notebook name; it does not change the color of anything else.

- **Copy Link to Notebook**: You can copy the link for one notebook into another notebook. By doing this, you can refer to that other notebook and have an easy and quick way to access that notebook. For example, if you have an employee notebook, you could use Link to another notebook on Safety.

- **Pin Notebook to Start**: Access your favorite notebook(s) from the Windows Start menu. Right-click on your favorite notebook and choose **Pin Notebook to Start**. This notebook will then be included in the Start menu tiles:

Figure 2.14 – Notebooks pinned to the Start menu

- **View Deleted Notes**: When you delete a page or a section from a notebook, it will go to **Deleted Notes**. The **View Deleted Notes** option is a quick way to see all that has been deleted from that notebook. You can restore that deleted information or delete it permanently.

There is a lot more you can do with your notebooks when you take advantage of the right-click menus. From notebooks, we go to sections and see what right-click options are available there.

Right-clicking a section name

When you right-click on a section name of a notebook, you will see the following menu:

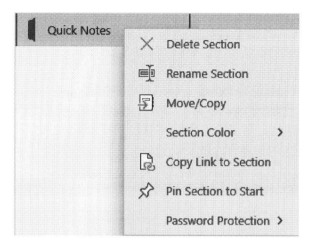

Figure 2.15 – Right-clicking a section of a notebook

The section's right-click menu gives you the following choices:

1. **Delete Section**: When you choose to delete a section of a notebook, you are also deleting all the pages in that section. This section will show in your **Deleted Notes** area, so you can recover the section if necessary.

2. **Rename Section**: If you choose to rename a section, it will be renamed everywhere. A renamed section will show with the new name on all your devices and for anyone else that is sharing that notebook.

3. **Move/Copy**: With this right-click, you can move or copy any section to any other notebook(s). Once you choose this option, you will be prompted with notebook names. Select the appropriate notebook for the move or copy.

4. **Section Color**: To make your sections stand out from each other, you can assign a color to that section. There are 16 colors available to you. This color applies to the section tab beside the section name; it does not change the color of anything else.

5. **Copy Link to Section**: You can copy the link for one section into another section (of the same notebook or another notebook). By doing this, you can refer to that other section and have an easy and quick way to access that section.

6. **Pin Section to Start**: Access your favorite section of a notebook from the Windows Start menu. Right-click on the section and choose **Pin Section to Start**. This section will then be visible in the Start menu tiles.

7. **Mark as Read**: This option will only show in the right-click menu if something in that section has changed. This change could have been done by someone else who is sharing the notebook with you. Where there is a change in a section, that section name will appear in bold. Once you have read all the pages that are in bold, this option for **Mark as Read** will disappear. If you made the changes on another device, then you may choose to use this **Mark as Read** option without having to click on each page that is updated (showing in bold).

8. **Password Protection**: Creating password protection on a section could be a good idea if you are sharing a notebook but do not want everyone to view or access a particular section. A **password** is also a way of creating an extra layer of security on your information. Right-click a section to attach a password. Once you have a password on a section, you will have access to more choices:

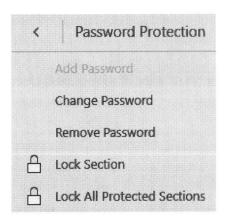

Figure 2.16 – Password protection for a section

Just like with notebooks, there are plenty of choices for how you can work with your sections by using the right-click menus.

From sections, we go to pages next and see what right-click options are available there.

Right-clicking a page name

When you right-click on a page name, within a section of a notebook, you will see the following menu:

Figure 2.17 – Right-clicking on a notebook page name

The right-click menu of the page name gives you the following choices:

1. **Delete Page**: Delete the page of a notebook with this right-click. This page will show in your deleted notes so you can recover the page if necessary.

2. **Rename Page**: If you choose to rename a page, it will be renamed everywhere. A renamed page will show with the new name on all your devices and for anyone else that is sharing that notebook.

> **Important Note**
>
> Cut, Copy, Paste work the same as any program, in helping you to copy or move information.

3. **Move/Copy**: With this right-click option, you can move or copy any page to any other section and/or notebook. Once you choose this option, you will be prompted with section and notebook names. Select the appropriate section or notebook for the move or copy.

4. **Make Subpage**: This option is only available if you have more than one page in your section and you are not on the top/first page (of that section). When you choose to make a subpage, you are grouping your pages together. This is beneficial if you have a long list of pages in a notebook and you want more organization for those pages. Once you create a subpage, you will see the following options added to the right-click menu (only when you are on those subpages):

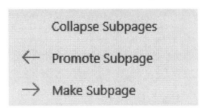

Figure 2.18 – Right-click pages menu for subpages

5. **Copy Link to Page**: You can copy the link for one page into another page within the same section and notebook or to another section and notebook. By doing this, you can refer to that other page and have an easy and quick way to access that page from a different location.

6. **Set as Default Template**: If you create a page with colors and/or lines, you may want that look to be the default template. A **default template** only applies to the current section of your notebook. The default template can also include words on it. Refer to *Chapter 4, Entering Information into Your Notebook*, for more on this topic.

7. **Pin Page to Start**: Access your favorite page of a notebook from the Windows Start menu. Right-click on that favorite page and choose **Pin Page to Start**. This page will then be visible in the Start menu tiles.

8. **Mark as Read**: This option will only show in the right-click menu if something on the page has changed. This change could have been done by someone else who is sharing the notebook with you. Where there is a change on a page, that page name will appear in bold. Once you have read the page, this menu option will change to read **Mark as Unread**.

9. **Page Versions**: This will show in the right-click menu of a page as long as there have been changes to that page. *If you are on a brand-new page, this option will not appear in the right-click menu.* When you choose **Page Versions**, you will see a listing on the right side of your screen showing each date and time that the page has changed. Click on any of the entries to view the changes. If you want to retrieve a past version of the page, click on the **Make Current Page** button (while on the appropriate past version). This will replace the current version of the page with a past version.

10. **Translate Page**: Use **Translate Page** to translate the text on the page from one language to another. You can choose the language to translate to.

11. **New Page Below**: Add a new page below the current page that you are on.

Once again, the right-click menus provide plenty of choices when working with the pages of notebooks.

From the page name column, we move on to the actual page to see what right-click options are available.

Right-clicking within a notebook page

There are many types of information that reside on a notebook page. When you use the right-click menu, your options will be based on what it was that you clicked on.

For instance, a different menu appears when you right-click on each of the following:

- A word or white space
- Selected text
- A PDF
- An image
- A file attachment
- A drawing or handwriting

When you right-click anywhere within a notebook page, you will see the following menu:

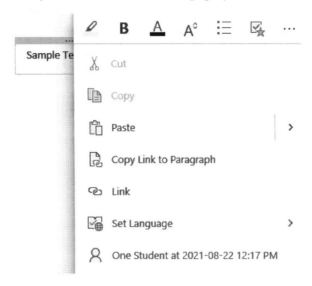

Figure 2.19 – Right-click menu on a notebook page

As we can see in the screenshot, you have the following choices:

1. **Shortcut toolbar**: Highlight text, bold text, and other choices are available at the top of this menu. These same choices are found on the **Home** toolbar.

2. **Cut**: This option is grayed out and unavailable until you select something on the page.

3. **Copy**: This option is grayed out and unavailable until you select something on the page.

4. **Copy Link to Paragraph**: You can copy the link for one paragraph onto another page within the same section and notebook or onto another section and notebook. By doing this, you can refer to that paragraph and have an easy and quick way to access that paragraph from a different location.

5. **Link**: If you right-click on a word and choose **Link**, you will be prompted to type in the address of that link. This link can be from a file (on **SharePoint**, **OneDrive**, or **Teams**) or from a website. Choosing the **Link** option will change that word into an instant link to that location.

6. **Set Language**: By choosing **Set Language**, you can have OneNote proofread the content in that language. For instance, if you set **Set Language** to **French**, then the words typed in will be corrected for spelling based on the French language.

The right-click menu changes on the notebook page based on what you have right-clicked on. The last example was for a right-click anywhere on text or a blank space on the page.

If you select text first, then the right-click menu changes to include two more options:

Figure 2.20 – Additional options when you right-click on text within a notebook page

These two extra options are as follows:

1. **Smart Look-up**: When you choose **Smart Look-up** on a word, you will see a **Smart Lookup** column appear on the right side of your page. This **Smart Lookup** includes the following:

    - A definition of the word

    - Excerpts from Wikipedia for the word

    - A web search of that word

2. **Translate**: This translates the text in the selection from one language to another. You can choose the language to translate to.

Aside from text in your notebook pages, you can also have PDFs inserted into your pages.

Important Note

Note that when you insert a file into a notebook page as a printout, OneNote converts this file to a PDF.

If you right-click on a PDF on your notebook page, you will see the following menu:

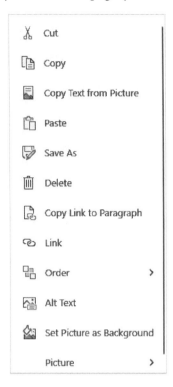

Figure 2.21 – Right-click menu for PDF within a notebook page

Some of the unique choices from this right-click menu for a PDF include the following:

1. **Copy Text from Picture**: Choose this option so that you can copy the text from the PDF. After you copy the text, click on a new location and paste the text to that location. This is an amazing way to extract text from a PDF! *This option may also be valuable to use if you right-click on a picture that has words on it.*

2. **Save As**: Take the PDF that is in the notebook page and save it as a file. You will be prompted about where to save this file.

3. **Delete**: Delete the PDF image from the notebook page.

4. **Order**: Because a PDF is like an image on your notebook page, you can overlap other drawings or text onto this image. Therefore, you may need to adjust the order of the element on the page. You will see another menu when you choose this option:

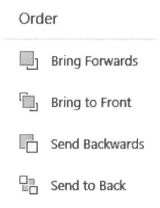

Figure 2.22 – Right-click submenu for the order of elements on the page

5. **Alt Text**: Create alternate text for the PDF so that it describes the PDF for people that cannot see the screen.

6. **Set Picture as Background**: If you set a picture or PDF as the background to your notebook page, you will not be able to move or edit this picture or PDF again. Rather than having a white background for your notebook page, you will now have this PDF or picture as the background. You can undo this, or you can choose this option again so that the PDF or picture is no longer the background.

7. **Picture**: This option is available to you if you want to resize your picture or move your picture using your keyboard. The arrow keys on your keyboard will help you resize or move your picture. The alternative to this is to use your mouse to move or resize the PDF or picture.

If you right-click on a file attachment on your notebook page, you will see the following menu:

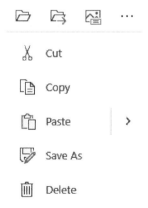

Figure 2.23 – Right-click menu for a file attachment within a notebook page

The unique choices from this right-click menu for a file attachment include icons at the top of the menu. The first two icons at the top of this right-click menu are **open this file** and **open this file with another app**:

- **Open this file** is best to use for any attachments that are created using programs you have on your computer, such as Word or Excel.

- **Open this file with another app** is helpful when you have to specify the type of program that is preferred for opening this file. This may be necessary when you have an image file and you have more than one program on your computer that opens and/or edits images.

If you right-click on an image on your notebook page, you will see the following menu:

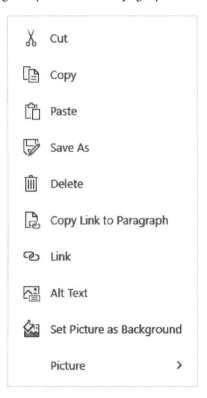

Figure 2.24 – Right-click menu for an image on a notebook page

Use this right-click menu to access the many options for images in your notebooks.

Images are similar to drawings and handwriting in OneNote, but there the right-click menu differs slightly. If you right-click on a drawing on your notebook page, you will see the following menu:

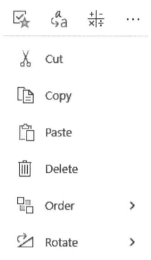

Figure 2.25 – Right-click menu for drawing on a notebook page

The unique choices from this right-click menu for a drawing include the following:

1. **Icons at the top of the menu**: They are options to add a tag to the drawing, convert handwriting to text, and the math option. Tags will be covered in *Chapter 6, Categorizing and Searching Notes*. Convert handwriting will be covered in *Chapter 4, Entering Information into Your Notebook*. The math option will be covered in *Chapter 8, Adding Shapes, Videos, Web Pages, and More to Your Notes*.

2. **Rotate**: This allows you to rotate the drawing, with these extra options:

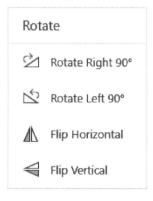

Figure 2.26 – Right-click submenu for rotating a drawing

There is a lot of information that can be stored in a notebook and with the help of the right-click menu, you can make almost any change possible.

There are two more places that you can right-click in your notebook and they are at the bottom of the screen: you can right-click on **Add page** and **Add section**.

Right-clicking on Add page or Add section

The **Add page** and **Add section** options seem to say it all, but there is a little bit more that you can do here. This is where the right-click menu comes in.

If you right-click on **Add page** at the bottom of the page column (or anywhere in the page column), you will see the following menu:

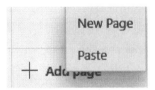

Figure 2.27 – Right-click menu for Add page

The two options are as follows:

1. **New Page**: This is another way to add a new page.

2. **Paste**: If you previously chose **Copy a Notebook Page**, you will need to paste that page using **Paste** from this menu.

Right beside the **Add page** button at the bottom is the **Add section** button. If you right-click on **Add section** at the bottom of the section column (or anywhere in the section column), you will see the following menu:

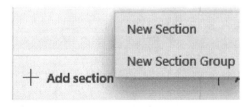

Figure 2.28 – Right-click menu for Add section

The two options are as follows:

1. **New Section**: This is another way to add a new section.

2. **New Section Group**: Create a section group so that you can organize sections that belong together into a group. *Figure 2.29* shows a section group entitled **Example Group** that contains four other sections that are underneath and indented:

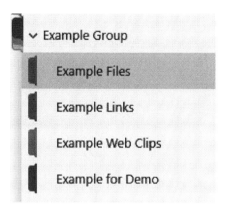

Figure 2.29 – Example of section group

Unless you right-click, you may miss the exceptional extras that OneNote gives you for the organization and customization of your notes. There are over 60 options available to you from the right-click menus, so this is a must in OneNote.

On a computer, the screen, toolbars, and right-click menus help you access the power of OneNote. But the power of OneNote goes beyond your computer; you can use OneNote on other devices, and when you start to open up OneNote on these other devices, the true potential of what you can do and what you can access is unlimited.

Let's take a look at how OneNote looks to you on a smartphone screen.

Understanding the layout of the OneNote screen on mobile devices

Mobile devices, or smartphones, are attached to most of us all the time, so it seems natural for us to want to store or retrieve notes from this device. The screen for your phone is a lot smaller than the computer screen so it is no surprise that the menus and layout are a lot different.

Once you install OneNote on your smartphone, your screen will look similar to the following:

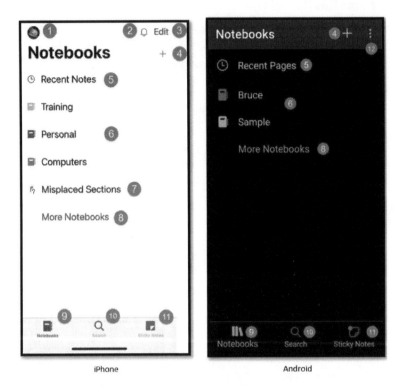

Figure 2.30 – iPhone and Android screens for OneNote

The screen shown in *Figure 2.30* is the first screen you will encounter for OneNote on your iPhone or your Android phone. The parts of this screen are as follows:

1. **Account icon**: The account icon in *Figure 2.30* is a picture that represents the Microsoft account that is logged in. This account icon could just have initials in it instead.

2. **Notifications bell**: The notifications bell will show a number beside it if there are any notifications for the notebooks you are logged into on your iPhone.

3. **Edit**: The **Edit** option will let you edit the order of the notebooks showing on this screen. You can also change the color of the notebook icon with the **Edit** menu, and you can close a notebook if you do not wish to see it on the iPhone screen.

4. **Plus sign**: Use the plus sign to create a new notebook.

5. **Recent Notes**: Once you start working in your notebooks, you can access the recent notes that you viewed, added, or edited.

6. **Notebook names**: This example shows three notebooks on the iPhone: **Training**, **Personal**, and **Computers**. The Android notebooks are as follows: **Bruce** and **Sample**. When you first install OneNote, you will not have any notebooks showing until you open them or add them.

7. **Misplaced Sections**: Misplaced sections can appear if you close a notebook or if a notebook is deleted from the cloud and you still had local changes on this device. Because these changes cannot be synced, you should move any content that you want to keep to another notebook or delete it if you do not need to keep it.

8. **More Notebooks**: Open up more notebooks using this option. If you created more notebooks on another device and want to access them on your smartphone, **More Notebooks** will show you all the notebooks that you can choose from. When you see the list of notebooks, click on the notebook you want to see, and it will appear on your iPhone notebooks screen.

9. **Notebooks**: The **Notebooks** icon in *Figure 2.30* is purple because this is the active screen we are looking at, showing the notebooks available to us in OneNote. If you choose **Search** or **Sticky Notes**, then the **Notebooks** icon here will change to gray.

10. **Search**: Use **Search** to search for any word or phrase in your notebooks.

11. **Sticky Notes**: If you are a fan of sticky notes, then you might like this digital version on the smartphone. Choose **Sticky Notes** and start typing. You can change the color of your sticky notes as well:

Figure 2.31 – Sticky Notes screen in OneNote, on the iPhone

12. **Three-dots menu**: On Android, this menu gives the options of **Sync Settings**, **Settings**, and **Send feedback to Microsoft**.

Now let's work with our notebooks on the smartphone. Once you select a notebook from the initial OneNote screen, you can continue to a section, and then a page.

On the **Sections** screen, you will notice the same **Edit** option at the top right of the screen (see *Figure 2.32*), and this will let you move the sections around or change the color of the section tabs:

Figure 2.32 – Top of Sections screen on iPhone

Just like you can add a notebook on your smartphone, within the **Sections** screen you can click on the plus (+) button to add a new section. The three dots at the top of the **Sections** screen is your menu; in this menu, you will have the option to share the notebook or to view the settings.

The Settings screen for OneNote on your iPhone

The **Settings** screen on your iPhone has a number of choices available to you:

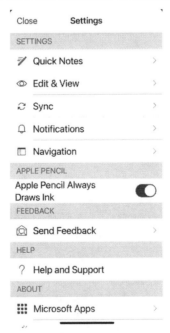

Figure 2.33 – Settings in OneNote, on the iPhone

Here is a description of each setting, in order as they appear in the menu:

- **Quick Notes**: Choose where you want to have recent notes available to you on the iPhone and what notebook will contain **Quick Notes**.

- **Edit & View**: In this menu option you pick the font style and size. You also have the option of turning any of these features on or off:

  - **Check Spelling**

  - **Hide Authors**

  - **Capitalize the first letter of sentences**

  - **Save photos as a PDF**

- **Sync**: By default, autosyncing attachments is turned on. You can choose to turn this off. With this option on, you can see attachments and images in your notebooks even if you are offline.

- **Notifications**: Choose how you want to show notifications for changes in your notebooks. Do you want a banner or badge app icon? You can also choose which notebooks you receive notifications for.

- **Apple Pencil Always Draws Ink**: This is a great feature to have on so that every time you use your Apple pencil, OneNote switches to drawing mode.

- **Send Feedback**: Send feedback directly to Microsoft.

- **Help and Support**: Search for help or read support topics listed here.

- **ABOUT**: Find out what's new in OneNote and retrieve other technical information with this option.

Once you have reviewed all your settings and ensured they are set up right, let's move on to pages within the sections of your notebooks.

Tip

For information on settings for the Android, please refer to Chapter 14, Customizing OneNote Settings.

When you select a section, it will open up pages. Here is a look at the **Pages** screen in OneNote on the iPhone:

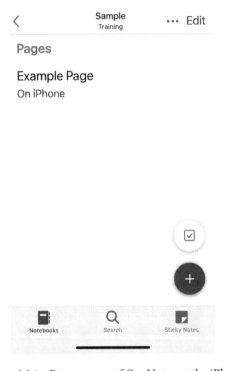

Figure 2.34 – Pages screen of OneNote, on the iPhone

The **Pages** screen is very similar to the **Sections** and **Notebooks** screens. One main difference is the plus (+) button is toward the bottom of the screen. There is also another feature available to you. Notice the checkbox button above the plus sign circle in *Figure 2.34*.

The checkbox button is a great way to create a checklist on your phone. This option is not available on Android devices. When you select this checklist option, you will see the following:

Figure 2.35 – Checklist example in OneNote, on the iPhone

With the list feature, you will need to provide a title for your list and then the items that you want to see on the list.

If you choose to add a normal page to your notebook rather than a list, choose the plus (+) sign. Here is what a new page will look like:

Figure 2.36 – Adding a new page in a notebook on iPhone

When adding notes in OneNote on your phone, you have access to a toolbar that can provide you with more than just typing. Here are the features you have on this toolbar:

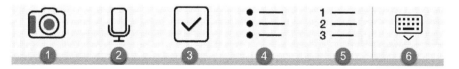

Figure 2.37 – Toolbar for adding a new page in OneNote, on iPhone

Let's go through them, from left to right:

1. **Camera**: When you choose the camera, you can insert a picture from the photo library on your phone or you can take a picture at that moment.

2. **Microphone**: Press the microphone button and it will start recording an audio file. This file will then be saved to the page that you are on.

3. **Checkbox**: Create your own checkbox tag. When you choose this option, the box will appear empty. Check the box anytime to show that item checked off.

4. **Bullet list**: Create a bullet list.

5. **Numbered list**: Create a numbered list.

6. **Keyboard**: Allows you to hide the keyboard, allowing more room to look at your page.

Aside from the toolbar in the middle of the page, you have more options at the top of your screen, appearing as follows:

Example Page

Figure 2.38 – Icons at top of page

Let's take a look:

- **Back arrow**: This will let you return to the list of pages for the section.

- **Squiggly line**: This represents drawing. Once you choose this squiggly line, you can draw with your finger or a pen (that is appropriate for your iPhone). You can add words (print or handwrite) or you can draw shapes or pictures. As you start drawing, you will see icons appear at the top that will help you. Choose **Done** when you are done drawing:

    - On Android, you will see a highlighter pen instead of this squiggly line.

- **Three dots**: This represents a menu of choices for this page:

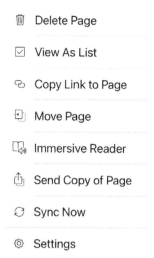

Figure 2.39 – Page menu for notes on iPhone

Some of the unique options in this menu include the following:

- **View As List**: With this option, you can change everything on the current notes page into a list. Checkboxes will appear in front of each paragraph of text as well as on each blank line. Change back to notes by choosing **View As Note** in the three-dots menu.

- **Copy Link to Page**: This option will copy a link for the current page that you can paste into an email. Only people that are sharing the notebook with you will be able to open this link.

- **Send Copy of Page**: This option will prompt you to send the page via Outlook (Outlook will need to be installed as an app on your phone) or with another app. If you choose another app, you will see the typical send choices, so you can send via text message, mail, as well as other choices provided. When you send a copy of a page, the page is sent as a PDF attachment.

If your page is a list and not a note, then you would have the following additional options:

- **View as Note**: With this option, you can change everything on the current list page into notes. Change back to a list by choosing **View As List** in the three-dots menu.

- **Email List with Outlook**: This option will send the list via Outlook (Outlook will need to be installed as an app on your phone).

- **Email List**: This option will send the list via your default email system on the iPhone. The list is emailed with the checkboxes and line items, as well as with a link to the OneNote page. Only people that are sharing the notebook with you will be able to open this link.

Aside from the menus provided, there is one more important thing you can do with the right touch gestures. You can slide to the left when viewing notebooks, sections, or pages.

To delete or close on the iPhone or iPad, the **slide to the left touch gestures** will let you delete a section or page. When you use this method on a notebook, your option will be to close a notebook:

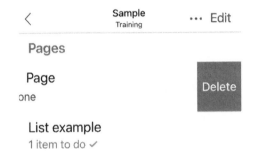

Figure 2.40 – Slide to left to delete a page (or section)

On an Android phone or Galaxy tablet, simply hold down on a notebook name and you will then see an option at the top right to close that notebook. If you hold down on a section or page, you will see a garbage can icon at the top right so that you can delete that section or page.

Your phone is a great place to work on your OneNote notebooks. In addition to typing in your notes, you have many options for working with your notebooks effectively.

If you need a bigger screen than a phone but don't want to jump onto your computer, then the iPad or Galaxy tablet is your next best bet. Let's look at how OneNote differs on the iPad or Galaxy tablet.

Understanding the layout of the OneNote screen on an iPad or Galaxy tablet

The OneNote screen on an iPad or Galaxy tablet has a lot to offer. Here is a look at the OneNote screen on an iPad:

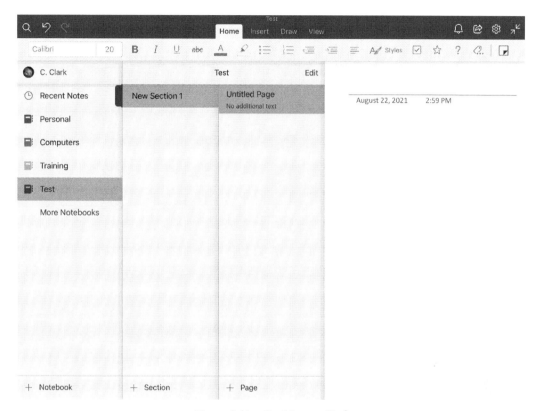

Figure 2.41 – OneNote on iPad

The Galaxy tablet screen is almost identical except for the following:

- The menus for **Home**, **Insert**, **Draw**, and **View** are only visible when you are viewing or typing onto the notebook page.

- The **Recent Notes** option, as shown in *Figure 2.41*, is displayed as **Recent Pages** on the Galaxy tablet.

- The magnifying glass, for the search tool, is on the top-right side of the screen, along with the undo and redo buttons.

The OneNote screen on the iPad or Galaxy tablet has almost everything that the computer has available. But what's different?

- The **Help** menu does not appear on the iPad or Galaxy tablet screen. But you can find **Help** listed in **Settings**. On the iPad, click on the **Settings** icon (the *gear*) at the top-right corner of your screen. On the Galaxy tablet, you will find settings in the three-dots menu at the top-right corner of your screen.

- The search, undo, and redo buttons have also moved; on the iPad, these buttons are always available at the top left.

On the iPad, when you start typing on your page, the columns on the left for the section and notebook will disappear. On the Galaxy tablet, the page listing also disappears. This way, you have plenty of room for typing. To activate these columns so that they show, tap on the left arrow that appears to the top left of your current page of the iPad. With the Galaxy tablet, use the three horizontal lines that appear on the top-left side of your screen.

The iPad and Galaxy tablet are convenient and great devices to use for recording notes in OneNote. Personally, I enjoy using the iPad for my notes because it is a nice size to work with and in addition to the pop-up keyboard, I can write or draw freehand with the touchscreen or an Apple pen (or stylus).

Summary

In this chapter, you have learned how to navigate on the OneNote screen of your computer, your smartphone, and your tablet. You have discovered dozens of options that are provided to you through the toolbars, right-click menus, and other shortcuts on the screen.

OneNote can be a powerful tool with the help of everything on these screens and menus. The added flexibility of changing to another device and still working on your notebooks is also a bonus.

In the next chapter, you will learn how to create notebooks, sections, and pages. The chapter will get you started on how to put your notebook together so that it is organized and easy to access information.

3
Creating Notebooks, Sections, and Pages

Microsoft OneNote is your key to organization. You simply need to decide on the best method of storing notes and related information to suit your needs. OneNote organizes your notes by providing you with the following divisions:

- **Notebook**
- **Section**
- **Page**

You can have as many notebooks as you wish. Some of these notebooks can be just for you, and some of them can be shared with others. Within each notebook, you have sections. And within each section, you have pages. Pages are where you record or capture all of your information.

In this chapter, we will focus on the following topics:

- How to create a notebook
- How to create sections in your notebook
- How to create pages in your notebook

By the end of this chapter, you will understand the difference between notebooks, sections, and pages. This will help you make the right decisions in terms of how to lay your notebooks out within OneNote so that everything flows naturally and is easy to access—not only for yourself but for anyone else you share a notebook with. So, let's get started with the first step: creating a notebook.

How to create a notebook

Before you create your first notebook, it is important to consider the full picture of the notebook's layout. This is so that you can decide how many notebooks to create and how to divide them up. In this section, we will explore the reasons why you might want to create a notebook.

Additionally, we will define the difference between a notebook and a section and help you to choose when to use one or the other. Whether you need to create a shared notebook so that others have access will also be discussed. Finally, we will look at the steps to create a new notebook on your computer or smartphone.

What to consider before creating your notebook

With OneNote, you have the opportunity to create unlimited notebooks that are divided into sections and pages. So, in what scenarios might you need a separate notebook rather than just one big notebook with many sections and pages? Before you create your first notebook, consider the following questions in order to decide:

- *Why do you take notes?* The topics you write about most will help you plan the best possible notebook structure. For example, you could be writing notes so that you can capture meeting discussions and to-do lists.

- *Do you record lots of meeting notes because you are part of a project or committee or department?* This could help you decide the name of your notebook. If what you record is shared with others, then your OneNote notebook can also be shared with them.

- *How many paper notebooks do you currently use?* Some people have multiple paper notebooks because each notebook has a specific purpose. This same logic could be used to create your digital notebook in OneNote, using different sections or pages to replace your different paper notebooks.

- *Do you have Word files saved that could be notes in a notebook?* There are a lot of files created in Word that are simply captured notes. Rather than creating those files in Word, that information could be written into a OneNote notebook. Perhaps the notebook could have the same name as the folder that held those files.

- *Do you receive emails with reference information that you want to keep indefinitely?* There are a lot of email folders full of valuable information that we don't want to lose. Why not take that information and create a notebook resource for yourself? There could be more than one notebook that is needed for this. For example, if you receive a lot of emails from human resources regarding vacation policies and your benefit structure, you might want to store this information somewhere that is easy to reference.

- *Do you need to share notes with others? Are you part of a team and using* **Microsoft Teams** *to share information?* Because Microsoft Teams is such a powerful collaboration tool, it is fitting that any notes that need to be shared with that team should be shared in a notebook within the team. When sharing notes, a notebook is a basic unit of sharing, so always create a new notebook when the set of people that should access notes are different. For example, if you create a notebook in Microsoft Teams, then that notebook is immediately set up as a shared notebook with all members of the team. Bear in mind that there might be various groups in your organization that share information within a separate Microsoft Team and, in doing so, would benefit from a shared notebook that only that group can see.

These considerations will help you decide on the division of your notes and how to organize them. It is important to know this so that you can create notebooks that flow and are easy to follow. There is no point moving emails or documents into a OneNote notebook and then having no idea how to find them again.

Another thing to consider is this: *Is the information you want to capture enough to make a notebook necessary, or is it just a section or page?* Let's dive into this next.

Should you make a notebook or a section?

A **section** is a way to divide up your notebook. In OneNote, you cannot have a notebook without a section. Within each section, you have pages. So, a section is a great way to group pages together. Looking at the hierarchy of OneNote, we have a notebook that is divided into sections, and those sections are then divided into pages.

Compare this to a main topic (the *notebook*) that has subtopics (the *sections*) and distinct information (the *pages*) within or about that subtopic.

Bear in mind that you can have as many notebooks in OneNote as you wish. Consider this example regarding how many notebooks and sections to have in OneNote:

1 notebook	5 notebooks
25 sections	5 sections
10+ pages per section	10+ pages per section

Table 3.1 – One notebook versus five notebooks

Looking at *Table 3.1, which scenario looks like it has a better flow?* This depends on your notebook and section topics. Ultimately, it is up to you and what makes sense in your world. Think about how you like to organize information. Generally speaking, you will benefit from more than one notebook. Read on to find out why.

Once you have considered all of the reasons you might need to capture notes in OneNote, you will then have to decide the best layout of this information, and that layout starts with notebooks and sections. *When does a topic need to be a full notebook as opposed to a section of a notebook?* Let's explore some examples to help you understand this better.

Let's say you are in a small organization, and you are in the HR department. In this scenario, you could have a notebook that looks like this:

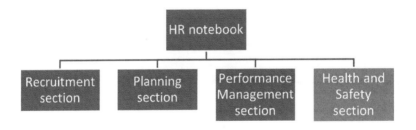

Figure 3.1 – An HR notebook example with sections

In *Figure 3.1*, we show one notebook for HR, which is divided into many sections. We need to decide whether this works best for us or whether we have a section, such as the **Health and Safety** section, which is so big that it should be its own notebook. **Health and Safety** could be its own notebook if we feel that this topic is large enough to need many subtopics that would become the sections.

Let's take the *Figure 3.1* layout of our notebook structure and show you an example of what this looks like in OneNote:

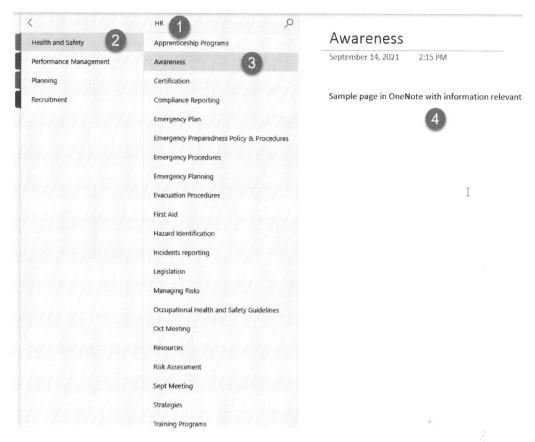

Figure 3.2 – An example HR notebook with sections and pages

Let's look at the details of *Figure 3.2*:

1. The notebook name is **HR**.

2. There are four sections in this notebook with the **Health and Safety** section being the currently selected section.

3. There are many pages in the **Health and Safety** section of this notebook. The **Awareness** page is currently selected.

4. The contents of the **Awareness** page are displayed.

There is no limit to the number of pages that are allowed in a section. The important factor is the ease of use and organization. We don't want to create a section with too many pages; if we have hundreds of pages in a section, they might be hard to navigate easily. We might also wonder the following: *should the pages be grouped together?* If there is a common theme with some of the pages, this is an indicator that a new section is necessary.

Let's look at an example in which a section from *Figure 3.1* is turned into its own notebook:

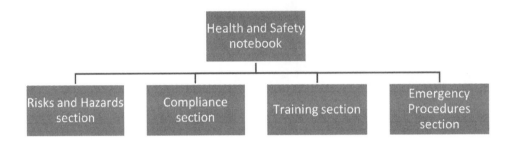

Figure 3.3 – The Health and Safety notebook example with sections

If the **Health and Safety** section is your responsibility, along with **HR**, then having a separate notebook is helpful.

Once again, let's look at this example in a real OneNote notebook:

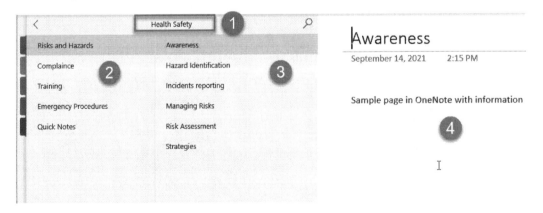

Figure 3.4 – An example Health Safety notebook with sections and pages

Following the numbering indicated in *Figure 3.4*, let's consider the following advantages of having this notebook:

1. *Figure 3.4* shows our new notebook called **Health Safety**.

2. With **Health Safety**, you can look at the important parts of this job and use them as your inspiration for creating sections. Our example of this, in *Figure 3.4*, includes sections for **Risks and Hazards**, **Compliance**, **Training**, and **Emergency Procedures**. Another reason that you might decide to create a new section is that there are many separate pages of information needed for each of these topics.

3. Notice that the page list is shorter in number **3** of *Figure 3.4* than it is in *Figure 3.2*. With **Health Safety** being its own notebook, there is an opportunity for us to divide up all the pages using sections in our **Health Safety** notebook.

4. There is lots of space to write about each topic that a page represents. In *Figure 3.4*, we have a separate page for **Awareness** that we can add information to.

In addition to using OneNote at work, there are many great examples of how OneNote can help you with notes in your personal life. Let's explore a personal notebook example next.

When you start using OneNote, there's a tendency to have one big personal notebook. Over a short period of time, you might find that one section of this personal notebook is becoming too big (and really warrants a separate notebook).

Figure 3.5 shows an example of a personal notebook with four sections:

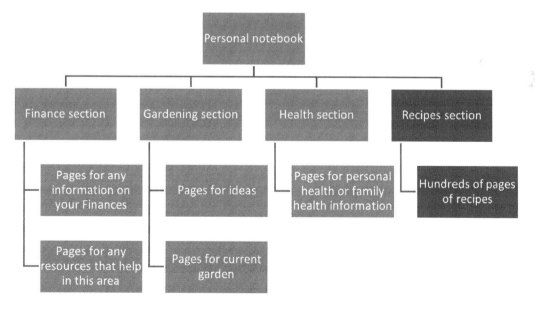

Figure 3.5 – A personal notebook example with sections

Any one of these sections in *Figure 3.5* could include dozens of pages or more. Let's say that the section for recipes is meant to replace the need for cookbooks or Googling recipes – over time, that could make this section very large.

Let's take the *Figure 3.5* layout of our notebook structure and show you an example of what this looks like in OneNote:

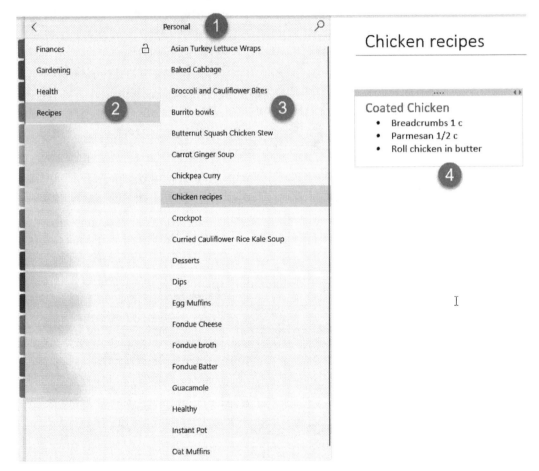

Figure 3.6 – An example Personal notebook with sections and pages

In *Figure 3.6*, the numbers represent the following information:

1. The notebook name is **Personal**.
2. There are four sections in this notebook. The selected section is the **Recipes** section.

3. There are many pages in the **Recipes** section of the **Personal** notebook. The selected page is **Chicken recipes**.

4. The page that is selected shows the actual **Chicken recipes**.

Figure 3.6 shows many recipes on the pages of the **Recipe** section. These pages will continue to increase in number as you add more recipes to your notebook. The more pages you add, the more organization you will need. Recipes are easier to read when you divide them into meaningful sections. Let's look at **Recipes** as its own notebook, as shown in *Figure 3.7*:

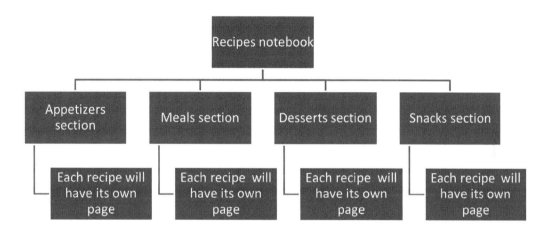

Figure 3.7 – The Recipes notebook example with sections

With this layout of the notebook, you know exactly where to go for the recipe that you might need. Therefore, it is easier to navigate. When you move to the **Appetizers** section, you will see many pages of appetizer recipes. If you want desserts, click on the **Desserts** section, and see the pages that are available there. Let's look at a real-life example of this **Recipes** notebook.

Here is an example of the **Recipes** notebook as it appears in OneNote:

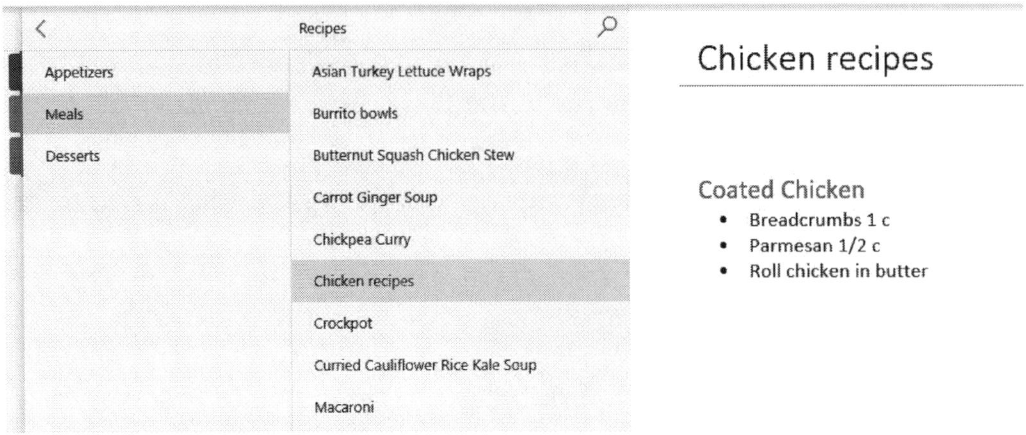

Figure 3.8 – An example of the Recipes notebook with sections and pages

As you look at the list of page names in *Figure 3.8*, you can see how easy it is to navigate from the **Meals** section to the recipe of your choice.

Whether a topic should become a notebook or a section is hard to determine unless you fully plan out the hierarchy of that topic. Figure out what the sections will look like and what example pages you could have in that notebook.

Another great option that is available when organizing your notebooks into sections is that you can create a section group. This means you can create a bit of a hierarchy for your sections, so you can start with a more general section group name and then have the specific names of the sections within that group.

Here is an example of the preceding **Recipes** notebook divided into section groups:

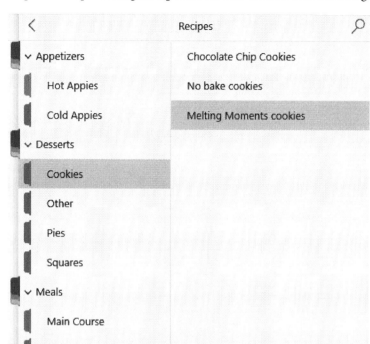

Figure 3.9 – An example of the Recipes notebook with section groups

To create a notebook with one or more section groups, you can follow these easy steps:

1. Right-click on **+ Section** at the bottom of the section column or right-click on any empty area of the section column. Please refer to *Figure 3.10* for the right-click menu:

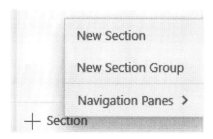

Figure 3.10 – Right-click on + Section to view these options

2. From the right-click menu, choose **New Section Group**. Type in a name for your group.

3. Then, you can drag existing sections into this group or add a new section while in this group, and that new section will go below the group name.

4. To expand or collapse the section group, simply click on the arrow beside the group name. For instance, in *Figure 3.9*, if you click on the arrow to the left-hand side of **Meals**, you can expand or collapse that section.

With the grouping of sections, you have just opened yourself up to so much more organization within your notebook. Plan for this in your notebooks where needed.

These examples were for one person to create notebooks for work or home. Let's move on to the scenario of more than one person needing to access the same notes. At work or home, it is possible that shared notebooks are necessary.

Should your notebook be shared?

Should your notebook be shared with others? And should it be part of a SharePoint site or your Teams app?

By default, when you create a notebook within Microsoft SharePoint or Teams, the notebook has the same name as the SharePoint site or the Teams name. When you share a notebook, all the sections and pages are shared. You cannot just share one page or one section. This could be a deciding factor in how you create notebooks.

Each department in your organization might need to share information in a notebook. If a number of people work together on projects or committees, then these groups might also benefit from their own shared notebook.

Based on the **HR notebook** example in *Figure 3.1*, if that notebook is shared with 10 people who make up the HR team, then all the sections and pages are available to those 10 people, too. However, if you need the safety officer of the organization to have access to the information on health and safety, and that information *only*, then you need to create a separate notebook to accommodate that (as shown in *Figure 3.3*). The **Health and Safety** notebook could be shared with the 10 people from the HR team as well as the 1 safety officer.

Is your topic (your information or your notes) a notebook or just a section? Do you need to share this notebook with anyone else? This is a crucial step to determine before you create your notebooks.

The next step is to create the notebook. Let's start by looking at how to create a notebook within OneNote on your computer.

How to create a notebook on your computer?

When you first install OneNote, it will create a notebook with your name on it. This notebook will be attached to the Microsoft account you entered when you installed OneNote. You might want to use this notebook as your personal notebook.

OneNote is meant for more than just one notebook, so let's look at how to create other notebooks.

Within OneNote on your computer, here are the steps for creating a notebook:

1. Click on the notebook name in the upper-left corner of your screen (under the toolbar). In *Figure 3.11*, the notebook's name is **Connie's Notebook**:

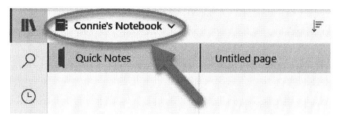

Figure 3.11 – Click on Connie's Notebook

2. Click on **Add notebook** at the bottom of this **Notebooks** column:

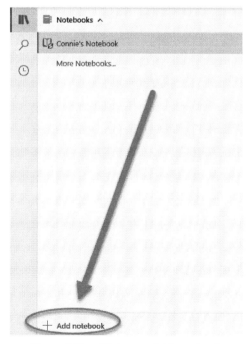

Figure 3.12 – Click on + Add notebook

3. You will be prompted for a new notebook name. Type in the name of your notebook. If you have multiple Microsoft accounts, those accounts will be listed below, click on the appropriate account so that the notebook is saved in the correct place. Choose your work or school account if the notebook is for work or school. Choose your personal account if your notebook is meant for you personally.

4. Once this notebook has been created, you will see the notebook name on the left-hand side. Additionally, you will see **New Section 1** and **Untitled page**:

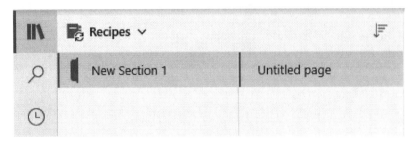

Figure 3.13 – A new notebook for Recipes

Note as you add a new notebook, it will go underneath any existing notebooks. The order of your notebooks can be adjusted, and this will be covered in *Chapter 7, Organizing and Easily Working with Pages, Sections, and Notebooks*.

Now that we are clear on how to create a new notebook, let's look at how to divide up this notebook into meaningful sections.

How to create sections in your notebook

Sections divide up your notebook. Be more organized and have a better flow with the help of sections. These sections will group the pages that house all of the information you are storing in your notebooks.

When you first create a notebook, a section is automatically created. Let's look at what we can do with this existing section.

Renaming a section in a new notebook

When you first create a notebook, you will see a section that is labeled **New Section 1**. You can rename this section as follows:

1. Right-click on the section labeled **New Section 1**.

2. Choose **Rename** and type in an appropriate name for your first section.

Your notebook should always have more than one section, so let's look at how to create more.

Creating a new section

The visual format of a section in a OneNote notebook is a **tab**. Consider tabs that you have used in your books or binders in the past and how they have helped you separate pages into meaningful sections, so that similar pages are together. Let's take advantage of this organization and create sections in our notebooks for pages that belong together.

Let's start by looking at how to add a section to a notebook while you are using OneNote on your computer.

Adding sections to notebooks while using OneNote on your computer

To create a new section in your notebook, perform the following steps:

1. At the bottom of the section column, click on the + **Add section** option:

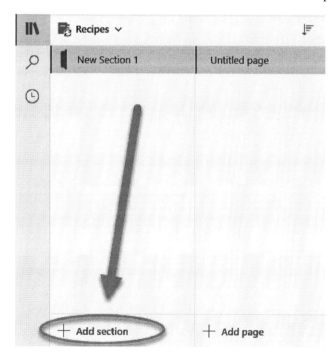

Figure 3.14 – Adding a section to the notebook

2. Type in a new section name and press *Enter* to complete.

Here is an example of four named sections within the **Recipes** notebook:

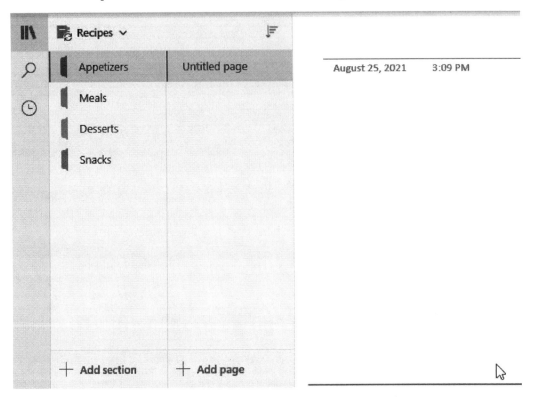

Figure 3.15 – Recipes with sections for Meals, Desserts, and more

As you add in a new section, it will show under any existing section. The order of these sections can be adjusted. This will also be covered in *Chapter 7, Organizing and Easily Working with Pages, Sections, and Notebooks*.

Let's look at how to add new sections to your notebook while you are in OneNote on your smartphone.

Adding sections to notebooks on your smartphone

To add sections in OneNote on your iPhone or Android smartphone, there are a few steps involved:

1. Choose the notebook that you want to add the section to.

2. On the sections screen, touch the plus (+) sign in the upper-right corner:

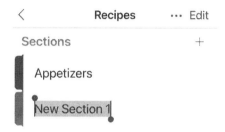

Figure 3.16 – Adding a new section to a notebook on the iPhone

3. On the iPhone, while **New Section 1** is highlighted, type in the name of the section. On Android, hold down the name of the section, and a screen will pop up for **Rename section**. Type the new section name in the space provided, and select the **Rename** button.

Now that we have the notebook and the sections, it's time to add pages and fill them up!

How to create pages in your notebook

Adding pages sounds easy in OneNote. However, a page in OneNote is not the equivalent of a piece of paper. There are no limits lengthwise or widthwise. Limits pertain to storage limits, that is, how much space you have for saving. If you are on SharePoint or OneDrive, your storage space would be quite large. This means you have room for lots of information on the pages of your notebooks.

Create separate pages in your notebook sections to organize separate pieces of information. Think of your notebook like a book, with each page of that book having a name and purpose within the section.

When you first create a notebook, a section is automatically created, and a page within that section is also automatically created. Let's look at what we can do with this existing page.

Renaming an existing page in a new section of your notebook

When you first create a notebook section, you will see a page labeled **Untitled Page**. The name of the page is the first line of text seen on the page. That first line is generally the page title on top of the creation date and time. You can name the page by typing in this space or you can rename it in the page list column.

Rename this page as follows:

1. Right-click on the page labeled **Untitled Page**.
2. Choose **Rename** and type in an appropriate name for your first page.

In addition to your notebook containing more than one section, your notebook sections should contain multiple pages. Let's look at how to create a new page in your notebook next.

Adding a new page

Adding pages is a very routine task in OneNote. When you have new information to introduce regarding the topic that is covered in your notebook section, then a page could be the best way to go about it. Whether you are sitting in front of your computer, or you are on the go with your smartphone or tablet, you can add pages to your notebooks.

Let's start by learning how to add a page to a section while working in OneNote on your computer.

Adding pages to notebooks while using OneNote on your computer

To create a new page in your notebook section, do the following:

1. At the bottom of the page column, click on + **Add page**:

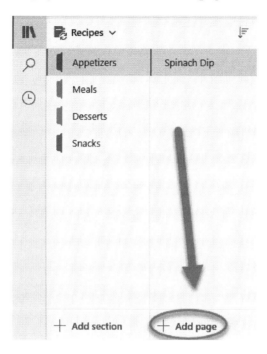

Figure 3.17 - Add page button

2. A new page shows up in the column, labeled **Untitled Page**.

3. Right-click on the page labeled **Untitled Page**

4. Choose **Rename** and type in an appropriate name for this page.

5. Repeat as needed.

As you add a new page, it will show under any existing pages. Additionally, you can create a page above an existing page by right-clicking on that page and then clicking on **New Page Above**. You may find this option depending on your device and this option may say *above* or *below*.

The order of these pages can be adjusted, which is something else you can look forward to in *Chapter 7, Organizing and Easily Working with Pages, Sections, and Notebooks*.

Let's look at how to add new pages to your notebook sections while in OneNote on your smartphone.

Adding pages to notebooks on your smartphone

To add pages in OneNote on your phone, follow these steps:

1. Choose the notebook and then the section that you want to add the page to.

2. Touch the plus (+) button at the lower-right corner of the screen:

Figure 3.18 - Add page button in OneNote on Smartphone

3. After pressing the *plus* button, you will be taken to a new page. Type in a title for this page. The title will become the page name.

Now all the fun begins with an empty page to be filled. How to set up your page for success is covered in detail in this book, so keep reading!

Summary

In this chapter, you learned how to create notebooks, sections, and pages in OneNote. You have seen how that is possible on your computer, your smartphone, or your tablet.

Planning the big picture of your OneNote notebooks is important, so take the necessary time to decide whether you should make a new notebook or simply a new section. How many pages you expect to have in a section could be one of the ways that can help you decide.

In this chapter, you also discovered that if you want to share information with others in your office, then you will need to create a notebook for that sharing. This notebook can be located in Teams or SharePoint, and we will look at these possibilities in *Chapter 11, Using OneNote Online with OneDrive, SharePoint, or Teams.*

Meanwhile, in the next chapter, you will learn how to enter information into your notebook. We will show you how different OneNote is for capturing information, and there is no comparison to other Microsoft programs such as Word or Excel.

Let the notetaking begin!

4
Entering Information into Your Notebook

Typing in OneNote is very different from typing in any other Microsoft program, and as an added bonus you do not even need to type – you can *handwrite* your notes in your notebook. In either case, there are no traditional page size boundaries. OneNote is very much like a giant whiteboard that you can write on. The limits of OneNote are restricted to the limits of your storage system. Your OneNote page can be as long or as wide as you want to make it.

To make a system like this work, OneNote introduces us to **containers**, which we can use to house our information on a page.

In this chapter, we will cover the following topics:

- Understanding how OneNote uses containers to capture information
- Giving yourself space
- Handwriting in OneNote
- Arranging your notes so they work well and look good
- Customizing the look of your notebook and creating notes faster

Whether you treat OneNote as your digital notebook or as a massive whiteboard, it is important to see how differently OneNote lets us capture information. When you type onto the page of your notebook, you will see containers being formed. Let's start by understanding how these containers can help you, or sometimes work against you.

Understanding how OneNote uses containers to capture information

Because OneNote acts like a giant whiteboard, you can literally type anywhere. Most of us are accustomed to typing along the left margin of a page, which you can do in OneNote, but you don't have to start there.

A container is created once you start typing. This container can start anywhere on your page, and you can move it anywhere, too. Let's see what it looks like to have a container for your information:

Figure 4.1 – Example container within your OneNote notebook

As shown in *Figure 4.1*, a container in OneNote creates a box around your information. This box will automatically expand with the information that you put inside it, as long as you do this properly. More on that in the *Where you click first makes all the difference* section.

Text is just one thing that a container can contain. The fun will begin with your containers when you start adding more to them. Let's explore that next.

What does a container in OneNote contain?

A container is similar to what other software, such as PowerPoint, calls **text boxes**. Just like a text box, a container can contain a flow of text, but in OneNote, each container behaves more like a Post-it on a page that can contain a mix of all the object types available in OneNote. So, along with text, containers can hold *anything* you add into your notebook, including the following:

- Pictures

- Outlook emails

- Tables

- Documents (Word, Excel, PDF, or any document that you can read on your device) and printouts of documents

- Audio or video clips

- Handwriting/drawings

In this chapter, we will refer to any of the aforementioned items or text as *information inside a container.*

So, if you have a blank notebook page, when exactly does a container get created? Here is a reference for how a container is started in OneNote:

- By typing text

- When inserting a table

- When inserting a file or printout of a document

- When recording audio

- When inserting a video

Sometimes, rather than a container getting created, an object is created on your page. An object is an item that can be sized or moved.

If there are no existing containers already on your page, or if you click on white space far away from an existing container, then the following activities will create objects:

- When you insert a picture or sticker

- When you draw with pens or shapes

- When you handwrite on your tablet or smartphone

If you type under that object, the text is placed in a separate container. This is important to understand because if you move a picture or drawing, the text will not move with it. The object could float over the top of existing containers when you make changes.

Let's look at a scenario so that we understand the difference.

In the following figure, we have inserted a sticker (picture) onto our notebook page in two different ways:

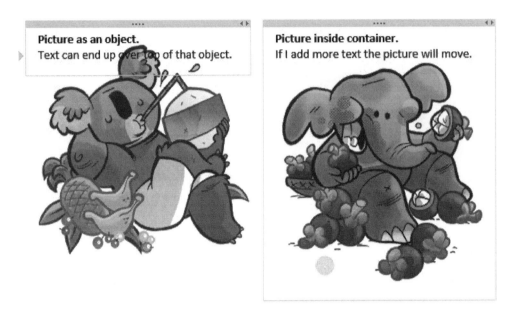

Figure 4.2 – Picture as an object or inside a container

In the preceding figure, on the left-hand side, where the picture is an object, we can type text in a container above the picture. But, if we add more text, the picture does not move. Text, or any information inside that container, can end up over the top of that object.

In *Figure 4.2*, where the picture is inside the container, the text in the container was already in place; then, the picture was inserted. We can type text in a container above the picture and if we add more text, the picture will move. The text will not go over the top of the picture that was created inside the container. Similarly, if we remove text, the picture will move up. So, you can see that if you want the text and pictures or drawings to be kept together (moved together if necessary), then type the text first and insert the picture or drawing under the text, keeping that picture or drawing in the same container. More on pictures and text will be covered in *Chapter 5, Best Practices for Creating Notes for Easy and Fast Retrieval*, and *Chapter 8, Adding Shapes, Videos, Web Pages, and More to Your Notes*.

Another important distinction about containers in OneNote is that they can be created anywhere, so where you click makes all the difference.

Where you click first makes all the difference

When you start typing text or inserting any information into OneNote, where you click first makes all the difference. You could click inside an existing container of information, or you could click outside an existing container and in turn be creating another container of information.

When you create more than one container for your information, these containers reside wherever it is that you created them. It's possible, for example, to click a couple of inches from the left margin of your page and then start typing, especially if you are trying to type beside something on the page.

See the following figure for an example of how this could look:

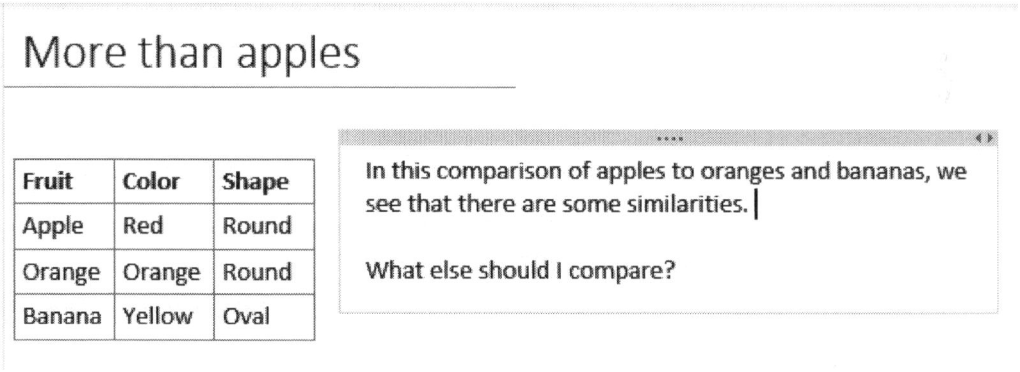

More than apples

Fruit	Color	Shape
Apple	Red	Round
Orange	Orange	Round
Banana	Yellow	Oval

In this comparison of apples to oranges and bananas, we see that there are some similarities. |

What else should I compare?

Figure 4.3 – Type text or insert a table on the page to create containers

Normally, you don't have to worry about the placement of text on a page, because in other programs, you have boundaries for where to start (that is, starting from the top within margins).

Let's go further with this scenario and show you what happens if you don't type text immediately below the current text on your page. The following figure gives us an example of this scenario:

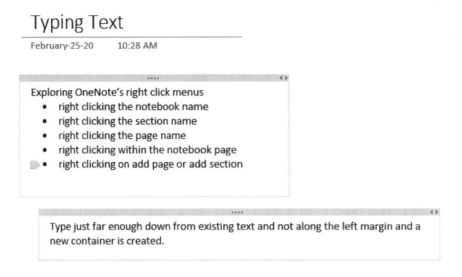

Figure 4.4 – Two containers of text written at separate times

The preceding figure shows how typing bits of information that are not immediately next to each other leads to having two different containers of information. If this is what you prefer, then great, otherwise you may find you have a mess on your hands.

So, let's learn about how containers work so this doesn't accidentally happen to you.

When typed text is placed in a container, hit the *Enter* key to continue typing, just as you would in Word or any other word processing program. Use the container to keep together any information that belongs together. The *Enter* key will give you the spacing between paragraphs but still keep you in the container.

Here is a test we will try. Click on an empty space on your page and look at the cursor. *Is the cursor by itself, or is there a container around the cursor and other information?*

Let's show you the results of this test in the examples within *Figure 4.5* and *Figure 4.6*. In the following figure, when you click on an empty space on your page, you see a cursor and there is no container surrounding it. This means you are typing into a new container:

Figure 4.5 – Cursor not in a container

In the following figure, when you click on an empty space on your page underneath existing text, you see a cursor with a container surrounding it. This means you are typing into the same container:

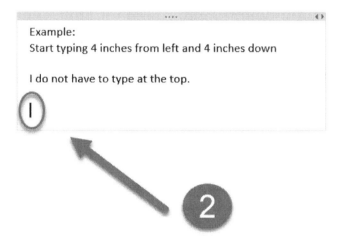

Figure 4.6 – Cursor in the container

So, why does it matter which container we are in? Well, there is no limit to how many containers you can create or type into on a page; it really comes down to ease of entry and the overall look of the information.

If all you are doing is capturing notes on one topic, then it is a good idea to stay in one container so those notes flow easily and line up properly for you.

When text does get placed into two separate containers, you do have the option of merging containers. Let's look at the steps for this next.

Merging containers

With the right steps, you can easily merge containers of information. Sometimes, we can click a little too far away from existing information, or we might have clicked a little further right on the page (when compared to a container above). See the following figure for an example of two containers that we accidentally created separately but should be merged:

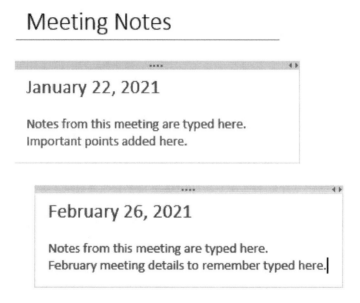

Figure 4.7 – Two containers that need to be merged as one

Follow these steps to merge the containers from *Figure 4.7*:

1. Hold down the *Shift* key on your keyboard.
2. Move your mouse to the top of the second container until you see the four-headed arrow for moving.
3. Click and drag that container into the bottom of the first container. Remember, you are still holding the *Shift* key while you are dragging the container. When the containers are merged, you will see a container border go around this second piece of information so that it is merged with the first container of information.

See an example of this in *Figure 4.8*:

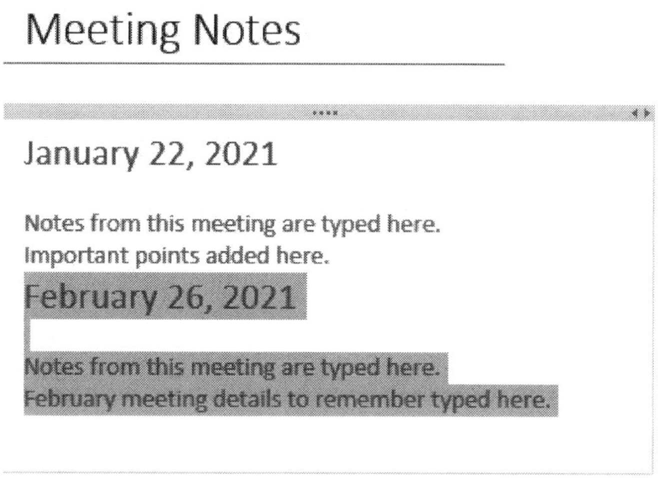

Meeting Notes

January 22, 2021

Notes from this meeting are typed here.
Important points added here.

February 26, 2021

Notes from this meeting are typed here.
February meeting details to remember typed here.

Figure 4.8 – Two containers merged as one

Hooray! Merging works and is a great fix! Although you can type text just like in a word processing program, the containers make this text unique. An advantage to these containers is that the container can be sized or moved. If you do not like how much room the container of information is taking on the page, you can make that container bigger or smaller. Similarly, if you do not like where the container is positioned on the page, you can move it.

Let's look at how to move a container, and then we will explore sizing.

Moving a container

Because you can click anywhere to start a container, you may decide you do not like the location you started in; the good news is, you can move it.

When you move the container, you are moving everything inside that container at the same time. So, that could mean you are moving one word, 10 paragraphs of text, tables, or any assortment of information, as outlined in the *What does a container in OneNote contain?* section.

If you want to move a container, do the following:

1. Click on the border of the container, and when the four-headed arrow appears, drag the container to somewhere else on the page.
2. When you let go of the mouse, the container will be in a new location on the page.

In the beginning, you may find yourself moving containers to the left side of the page so that you're typing lines up like a normal typewritten page. Or if you accidentally started two containers of text and you want them to be lined up together, you can move them.

Sometimes moving the container is not enough; you need to resize that container, so it fits better in relation to everything else on your notebook page.

Resizing a container

Remember, your notebook page is like a whiteboard, and you can add information across the page or down the page. If you place more information on your page, you may want to size the existing information, so it is easier to read or follow.

You may also want to size a container because, after you have placed everything in that container, you realize it is too wide. If you size it, you get rid of the white space and you can easily move another container of information to be beside it.

Sizing is also a good thing to do when preparing for printing. You size the containers so that they fit better on the printed page. You will learn about printing in *Chapter 12, Printing and Sharing with OneNote*.

When sizing a container, you have the option to make it wider or narrower. There is no option to make the container longer.

Follow these steps to size a container:

1. Click inside the container to select it.

2. Once you see the right border of that container, hover your mouse over it.

3. Click and drag with your mouse on that border when you see the double-headed arrow, as follows:

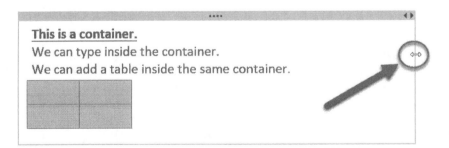

Figure 4.9 – How to size a container

Keep in mind that OneNote does automatically size containers for you, so you should not resize unless required.

Aside from moving or sizing your containers in OneNote, you can use a feature on the **Draw** toolbar to insert a space where needed.

Giving yourself space

If you have separate containers of information on your page and you are doing a lot of editing, then you may find you need to add space between the containers or take space away.

Insert Space works between containers, as well as objects that are not in containers, to fix any spacing problems. You can insert space vertically or horizontally. Although the feature is called Insert Space, you can also use it to reduce the space between containers.

> **Fun Fact**
>
> The OneNote team internally called this the *Wiping tool* for the longest time. It makes sense, as it started as a *wiper* to push everything down the page; but, at some point, the tool was modified to work either way – adding space or shrinking space. The *wiper* analogy just didn't work well anymore, but the OneNote team never really found a name that made sense – so it stuck with Insert Space, even if that's not all it can do.

Although you know how to move a container, sometimes there are too many containers to move. The Insert Space feature helps us by quickly adding (or removing) extra space, while at the same time moving the other containers appropriately.

Let's look at an example of how this works:

- If you add space between two containers, then you will be moving the lower container further down the page (and further away from that first container).

- If you take away space between two containers, then you will be moving the lower container further up the page (and closer to that first container).

Insert Space will also work within one container. In other words, if you feel like you need more spacing within your container, you can use this Insert Space feature. When you add space within one container, it will separate that one container into two containers.

Let's look at the steps you need to follow to add space within a container or between containers:

1. Click in the area of the notebook page that needs more space.

2. Click on the **Draw** menu.

3. Click on the Insert Space icon in this toolbar:

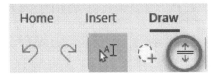

Figure 4.10 – Insert Space icon on the Draw toolbar

4. Your cursor will now change to a horizontal line with an arrow in the middle. Click and drag the arrow with the line downward to create the space you want:

Figure 4.11 – Insert Space guide bar to help you add space between containers

If you need to decrease space between containers, do the following:

1. Repeat *step 1* to *step 4* from the previous instruction list.

2. Click at the bottom of the empty space you want to eliminate.

3. Click and drag the arrow with the line up to create less space between containers or objects.

> **Important Note**
> To reduce space across the width of the OneNote page, you will follow these same steps but with the help of a vertical spacing line. The vertical spacing line will only show on the far-left side of the OneNote page.

Now that we know how OneNote works with text, drawings, or any information we add to our notebooks, let's take a look at how we can handwrite in OneNote.

Handwriting in OneNote

The OneNote notebook application is meant to mimic your paper notebook, *so what better way to do that than to capture handwriting?* Handwriting, printing, or drawing is best done on a smartphone or tablet, but it is possible to use a mouse on a computer to handwrite or draw.

Let's look at how handwriting or drawing works on these different devices. We'll start with the computer.

Handwriting in OneNote on your computer

When using a computer that does not have touchscreen capabilities, you can still draw or handwrite within OneNote.

Follow these steps to handwrite or draw in OneNote on your computer:

1. Click on the **Draw** menu.
2. Click on any of the pens shown. You have many colors to choose from.
3. Click anywhere on the page to start.
4. While holding the left button down on the mouse, simply move the mouse to draw, handwrite, or print.
5. The drawing or handwriting will stop when you let go of the button.

In addition to handwriting, you can also draw shapes, such as lines, arrows, boxes, or circles. These shapes can go around or over the top of anything that is already on the page. More detail on creating shapes will come later, in *Chapter 8, Adding Shapes, Videos, Web Pages, and More to Your Notes*.

Now that you know how to handwrite or draw using your mouse on the computer, let's try this on a tablet.

Handwriting in OneNote on your tablet

Handwriting or drawing is so much easier when you have a touchscreen. You can draw with your fingers, an appropriate pen, or a stylus. The tablets we refer to here are the **Apple iPad** and **Microsoft Surface**. Let's start by looking at how to handwrite with touch, no pen needed.

Handwriting with touch

By default, when you are using your tablet or iPad, OneNote does not have you in **Draw with Touch** mode. Instead, you have to tell OneNote that you want to do this by selecting **Draw with Touch**.

Follow these steps to handwrite or draw in OneNote on your tablet:

1. Select the **Draw** menu.

2. Change the Drawing mode to **Draw with Touch**:

    - On an iPad, choose the following icon:

Figure 4.12 – Draw with Touch icon on an iPad

    - Once selected, turn **Draw with Touch** on. Repeat the same process to turn off touch mode.

    - If on a Microsoft Surface tablet, choose the following icon:

Figure 4.13 – Draw with Touch icon on Microsoft Surface

    - Once you select this icon, it is shaded. To turn off **Draw with Touch** mode, choose this icon again.

3. Select a pen from the **Draw** toolbar and choose the color you wish to draw with.

4. Anywhere you touch or move your finger on the screen will create a drawing or some handwriting.

Although this refers to Draw with Touch, you can use an appropriate pen that has a rubber stylus in the same way that you would use your finger to draw or handwrite.

A **stylus** is like a generic pen for your tablet. It does not work the same as the pens that are built for the device you use. Let's look at handwriting with these pens next.

Handwriting with a pen

When you use a pen that is meant for your tablet, you will have different results with handwriting and drawing. Apple has created the **Apple Pencil**, which you can use with your iPad, while Microsoft has a **Surface Pen** to use specifically with the Microsoft Surface tablet.

The benefit of using these particular pens is that once the pen touches the surface of the appropriate device, you are in Drawing mode. You can draw, handwrite, or print. The feel of these pens is meant to emulate you holding a pencil to your notepad. Notetaking should seem more natural.

Follow these steps to handwrite or draw in OneNote on your tablet with a pen:

1. Choose the **Draw** menu.
2. Select a pen from the **Draw** toolbar and choose the color you wish to draw with.
3. With the appropriate pen, freely create your drawing or handwriting.

From handwriting on tablets, let's move to learning how to draw or handwrite on your smartphone.

Handwriting in OneNote on your smartphone

Working with OneNote on your smartphone is fast and convenient. If you quickly want to draw or handwrite on a page of your notebook that is super easy.

Follow these steps to handwrite or draw in OneNote on your smartphone:

1. Open up a page of your notebook.
2. Tap on the squiggle icon at the top right of the page:

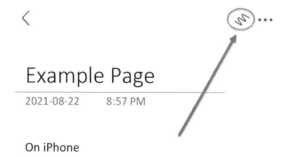

Figure 4.14 – Switch to drawing on a OneNote page on your iPhone

If you're on Android, the draw icon looks like a felt marker tip:

Figure 4.15 – Switch to drawing on a OneNote page on your Android phone

3. You can use your finger or a stylus pen to draw or write on the page of your notebook. Also, at the top of the screen, you will have a new toolbar so that you can choose a thicker pen or an eraser, the lasso, and the undo options.

4. When you have finished writing or drawing, tap on **Done** at the top right of your screen.

Now that you know how to draw or write in OneNote, let's look at reversing that with the **Eraser** or **Undo** feature.

Using the Eraser or undo feature

Whether you are using a computer, tablet, or phone, you can easily change your mind about what you have drawn or written:

- Use **Eraser** on the **Draw** toolbar to erase any drawing or handwriting on the screen.

- Or, you can undo using the undo icon on the **Draw** toolbar; this is the first icon that looks like a curved arrow (on an iPad, it is above the toolbar).

If you are using the Microsoft Surface Pen, then the tip of that pen is an eraser that you can use. Other pens may have a built-in eraser feature as well, so check the instructions for your pen.

Rather than erasing or undoing your handwriting, let's look at how you can convert your handwriting to typed text.

Converting handwriting into typed text

It may seem more familiar or comfortable handwriting in your OneNote notebook, but typed text is easier to read and more universal. So, OneNote has built into their framework the ability to convert your handwriting (or printing) to typed text. Please note that this is not an exact science and, although OneNote is quite good at reading a lot of handwriting styles, it is not perfect.

Here are the steps for converting handwriting to text:

1. From the **Draw** toolbar, choose the **Lasso** icon to select the handwriting:

Figure 4.16 – Lasso icon on the Draw toolbar

2. With your mouse, click starting above the top edge of one corner of the handwriting. Drag the lasso to the opposite corner. Try to give yourself extra room above, below, left, and right of the handwriting so that you can get everything selected with the lasso. The example in *Figure 4.13* is handwriting for my name, Connie:

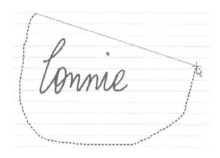

Figure 4.17 – Lasso formed around handwriting

3. Once the lasso goes around all the handwriting, let go of the mouse button. This will put a dashed box border around the handwriting.

4. From the **Draw** toolbar, choose **Ink to Text** to convert the handwriting to text.

> **Important Note**
>
> On a touchscreen, rather than having to use your mouse for the lasso, you can use Touch mode or the appropriate pens to do the selecting. When using a pen, there is often a button dedicated to selecting.

Handwriting in OneNote is a great feature that you can use on your computer, your tablet, or your iPhone. If you change your mind about handwriting, you can either erase it or convert it to text.

Now, we move on to our typewritten text notes and take a look at some ways we can make those notes look better.

Arranging your notes so they work well and look good

Learn basic formatting for text in OneNote, as well as highlighting and using styles. Just as you can format text in your favorite Word document or Excel spreadsheet, you can also format your notes in OneNote. The icons on the **Home** toolbar for text formatting are very similar to the icons you see in other Microsoft programs.

Let's start with the basic text formatting choices for our notebooks.

Basic text formatting

Format your text before you type or after. If you format your text after you have typed it, then you need to select that text first.

Formatting your text could be related to the font or to the actual positioning (aligning) of that text. Let's look at our font choices first. Font-related choices in OneNote are located on the **Home** toolbar; please refer to *Chapter 2, Screen Layout and Toolbars*, for a full description of toolbar icons.

A popular way of working with text in a paper notebook is to highlight the text. OneNote provides this highlighting option and helps you to make your text stand out.

Let's look at your highlighting options in OneNote.

Highlighting text in your notebook

Yellow highlighters are the tool that helped most of us make it through school and studying. Yellow is just one of 40 colors available to you in your OneNote notebooks:

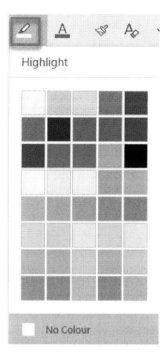

Figure 4.18 – 40 colors available for highlighting text

If you are working with black text, then the lighter highlight colors work best. Note at the bottom of this dropdown is the option for **No Colour**.

When you choose a highlight color (other than yellow), that color is available from the highlight icon, and you don't need to select the color again. That color will be reset to yellow once you close OneNote and then open it back up again.

If you highlight text and change your mind later, then you can select that text and choose **Highlight | No Colour**.

Highlights prove to be a very visual way to format your text, but if you are looking for a consistent method of titles and sub-titles, you want to look at styles for that job.

At the far right of the **Home** toolbar is **Styles**, so let's look at this feature next.

Using styles in OneNote

Styles are pre-formatted text and are a common feature in many Microsoft programs (as well as many other applications).

Rather than changing the size, the style, and the color of your font, Styles puts all this together for us.

In addition to the **Normal** style, in OneNote, you have 10 other styles to choose from. You cannot customize these existing styles or add any new ones. A popular use of styles is for titles or headings. In OneNote, you have six heading styles.

The drop-down menu for **Styles** gives you a preview of what the style will look like when applied to your text. *Figure 4.19* shows you the **Styles** drop-down menu:

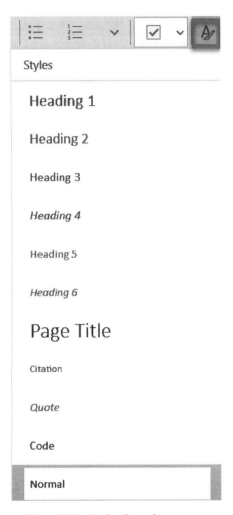

Figure 4.19 – Styles drop-down menu

Another special thing about **Styles** is that it is assumed you are applying a style to a paragraph (or heading), so you do not need to select any text first! The style stops when it sees a hard return, in other words, you press *Enter*.

Here is an example of how to apply a heading style to existing text on your page:

1. Click *anywhere* on the text; you do not need to select the text:

    -   If you have one word on a line, the style will be applied to that one word.

    -   If you have two or more words on a line, the style will be applied to all the words on that line.

    -   If you have a paragraph, the style will be applied to the entire paragraph.

2. Click on the style icon from the **Home** toolbar.

3. Choose the appropriate style, such as **Heading 1**.

4. Your text on that line or in that paragraph will change to look like **Heading 1**.

Styles help make your notes easier to read. Styles also give a more professional and consistent look to your notes. In the next section, we will be talking about more ways to enhance notebooks and produce notes faster.

Customizing the look of your notebook and creating notes faster

A great way to customize the look of your OneNote notebook is to change the background of the notebook page you are working on. You can change the page color or add lines to the notebook page.

Let's start by changing the page color.

Changing the page color of your notebook page

When you change the color of a notebook page, you are giving that page a different look. You can color-code your pages. For instance, all the meeting notes are in blue, and meeting agenda pages are in green. At a glance, you will immediately know what note page you are on and what it is about.

Follow these steps to change the background of your page to a new color:

1. Click on the **View** menu.

2. Select **Page Color** from the **View** toolbar.

3. There are 16 colors shown in the drop-down menu, but you can choose more colors if you wish. To start with the colors provided, click on one of the colors shown.

4. Your note page will change color. This affects only the notebook page you were on; no other pages are colored.

5. If you want to color multiple pages at one time, *Ctrl + click* on each page, then click on **Page Color** and the color of your choice. If all pages are next to each other, you can use the *Ctrl + click* method. This will change all pages selected.

6. If you no longer want a color background on the page, go to the page color icon, and choose **No Fill**.

If you print your note page, any page color chosen as a background will not print.

Another exciting way to change the look of your notebook page is to add rule lines to the page. Let's look at **rule lines** next.

Adding rule lines to your notebook page

Do you need lines in your notebook? The answer to this could depend greatly on what is on the page. If you are drawing on a notebook page, handwriting on the page, or positioning images, having lines could be a real advantage. If you intend to handwrite with a pen in OneNote, it is recommended that you use one of the rule line choices. Having rule lines will make your page look tidier and will help OneNote better recognize your text.

Follow these steps to add rule lines to your notebook page:

1. Click on the **View** menu.

2. Click on **Rule Lines**. There are several choices available for **Rule Lines**:

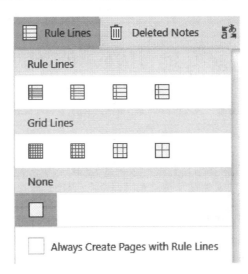

Figure 4.20 – Rule Lines drop-down menu

3. Click on the example of the lines that you prefer.

4. Your note page will change to show these lines as a background. This affects only the notebook page you were on; no other pages will have lines:

    ▪ If you want to add lines to multiple pages at one time, *Shift + click* on each page, then click on **Rule Lines** and the line style of your choice. This will change all pages selected.

5. If you no longer want rule lines on the page, go to the **Rule Lines** icon, and choose **None**.

If you print your note page, the rule lines you've chosen for your notebook page will print.

Another option available in the Rule Lines drop-down menu is **Always Create Pages with Rule Lines**. If you check off the box beside this option, then whenever you add a new page into your notebook it will have the Rule Lines style you selected. This feature turned on will affect all your notebooks unless there is a default template in place.

If you need to type the same type of notes over and over again, you can create a **default template**. This default template could have a specific page color attached to it, as well as rule lines and typed information.

Let's take a look at how to set up a default template next.

Setting up a default template

So much time can be saved on typing when you create a notes template. Plus, you can have the color of the note page and rule lines built into that template as well. A default template is attached to whatever section of your notebook you are in at the time of the creation of the template. In other words, no other sections or notebooks will be affected.

Create a notes template for any recurring notes that you create. An example of this might be **Meeting Agendas** and **Meeting Minutes** within the **Project** section of your notebook. In this template, you can have everything laid out that is repeated and then you can just fill in the blanks with the new information.

Follow these steps to create a default template:

1. Choose the notebook and section where you want the template to be located.

2. Create a page in that section.

3. Populate the page with any headings or text that is repeated. Change the page color and/or add rule lines to the page.

4.   Once the page template is complete, right-click on the page name in the page column. Choose **Set as Default Template** from the drop-down menu. That page is now the default page for that section of your current notebook.

5.   Click on **Add Page** at the bottom of the page column.

6.   The new page will have all the text, headings, and other details that you stored in the template.

7.   Type new information onto this page.

8.   Change the title of this page to be more specific to what the page is about (otherwise this page title and name will be the same as the template page title and name).

If you need to override this **Default Template** page in the future, repeat *step 2* to *step 4*. You can create a default template on a blank page if you wish to reset it to what it was in the beginning.

There's no need for a blank page now that you know about default templates, page colors, and rule lines. You now know how to make your notes more interesting and unique.

Summary

In this chapter, you learned how to enter information into notebook pages and work with the containers on those pages so that everything flows well and looks good. When the spacing is not right, you discovered how to insert space to move containers closer or further apart.

Surprise! OneNote is not just for notes that are text. You learned how your pages could include images, videos, and documents. And to make you more at home with this type of notebook, you found out how easy it was to draw or write, no matter what device you were using. Then, the miracles of this OneNote technology allowed you to take your handwriting and convert it to text – wow!

Furthermore, you learned how to pretty up your notes with highlighting and styles, as well as discovering how to create visually unique notes with rule lines and page colors. And lastly, you were introduced to default templates, the best shortcut to creating any notes you type regularly, such as meeting notes or meeting agendas.

All this helps you to add valuable information onto the pages of your notebooks. In the next chapter, we will explore the best practices for creating notes so that you can retrieve and access those notes faster.

Section 2: Navigating, Searching, and Shortcuts within Notebooks

A notebook within OneNote is more than just a collection of notes. It becomes a reference that you can rely on to find anything fast. If you think of something and write it down (in OneNote), you will be able to remember it and retrieve it quickly with OneNote. In this section, you will learn how to navigate through OneNote with ease, how to search for virtually anything, and how to save time with shortcuts.

You'll learn how to copy or move information easily within your notebooks or from notebook to notebook and learn valuable tips for creating notebooks with sections and pages that flow logically and are well organized.

You'll discover how to apply tags to your notebook pages so that your notes stand out and are easy to search.

You'll also learn how to move, copy, rename, or delete any part of your notebook(s) and see how to access a notebook from any device you own. We'll also find out how to password protect or color code our notebooks.

This section comprises the following chapters:

5

Best Practices for Creation and Easy Retrieval of Notes

When taking on a new application, it is best to give it some thought—*how can you effectively use that application in your everyday work?* Let's face it, we are learning about a new application because it is going to make our life easier. However, to do this, we should set some ground rules. In this chapter, you will discover ideas regarding how to build best practices for your notebooks, and as a result, create a better system for yourself and others.

In particular, in this chapter, we will cover the following topics:

- How moving or copying in OneNote behaves differently
- Keeping the end in mind
- Creating a system of best practices for sharing

So, let's get started with the fundamentals of moving and copying information within OneNote.

How moving or copying in OneNote behaves differently

In every program, the ability to copy or cut information from one place to another is essential. It seems like a simple enough task, but within OneNote, it takes on a different twist.

With OneNote, there are many choices for where you can copy or cut and paste information. You can copy or cut from one location on a page to any of the following:

- A different location on the same page
- Different pages in the same section of the current notebook
- Different pages in a different section of the current notebook
- Different pages in a different section of a different notebook

Another special part of OneNote to consider is its **containers**. When copying or moving (cut) information, you can copy or cut either part of the information in a container or the entire container.

Let's look at how to copy the contents of an entire container.

Copying the entire container

It is easy to copy everything inside a container. You just need to position your mouse in the right spot, and you have everything selected. Here are the step-by-step directions for selecting the entire container:

1. Move your mouse to the top of the container, and when you see a four-headed arrow, click to select everything in the container. The following screenshot shows the four-headed arrow at the top of the container:

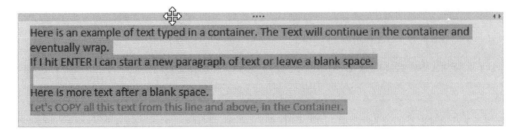

Figure 5.1 – Selecting the entire container when you see the four-headed arrow

2. Right-click to access a menu of choices for this container. Choose **Copy**.

Now that the information has been copied, let's consider how you can paste this information onto a page. This could be a page in the current section of your notebook or another location, as listed in the bullet points at the beginning of this section. The following table shows what happens if you paste in a container or outside of a container:

The location where information is pasted	Where to right-click and paste
Underneath the existing text and in the same container	Right-click slightly below the existing text and close to the left-hand edge of the container. After you right-click, choose **Paste** to have this copied text in the container.
In a different container	Right-click at least an inch below the existing text or to the right-hand side of the existing text. Then, choose **Paste** to paste this copied text in a new container.

Table 5.1 – Pasting information into the same container or a different container

3. Right-click inside the container or outside of the container, as described in *Table 5.1*, and choose **Paste**.

If you don't need to copy the entire container, you can copy and paste any amount of information. When you paste that partial information, you can follow the same steps as outlined in *Table 5.1*.

When working with pictures in OneNote, there are several things to bear in mind. Let's look at how to properly copy or cut and paste pictures next.

Moving pictures to a better spot

Having pictures and text is a popular combination in a OneNote notebook. Unfortunately, this is one area that I often see my students struggle with. After placing a few pictures on their page, my students notice that these pictures do not line up. Alternatively, another issue could be that these pictures simply do not stay with the text they are referring to. This is why it is important that you learn how to cut (or move) these pictures from wherever you don't want them to be, and then paste them to a better location on the page.

Let's look at some examples of where a picture can be placed alongside existing text.

If you want your text to always include the picture, then place the picture in the same container as the text. The following screenshot shows an example of the picture and text in the same container. Notice the container box surrounding both the picture and the text:

Typing text in a container is what OneNote does. You can place more than text in this container. A picture is something you can add. You can have a picture inside this container, on top of this container, beside or under this container.

Figure 5.2 – A picture inside a container, underneath the existing text

To place the text and the picture together, as shown in *Figure 5.2*, perform the following steps:

1. Assuming you have this picture somewhere else on your page, the first step is to copy the picture. Right-click on the picture and choose **Cut**.
2. Click at the end of your text, or press *Enter* to create a blank line.
3. Right-click and choose **Paste** to move the picture into this container.

Our next example, as shown in *Figure 5.3*, is of a picture that has been placed underneath a container consisting of text. If you move this container, the picture will not move with it. However, if you add more text, then that container with text will get bigger and the picture will move down. In other words, if you add two more paragraphs of text to our example in *Figure 5.3*, the text will not cover the picture. Instead, the picture will move as the text container gets bigger:

Typing Text in a container is what OneNote does. You can place more than text in this Container. A picture is something you can add. You can have a Picture inside this Container or on top of this Container or beside or under this Container.

Figure 5.3 – A picture underneath a container of text

To place the text and the picture together, as shown in *Figure 5.3*, perform the following steps:

1. Right-click on the picture and choose **Cut**.

2. Click at least two lines after your text so that you are not clicking inside the existing text container.

3. Right-click and choose **Paste**. This picture should not be in the text container.

4. If you click on this picture, it will be treated as an object that can be moved or resized. Notice the *dashed* lines around the picture; there is no thick grey top line like a container.

If you are moving pictures (or objects) around on a page that has text containers, be careful. You could accidentally cover your text with a picture.

It's important to understand how to effectively copy and paste within your notebook pages so that your information lines up and does not overlap.

Next, we will look at how to move information from one page of your notebook to another page, section, or notebook.

Moving information to different pages, sections, or notebooks

As you start to use OneNote more often, you will create more pages, more sections, and more notebooks. In doing so, you might find yourself rearranging information. You might want to move or copy existing information onto different pages within the current section of your notebook, into different sections, or even different notebooks. You can move anything in OneNote virtually anywhere you choose. Let's start by looking at moving information from one page of your notebook to another page.

Moving information to a different page

If you decide the notes or information you have on a particular page of your notebook are better suited on another page, no problem. We can easily cut and paste from one notebook page to another. To move information to another page, follow these steps:

1. Select the information you want to move from the page. You can select an entire container, any amount of information inside a container, or multiple containers and objects on the page.

2. Right-click on the selection and choose **Cut**.

3. Click on the page that you want to move the information to. Then, click on the page at the appropriate location for the move to take place.

4. Right-click and choose **Paste**. Your information has moved to a different page.

The same process applies to moving content to other sections or notebooks; simply navigate to the appropriate page in other sections or notebooks and paste the information onto that page. Next, we will look at how to copy, cut, and paste in OneNote using your smartphone or tablet.

Using OneNote on the smartphone or tablet to cut, copy, and paste

While on your smartphone or tablet, you might want to make changes to your pages by moving or copying information.

But before we get into moving or copying information, let's make sure you understand how to select the information within OneNote on your smartphone or tablet.

Selecting in OneNote while on your Apple or Android devices

To successfully move or copy, it is important you understand how to select within OneNote on an iPhone, iPad, or Android. Here is a list of tips on how to select:

- Click anywhere on the page, and you will see a container box or the borders around a picture appear (if you have selected a picture).

- When a container box appears around the information, select the top of that container (*the thick grey line*) and this will select everything within the container.

- If you press down within that container, you will be prompted to **Select** or **Select All**, as shown in *Figure 5.4*. Choose **Select** and it will select the word you are on. The **Select All** option will select the current paragraph in the container. On Android, you will only see the **Select All** option. So, you can press down on a word, which will select that word.

Objects that are selected will have a toolbar pop up with choices, such as cut, copy, and delete. Additionally, you will see a four-headed arrow in the middle of that picture. You can select this four-headed arrow and drag the picture somewhere else on the page:

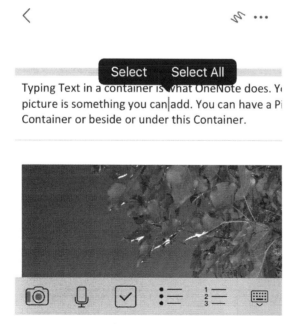

Figure 5.4 – Selecting on the iPhone or iPad

Now that you know the tips on how to select while using the smartphone or tablet, let's dive into cutting, copying, and pasting.

Copying or moving information in OneNote while on your smartphone

Copying information or moving information with cut, copy, and paste is virtually the same process as on the computer. Here, the difference is in the prompts provided when you select text, images, or an entire container of information. To move information to another page, follow these steps:

1. Select the information you want to move from the page. You can select an entire container, any amount of information inside a container, or multiple containers and objects on the page.

2. A toolbar menu will be shown on the screen; choose **Cut**.

3. If on an iPad, choose another page from the page column on the left-hand side. If on an iPhone, use the arrow icon (on Android, use the three horizontal lines) in the upper-left corner to see your pages, then choose a page.

4. Select somewhere on the page, of your choice, to place the text or information that you are moving. Select by touching the screen.

5. Touch the screen a second time and you will be prompted to paste the information; choose **Paste**. On Android, hold down onto the screen to see **Paste** pop up as an option to choose. Following this, your information will move onto this page.

In addition to moving information from page to page in your notebook, you can move to different sections or different notebooks altogether. Follow these same steps and change the destination.

Although the aforementioned examples have focused on moving information, you can use copy instead of cut to copy information.

Now that we are clear on how to successfully copy and paste within our notebooks, we have the fundamental maneuvering in place.

Let's move on to some best practices for creating our notes so that retrieval is easy and fast. The first best practice we will talk about is how to keep the end in mind when working with your notebooks.

Keeping the end in mind

As you create each notebook, not only do you need to plan out the structure, as you learned how to do in *Chapter 3, Creating Notebooks, Sections, and Pages*, but you also must keep the end in mind. Remember that as you populate your notebooks with all sorts of great information, you will want to access that information quickly and easily in weeks, months, and even years from now.

So, here is a list of tips to bear in mind:

- **Make sure your notebooks flow**: Once you land on the notebook name, you'll see the available sections. Ensure that this list of sections makes it easy for you to identify exactly what you will find there and where to go next. Then, in each of the sections, you have the pages listed. Again, once you select a section, the list of pages should make sense, and it should be easy for you to select the page that you need. Here is an example of the **Health Safety** notebook:

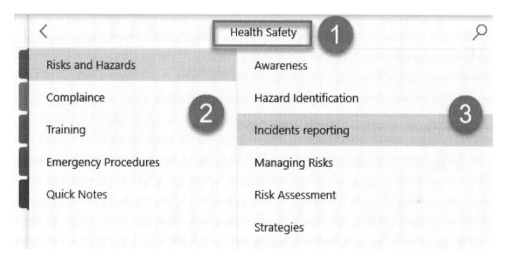

Figure 5.5 – An example of how a notebook should flow

Now, let's look at how the notebook should flow:

I.   As shown in *Figure 5.5*, select the **Health Safety** notebook (**1**).

II. Next, you will need to decide the right section (**2**) to go to. In our example, we choose the **Risks and Hazards** section.

III. Then, in that section, we see a list of pages (**3**). These pages should relate to the section and the notebook we are in. It should be easy for us to determine how to get to a page because our notebooks flow naturally.

- **Use more than one notebook, use more than one section, and use more than one page**: Take advantage of all the ways OneNote offers you to segment your information. Don't have one notebook with one section and 2,000 pages—that's not giving you the order you deserve.

Break up your thoughts. Let's imagine that you start with a page and enter information onto that page, but at some point, you might find that your page covers too many different things. Break up this page into other pages. You might need to do this relatively often. Add more pages, and rearrange your notes onto the appropriate pages whenever you see fit:

- Although you are on a notebook page, you can create as many containers of information as you wish. There are advantages to keeping as much information together as possible in one container. You can copy or cut that entire container with one click. Additionally, you can quickly format all the text in that container so that it has the same look.

- Organize your thoughts with OneNote. Gone are the days of trying to remember stuff. Use OneNote to jot down ideas or thoughts as you have them. Then, search out more information to add later.

- Develop some form of consistency for your notes so that you can easily go back to a past note to search for that piece of information. For example, if you use notes to capture information about your projects and each project has a unique project number, make sure you consistently add that project number in your notebooks so that you can search for it later.

  Consistency is also important because of the search capabilities of OneNote. If you consistently use the same terms to describe something, you can then find that term easily throughout your notebook(s). For example, if I use the word *customer* on some pages and then have the word *client* on other pages, my search results for either word will not be accurate.

- Don't try to make OneNote something it is not. Some people start using OneNote and then wonder how to print out their pages with page numbers and headers and footers, just like Word. While it is possible to print from OneNote, and it is possible to fit everything onto a page printout, OneNote is not very resilient in this area. If you only want to print, then you might need to go back to Word. However, if you are ready to save the trees and go paperless, then use OneNote, and use it differently. Don't treat OneNote like Word; they are from the same family, but they are not twins. If you really want to treat your OneNote page like Word, then stick to one container and type within that container.

- Diarize your entries. On a page of your notebook, you might find that you will continue making notes on a topic for a long time. If it is helpful to know the last entry date of your notes, then add in a date before that note:

  - To enter today's date, use this keyboard shortcut: *Alt + Shift + D*. This will display in the same format as your computer date (the date at the lower-right corner of your PC).

  - To enter today's date and time, use this keyboard shortcut: *Alt + Shift + F*.

  - The date and time on your notebook page reflect when you created that page. Unfortunately, at present, there is no way to change this page date and time. If you do not want to see this date or time, you can delete it. To delete the date at the top of the page, click on the date, then hit *Delete* from your keyboard. Follow the same steps for the time.

- Decide what you truly want to use OneNote for and stick to it. If you currently have a paper notebook for project *X* and want to use OneNote to replace that paper notebook, then do the following:

  - Take all the existing notes about project *X* from that paper notebook and scan them, take pictures of them, or retype them so that they are in your OneNote notebook.

  - Then, throw away the paper notes on project *X*. If you can't throw away those paper notes, then you are not truly committed to changing to the OneNote digital notebook. Give yourself a few days if that makes it easier, but throw out the paper notes.

  - Attend all meetings for project *X* with a device that allows you to capture your notes in OneNote. This device could be your phone, tablet, or laptop. If this is not possible at all, then use paper to transcribe those paper notes into OneNote after the meeting.

Don't be afraid to push the boundaries of your notebooks

Since OneNote does not limit you to the boundaries of a page, use this extra space to be creative. Capture things together in a new way. Some ideas for you to consider include the following:

- After you add notes, don't be afraid to mark them up with more details. The following screenshot is an example of this:

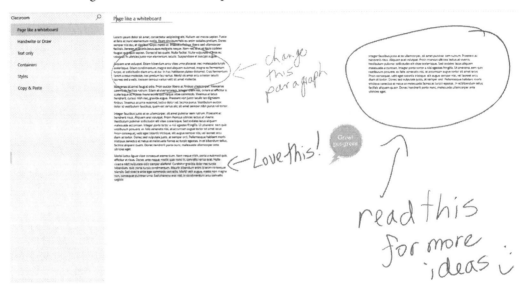

Figure 5.6 – A notebook example with text and lots of markups beside the text

- Use a page for brainstorming ideas. In *Chapter 8*, *Adding Shapes, Videos, Web Pages, and More to Your Notes*, you will learn how to draw all of these shapes onto your pages. The following screenshot shows an example of a brainstorm page:

Figure 5.7 – A notebook example for brainstorming ideas

- *Have you ever seen a wall of sticky notes?* This is popular for brainstorming ideas or planning out projects. You could create something similar within your notebook pages.

- Take advantage of the camera on your smartphone or tablet and take a picture while you are on a page of your notebook. That picture will appear immediately on the page, and you can type text beside it so that you can search for that text later on. The following screenshot is an example picture page:

Property visits Summer 2021

Giant fern growing at back of property xyz, July 1 2021.

Front of property xyz, July 1 2021.

Partial tree stump at property abc, August 1 2021.

Ferns starting to grow at property 73JK, August 15 2021.

Figure 5.8 – A notebook example for pictures and text

- OneNote can help you capture any notes, not just formal information. Every company has its standard protocols and documentation that needs to be adhered to, *but if the notebook you are using is your own, what can you add that will help you?* Aside from the standard company project numbers or codes, also take the time to go beyond this. In your notebooks, you don't have to be overly formal with everything. If you want to describe a project in your own words or add a note regarding how this project is going or how you feel about it, or anything else that is going on in your mind that is worthy of noting, note it. Unless your company tells you otherwise, use your own words so that you can find your own notes.

Be careful when using a version of OneNote that is part of a company license. If you use a notebook for jotting down personal notes, the company can take over those notes.

These ideas for your notebook pages should get you excited about everything that you can create. Start picturing or thinking about what your OneNote world will look like, and then you will be more than ready to jump in.

Just as these best practices are important for your own notebooks, it is equally important for notebooks that you share with others. You will want to lay down expectations and systems. In the next section, let's look at how to create a shared notebook system.

Creating a system of best practices for sharing

When you share a notebook with others in your organization, everyone has the same ability to add, edit, and delete. Unless your IT infrastructure changes these permissions, this is what sharing means in OneNote.

So, if everyone can update a notebook, you need to have some order and best practices in place.

One good practice for sharing a notebook that includes many people is to clearly outline the purpose of that notebook. Name one of the pages of each shared notebook as *the best practice guide* or something similar. Be consistent with the location of this best practice page and the content. This is so that everyone understands how to contribute to the notebook.

The following is a list of ideas regarding what can be included in a shared notebook best practice guide:

- *Can everyone add information at the same time?* Technically, they can, but you should decide whether this makes sense or not for your notebook's purpose.

- *How can each person sharing that notebook add information*? Outline whether each person should simply type underneath one another's text, or should they update certain pages or sections?

- Outline the best way to organize the notebook for the shared group. Describe how the organizations' sections work, including what pages to expect in each section and what to include on those pages.

- *Who are the organizers of the notebook?* These are the people tasked with the job of adding more pages and sections. Although everyone in the shared notebook will have the power to add more pages and sections, you can delegate this responsibility to a select few. You can further describe why someone would add a new page or a new section, and outline the criteria for doing this (unless it is obvious).

In a shared notebook, it is a good idea to have saved templates for the pages so that page creation is not only fast but also consistent. In these page templates, you can outline what is to go on the page and where it is to be entered, such as a form or a fill-in-the-blank system.

Color coding your pages could also work well when sharing with others. This way, you can easily verify whether other members are on the correct page of the notebook. For instance, in a remote meeting, you could say *I'm not sure if you are on the same page as me; is your notebook page blue?*

Summary

In this chapter, you learned the best ways to cut, copy, and paste in OneNote so that the information you are working with lands in the right place. We discovered how pictures can be especially tricky and how we have to consider whether we want the picture alongside the text, in the same container, or outside the text container. Additionally, we explored how easy it is to cut, copy, and paste on our smartphones and tablets. With these fundamentals under our belt, we moved on to best practices. We chalked down a long list of ideas for your notebooks and best practices to consider so that you can create notebooks that work well for you. Finally, we talked about shared notebooks and the best practices to consider so that everyone benefits.

Now that you have a handle on how and what to put in your notebooks, in the next chapter, we will introduce you to categorizing and searching your notes. You will learn how to categorize with tags so that your notes stand out and can be searched easily.

6
Categorizing and Searching Notes

Let's face it – the reason you may love your paper notebook is that you have all those special markings in it, telling you what to do next. You may have created empty checkboxes as a reminder to do things that you can check off. Or maybe you've put a question mark beside something so that you can be prompted to look it up later. Super important information may have been worthy of a star in your notebook. Well, you can do all of that and more in your digital OneNote notebook with a feature called **tags**.

With tags, you have a fast and easy way to categorize your notes. In this chapter, you will learn how to set up a system of tags to mark your notebook in a way that works well with your personality and your work or home notebook needs.

In this chapter, we will cover the following topics:

- Understanding the importance of tags in OneNote
- Using tags, creating tags, and tag shortcuts
- Working with tags – finding them, removing them, and completing them
- Searching for notes in OneNote
- Accessing your recent notes quickly

Let's start by understanding what tags are and how important they are to your notebook structure.

Understanding the importance of tags in OneNote

Tags in OneNote are a great way to mark up your notes so that they stand out visually on the page. It is this feature that makes OneNote a better choice than using Microsoft Word or notes on your smartphone. A tag is either a symbol that is placed by your information in OneNote or a color highlight that's placed on top of the text. Using tags, you can easily create checklists and highlight information in many ways, making it easier to search for it when necessary.

Not only does OneNote provide several tags for you to use, but you can also create some yourself.

Let's look at using the available tags and creating some tags.

Using tags, creating tags, and tag shortcuts

OneNote gives us a list of tags that represent popular symbols or methods of highlighting text just as if you were using paper.

The tags that are provided by OneNote are shown in the following screenshot:

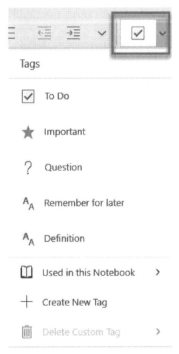

Figure 6.1 – Drop-down list of tags on the Home toolbar

The drop-down list for **Tags** is available from the **Home** toolbar. These tags are either symbol tags or highlight tags. The symbol tag will create a symbol or icon beside your information; it is the symbol that is shown in the menu in the preceding screenshot. The highlight tags will apply a color highlight to your text.

You can apply tags to any information on your page. The exception to this is the highlight tags, which only work with text. Usually, you apply the tag after you have created the information in OneNote. However, the **To Do** tag is an example of a tag that you may want to create before you start typing.

Let's look at some examples of how each of the tags listed in the preceding screenshot can be used in your notebook. Because the **To Do** tag is listed first, we will start with the following example:

This week's priorities
Create agenda for next week's meeting
Prepare presentation for client abc
Send notes to Joe
Call Mary about the proposal

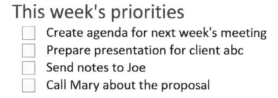

Figure 6.2 – Example of using To Do tags as a to-do list

As we can see, **To Do** tags can be used to create a to-do list. You could create to-do lists in one or more of your notebooks so that they are grouped within that notebook or section topic.

The **To Do** tag can also be applied to any text on an existing page of notes so that you can easily find what you have to do (as it is mentioned in that text), as follows:

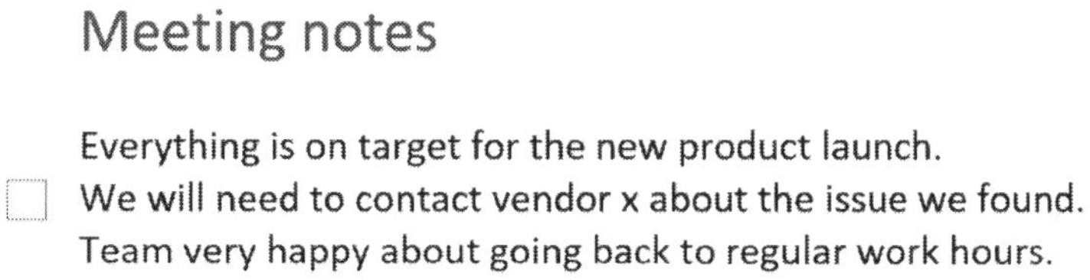

Meeting notes
Everything is on target for the new product launch.
We will need to contact vendor x about the issue we found.
Team very happy about going back to regular work hours.

Figure 6.3 – Example of using the To Do tag within our page notes

In addition to the **To Do** tag, we have several other useful tags that we can use in our notes. Let's look at a few more of these now:

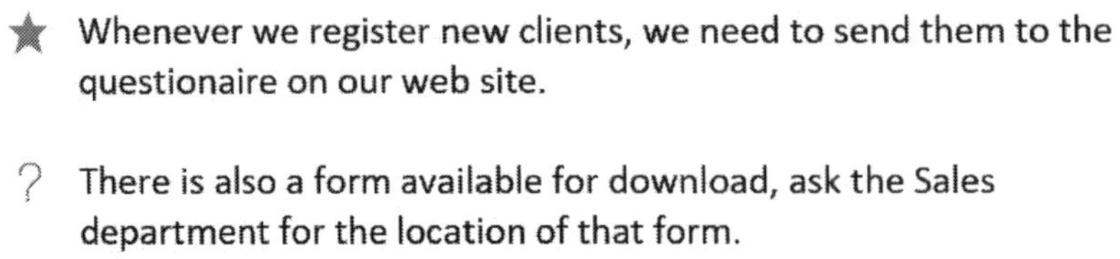

★ Whenever we register new clients, we need to send them to the questionaire on our web site.

? There is also a form available for download, ask the Sales department for the location of that form.

Figure 6.4 – Examples of an Important tag and a Question tag

In the preceding screenshot, the **Important** tag is shown as a star, while the **Question** tag is shown as a question mark.

Now, let's look at the tags that highlight your text:

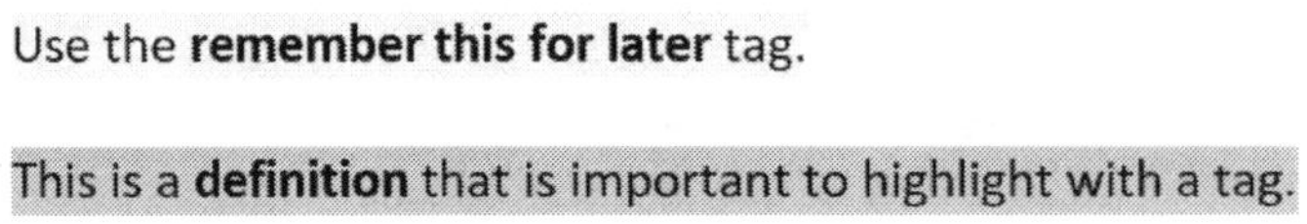

Use the **remember this for later** tag.

This is a **definition** that is important to highlight with a tag.

Figure 6.5 – Example of a Remember this for later tag and a Definition tag

The tags in the preceding screenshot are extra special because when they're applied, they highlight the relevant text and also the entire paragraph of text.

Now that you know what tags look like, let's learn how to apply them to notebook pages.

Applying tags to your information in OneNote

Applying tags to your information in OneNote is very easy. Follow these steps:

1. Start by clicking anywhere on the line of text where you want to apply the tag.
2. From the **Home** toolbar, click on the arrow beside the **To Do** tag icon.
3. Click on any of the tags listed in the drop-down menu, as shown in *Figure 6.1*.
4. Your information will change so that the tag is on the left (if it is a symbol) or the text is highlighted if you choose either of the highlighting tags.

You can pick more than one tag to apply to the same information if you wish.

The tags list is not that long, so you may want to create some tags yourself. We'll do that next.

Creating tags in OneNote

Besides the tags provided by OneNote, you may want to create some tags. Think of it as a personal symbol so that you can mark something and then easily notice it as you skim the page.

Your tags could center around projects or work you are currently undertaking. To get you inspired, here is a small list of ideas for tags:

- Ask the boss (you can use the boss's name)
- Delegate to my staff (you may have more than one of these, so you can specify different people for delegation)
- ABC Project task
- An idea for a book (or event or anything you are constantly thinking about that needs fresh ideas)
- Discuss at the staff meeting
- Buy or purchase later
- Post on social media

Remember that tags are searchable, so this will let you bring all the notes that have the same tag together. For example, if you use the **Discuss at the staff meeting** tag, then before the staff meeting, you can search for this tag, and it will find all occurrences of it throughout your pages, sections, and notebooks.

Now, let's learn how to create a tag.

Creating a tag

Follow these steps to create a tag:

1. From the **Home** toolbar, click on the arrow beside the **To Do** tag icon.
2. Click on **Create New Tag** from the drop-down menu.

3. You will be prompted for a **tag name**. Type your tag name in the box provided:

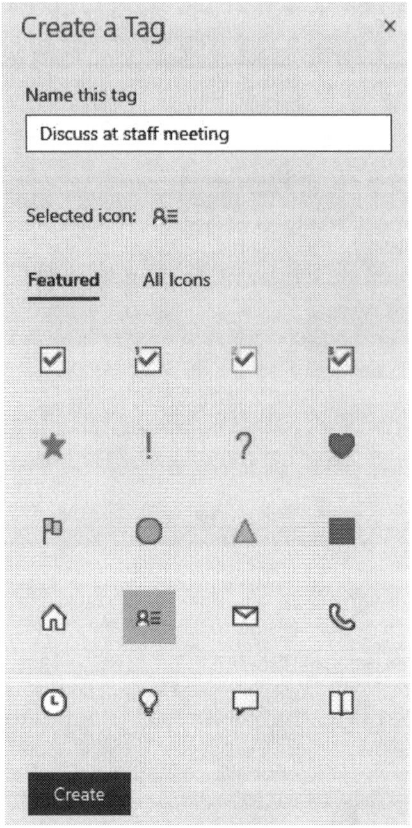

Figure 6.6 – The Create a Tag dialog box

4. As shown in the preceding screenshot, you can pick an icon or symbol for a tag from the **Featured** list. Alternatively, you can click on **All Icons** and choose from a larger list.

5. Once you have chosen your icon, click on the **Create** button.

6. Go back to the **Tag** drop-down menu and notice your new tag name under the default tag names. As you create more tags, you will see a scrollbar appear on this drop-down menu, so remember to use that as you expand your tags.

7. Follow the steps provided in the *Applying tags to your information in OneNote* section so that you can use your new tag on notes or any other information on the page.

When you're working with tags, there are some shortcuts that you can take advantage of. Let's check them out next.

Tag shortcuts

Over time, you may find yourself using tags quite often, so rather than going to the menu to select a tag, you can memorize the shortcut.

All the tag shortcuts use the *Ctrl* key on your keyboard and a number that represents where the tag is in the drop-down list. The following table shows some examples of the available tag shortcuts:

Tag Name	Shortcut Key
To Do	*Ctrl + 1*
Important	*Ctrl + 2*
Question	*Ctrl + 3*
Remember for later	*Ctrl + 4*
Definition	*Ctrl + 5*

Table 6.1 – Shortcuts for tags

So, in the future, if you want to show a **To Do** tag beside your text, simply press *Ctrl + 1*. Similarly, use the appropriate shortcut combination for the other tags and before you know it, you will have it memorized.

You can also use shortcuts for tags you create. Let's find out how.

Shortcuts for tags you create

Each time you create a new tag, it will appear in the menu. It will appear in the menu after the default tags and in the order that you added it.

Let's say that the first tag you added was the **Discuss at the staff meeting** tag. It will be placed under the **Definition** tag and the shortcut will be numbered accordingly. If you create a tag for **Ask the Boss**, then that tag will be next in the menu. The following table shows how the shortcut keys will be assigned to your new tags:

Tag Name You Created	Shortcut Key
Discuss at the staff meeting	*Ctrl + 6*
Ask the Boss	*Ctrl + 7*

Table 6.2 – Shortcuts for tags you created

This is a pretty easy system. Keep your favorite tags near the top so that it's easy to see them in the menu and easy to remember the shortcut associated with them.

Unfortunately, the shortcut keys only work until *Ctrl + 9*, since *Ctrl + 10* would appear as *Ctrl + 1*.

Now, let's take a closer look at how we can work with these tags.

Working with tags – finding them, removing them, and completing them

Once you have your tags in place, you may want to make changes to them. In this section, we'll learn how to change tags, find tags, and complete tags (that need to be completed).

Working with checkbox tags

Starting with the tags that tell us about the tasks that need to be completed, we have the **To Do** tag, which is a checkbox that's part of the default tags in your **Tag** drop-down list. When you create a tag, you can also create a checkbox tag, just like the **To Do** tag check box.

And just like you would expect with any checkbox, you can checkmark the box when you finish the task. Here are some details about how the checkbox works:

- If you have a checkbox tag, then to checkmark the box, simply click on the box.

- To clear the checkmark from the box, click inside the box once more.

- From the **Home** toolbar, you can click directly on the **To Do** tag. You do not need to use the arrow and drop-down menu to choose the **To Do** tag. Click directly on the **To Do** tag, which is the checkbox icon, as shown here:

Figure 6.7 – The To Do tag on the Home toolbar

- If you click on the **To Do** tag from the **Home** toolbar a second time, a checkmark will be placed in the box. Alternatively, you can click inside the box.

Removing a tag may be necessary at times, so let's learn how to do that.

Removing a tag

If you no longer need a tag beside your information, you can remove it.

To remove a tag, click on the line where the tag appears and do one of the following things:

- For a checkbox tag, if the box is checked, click on the appropriate checkbox tag from the tag drop-down menu. Alternatively, use the shortcut key that's been assigned to that tag.

  For example, to remove the **To Do** tag when it has a checkmark in the box, press *Ctrl + 1*.

- For a checkbox tag, if the box is not checked, check the box, then click on the appropriate checkbox tag from the tag drop-down menu. Alternatively, use the shortcut key that's been assigned to that tag.

  For example, to remove the **To Do** tag when there is no checkmark in the box, press *Ctrl + 1* twice.

- All other kinds of tags can be removed by clicking on that tag a second time from the tag drop-down menu. Alternatively, use the shortcut key that's been assigned to that tag a second time.

  For example, to remove the **Important** tag with a shortcut key, press *Ctrl + 2*.

- *Ctrl + 0* (zero) removes all the tags from the current paragraph or object. For example, if you have the **To Do** tag on a line and you don't want it there anymore, you can press *Ctrl + 0*. Alternatively, if you added a checkbox tag and a star tag beside your text and didn't want either tag anymore, *Ctrl + 0* would make both tags disappear.

If you wish to keep your tags, it can be beneficial to search for them. Let's learn how to find them.

Finding your tags

Finding your tags or searching for tags is one of the biggest advantages of creating tags in the first place. By tagging your notes, you are showing that you want to go back to some of the information on your pages. These tags do not have to be on the same page, in the same section, or even in the same notebook. You can search for tags no matter where they are placed.

You can search using the magnifying glass at the top left-hand side of your screen. The location may vary slightly, based on the device you are using. The following screenshot shows an example of where the search icon could be on your screen:

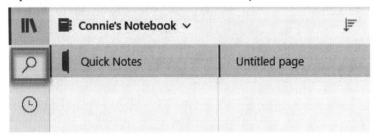

Figure 6.8 – Magnifying glass for searching

On smartphones, the search icon (the magnifying glass) will be at the bottom of the screen.

To search for tags, follow these steps:

1.   Click on the magnifying glass icon:

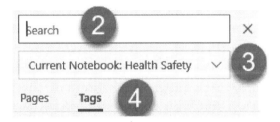

Figure 6.9 – Search box choices

2.   Type the name of the tag in the search box, as shown in the preceding screenshot. If you are unsure of the name of your tag, go to the **Tag** drop-down menu via the **Home** toolbar to find the name of the tag listed beside the symbol of the tag.

3.   Choose where you are searching for the tag. Your choices are as follows:

    - **All Notebooks**

    - **Current Notebook**: Notebook name shown

    - **Current Section**: Section name shown

    - **Current Page**: Page name shown

4.   Click on **Tags** instead of **Pages**.

5.   Select any page listed to see where your tag is located on that page.

The following screenshot shows what this search looks like, along with the results:

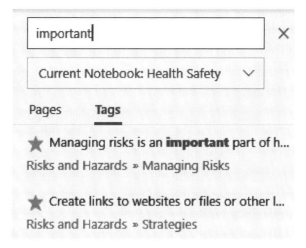

Figure 6.10 – Searching for important tags

In the preceding screenshot, we are searching for **important** tags. That search is looking in **Current Notebook: Health Safety** and the search is based on **Tags**. Two examples of important tags are shown here.

Clicking on a search result will take you to the exact page, section, and notebook that the result came from.

Instead of using the search magnifying glass icon, you can use the *Ctrl + F* shortcut to find information on the current page. If you want to search everywhere, you can use *Ctrl + E*.

In addition to searching for tags in your notebooks, you will most likely want to search for words or phrases. Let's take a look.

Searching for notes in OneNote

Just like you can search for tags on your pages, you can find any text that you entered. As you start to accumulate a lot of notes in your notebooks, searching for text becomes very helpful. Let's say that you know you wrote a note on that topic somewhere, but you just can't remember where to find it. To overcome this, you can search the notebooks on your computer, smartphone, or tablet.

Follow these steps to search for text or words in your notes:

1. Click on the search icon (that is, the magnifying glass).
2. Type one or multiple words into the search box.

3. Choose where you are searching for the word(s). Your choices are as follows:

    - **All Notebooks**
    - **Current Notebook**: Notebook name shown
    - **Current Section**: Section name shown
    - **Current Page**: Page name shown

4. Click on **Pages** to see the word(s) that was found on your notebook pages.

5. Select any page listed to see where on the page your word(s) has been found. The word will be highlighted.

Several search parameters are available that you can use to make your search more general or precise. Each search will find any page that contains the word (or words) you're searching for in the body or title of the page. When you're searching for one word, the search results can be a full match to that one word or a partial match to that one word.

The following table shows some examples of searches:

Example in Search Box	Result
training	training. trainings.
train	train. training. trainings.
safety training	Will find any page that contains both of these words in the body of the page or the title. These words do not need to be side by side; they can be anywhere in the text.
"safety training"	When you use double quotes around your words, you are asking for an exact match of whatever words are together in the quotation marks.

Table 6.3 – Search examples

Let's look at a few of these examples in OneNote:

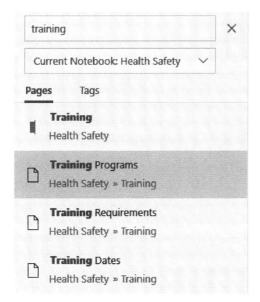

Figure 6.11 – Searching for the word "training" in the current notebook

In the preceding screenshot, the search in the current notebook finds four pages that contain the word training. Notice that the visible page shows the word **Training** in both the body and title of the page since both instances are highlighted.

Let's look at what happens when you search for two words:

Figure 6.12 – Searching for two words in the current notebook

The two words that are being searched for are not necessarily next to each other, as shown in the preceding screenshot.

If we had double quotes around these two words, then we would only get results showing that had both words together.

In addition to searching for words or tags that you have placed in your notes, you may just want to find the notes you've worked on recently. Let's look at this next.

Accessing your recent notes quickly

You can always find out what you worked on last with the **Recent Notes** feature that's available in OneNote.

The Recent Notes feature is updated with any notes that you edit.

Editing includes doing the following:

- Formatting of any kind, such as bold, highlighting, and using bullets
- Adding text or titles
- Changing text, objects, or anything in any container within a page
- Deleting anything from a page

If you click on a page, it will not be considered one of your **Recent Notes**:

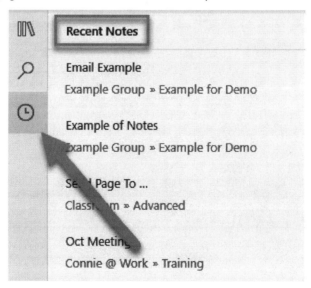

Figure 6.13 – The Recent Notes area in OneNote

Depending on your device, the **Recent Notes** area can be found by clicking on the clock icon, as shown by the arrow in the preceding screenshot. On your tablet or smartphone, the **Recent Notes** area can be found at the top of the Notebooks listing.

The order of the pages shown in **Recent Notes** is from the newest to the oldest. Click on any page listed to open that page and work on it.

Summary

In this chapter, you learned how to categorize your notes with tags and search for those tags with ease. You also learned how to search for any text that you have entered on a notebook page and how to easily get back to your recent notes.

With tags, you have an extra layer of organization available to you. You can create a list of to-dos on your notebook pages and keep track of what has been completed and what is left to do. Once you have written your notes, any tags or questions that you have marked as important will be easy to spot or search for. And if the appropriate tag isn't there, you can create it – the sky is the limit! You decide what other symbols, tags, or markings will be helpful for you to quickly revisit your notes. Another time-saver you learned about is the shortcut keys that are attached to tags, such as *Ctrl + 1* for the **To Do** tag.

All of this will help you set up a notebook that you can rely on and trust to get you to the information that is on your mind.

In the next chapter, you will go one step further in terms of organizing your pages, sections, and notebooks by learning how to color-code, sort, rename, and close or delete pages, sections, and notebooks.

All of this will help make navigating your notebooks even easier!

7
Organizing and Easily Working with Pages, Sections, and Notebooks

We all need to put all our notes in better order, don't we? In this chapter, you will find out how to work with your notebooks, sections, and pages to make them more organized and easier to spot. You can organize them alphabetically, or in any order that makes sense to you. You can color-code the notebooks and sections so that similar topics or themes are easier to spot. Because you can work on your notebooks on any device, it is possible that you only open up certain notebooks on certain devices.

In this chapter, we will cover the following:

- Moving, copying, renaming, or deleting a section or page
- Creating page or section groups
- Accessing your notebooks

- Password protection
- Working with colors and sorting within OneNote notebooks, sections, and pages
- Getting to a page, section, or notebook without opening OneNote first

Let's work on moving, copying, renaming, or deleting a section or page first.

Moving, copying, renaming, or deleting a section or page

What seems like a good idea for a section or page, in the beginning, could end up not being so after you have added many months' worth of notes. You are allowed to change your mind. OneNote has you covered.

Let's start by finding out how to change the sections in your notebook.

Changing the sections in your notebook

With a notebook, you can have multiple sections, and your sections can have multiple pages. You can work with these sections and pages in many ways. Let's start by exploring some of the things we can do with your notebook sections.

If you right-click on a section, you will see the following menu:

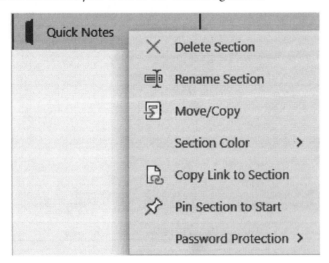

Figure 7.1 – Right-click menu of a section

We'll look at a few of the menu options in the upcoming sub-sections.

Renaming a section

If you don't like the name of your section, it is super easy to rename that section. Maybe you want to rename the section because you changed your mind on what it should be called. Or, maybe the pages in that section have evolved differently than you first imagined, so the section should be renamed accordingly. Whatever the reason, no problem, just go ahead and follow these steps to rename your section:

1. Right-click on the section that you want to rename.

2. Choose **Rename Section**.

3. Type in a new name.

This new section name will appear in place of the previous name, and if you have this notebook on other devices, the new section name will appear there as well.

Apart from renaming a section, you can also choose to move or copy a section.

Moving or copying a section

When you right-click on a section, another option you have is to move or copy a section into another notebook.

As your notebooks grow in size, you may notice that some sections of your notebook are better suited for a new notebook, so a move is needed. Moving a section from one notebook to another means you are moving all the pages in that section to a new notebook location. Let's look at the steps for moving a section:

1. Right-click on the section that you want to move.

2. From the menu, choose **Move/Copy**. A list of your current notebooks and any grouped sections will show on your screen.

3. Click on the appropriate notebook that you wish your section to move to. You could also choose to move your section into a grouped section that is listed.

4. Then, click on the **Move** button.

Your section is now moved to a new location. Follow the same steps to copy a notebook, instead click on the **Copy** button.

If you need to copy a section, then all the pages of that section will be copied to another notebook of your choosing. For instance, if you have several project notebooks and have created a **Project Guidelines** section in one notebook, you can save time by copying that section to your other project notebooks. A benefit of copying a section is that it copies all the pages within that section at the same time.

Deleting a section

When you delete a section, all the pages in that section will be deleted as well. These pages can be recovered after they have been deleted.

Right-click on the section you want to delete and choose **Delete Section**.

For instructions on how to recover a deleted section or page, refer to *Chapter 2, Screen Layout and Toolbars*. The **View** toolbar gives you access to these deleted notes.

Now that you've made some changes to the sections of your notebook, let's move on to the pages.

Changing the pages of your notebook

Pages are organized into sections of your notebooks. From time to time, you may want to move, copy, or delete a page from a section.

When you right-click on a page, you see many options for how you can change your page. See the following figure for the page's right-click menu:

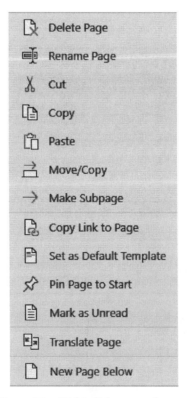

Figure 7.2 – Right-click menu of a page

First, let's look at how to move a page.

Moving a page

When you choose to move a page, you can move that page to a different section in the same notebook, or to a section of a different notebook. Follow these steps to move a page:

1. Right-click on the page that you want to move.

2. Choose **Move/Copy**.

3. Choose a different section, or choose a different notebook and section within that notebook.

4. Click on the **Move** button.

Rather than moving a page, you may just want to copy that page. Let's look at this next.

Copying a page

You can copy a page from a section of your notebook to another section in the same notebook. Or, you could choose to copy a page into a section of a completely different notebook.

Follow the same steps as listed in the previous section, except you will now choose the **Copy** button as the last step.

As your notebooks grow and you need better organization, take advantage of grouping sections or pages. Let's review how to do this next.

Creating page or section groups

A major strength of OneNote is its ability to help you stay organized. An example of this is grouping pages or sections, which provides another way to create order within your notebooks. Let's start with **section groups**.

Creating a section group

As you start to create sections within your notebook, you might want to organize sections together that are similar in topic or theme. Rather than having a long list of sections that you need to scroll through to find the one you want, create groupings.

The following figure is an example of how a section group can look:

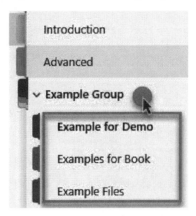

Figure 7.3 – Section group called Example Group

To create a section group, follow these steps:

1. Right-click beside the **+ Section** button at the bottom of the section column.

2. Choose **New Section Group**.

3. Enter a name for that section group.

4. Drag existing sections into this group. Or, if you are on this section group and choose **Add Section**, the new section will be added to the group.

In addition to the section groups, you have page groups to discover. Let's go there next.

Grouping pages together

Just as with sections, when you accumulate a lot of pages and need to improve the organization, then grouping your pages can help.

This grouping happens when you make an existing page a subpage of the page above.

The following figure shows an example of pages and subpages in the **Meetings** section of the **Health Safety** notebook:

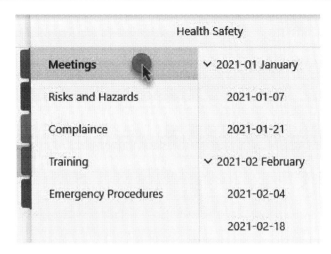

Figure 7.4 – Pages and subpages for January and February meetings

To create a **subpage**, follow these steps:

1. Right-click on a page that you wish to have listed underneath another page.

2. Choose **Make Subpage**. It will indent that page.

3. If you do not want that page to be a subpage anymore, then you can right-click on that page and choose **Promote Page**. Be careful not to promote a page that has a subpage under it. For example, in *Figure 7.4*, if you promote **2021-01-07**, then the page underneath for **2021-01-21** will become a subpage of that page. To ensure that this mistake does not happen, drag the subpage to the bottom of the subpages listed, then promote that page.

4. Once you have subpages, you can drag other pages into the subpage list.

With subpages, you can click on the arrow beside the top page so that you do not have to view the subpage list. In other words, you can collapse or expand the subpage groupings. The **Collapse** and **Expand** options are also available from the right-click menu.

There is so much potential with your notebooks, and many opportunities to change them as you go, to make them better.

When working with OneNote on any of your devices, it is important that you have the right notebooks available to you. Let's look at accessing your notebooks next, so you know how to have the right notebooks showing on your different devices.

Accessing your notebooks

Once you start creating notebooks and populating them, you may want to access those notebooks and all that information on other devices. You can open notebooks on other devices. When we refer to other devices, we are talking about how you can work with OneNote on not only your computer but also your smartphone or tablet. Opening a notebook in OneNote on another device means that OneNote will sync that notebook with that device. It is like adding an email account to your mail software, which will allow you to see these emails from that device every time you need to. In general, there is no need to close a notebook unless you are permanently done with it, or if you need space on your device.

When you use OneNote on these other devices, you will need to also open up the notebooks you want to work with on those devices. For example, if you create three new notebooks from your desktop computer that are stored in the cloud, then you can access those notebooks from that day forward on that desktop computer. When you go to OneNote on your smartphone, those three new notebooks will not be opened automatically. On the smartphone, you will need to choose which notebooks you want to see by choosing what notebooks to open. This example would apply to any tablets or other devices you want to use for OneNote.

Let's look at how we open a notebook on a different device.

Opening a notebook on another device

If you did not create the notebook from the device you are using to access OneNote, then you will need to open the notebook.

The steps to open a notebook are as follows:

1. Click on the arrow beside your current notebook, so that you can see the full list of notebooks currently opened on that device.

2. At the bottom of this list of notebooks is the **More Notebooks...** option, as shown in the following figure. Click on it:

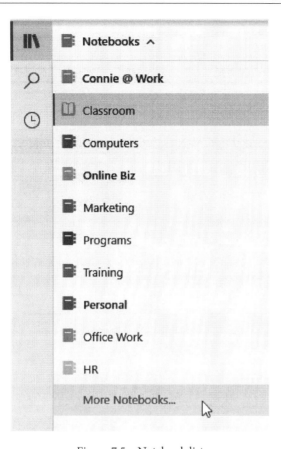

Figure 7.5 – Notebook list

3. When you choose **More Notebooks...**, you will see a list of notebooks available to you. You can use the search box to find the notebook name, or you can look through the list presented. The notebooks that you see here are based on the Microsoft account that you are logged into. If you have more than one Microsoft account, you can choose **Add Account** so that you can see notebooks that you have saved under a different Microsoft account. Once you find the notebook you want, checkmark the box beside that notebook and click on the **Open** button.

Now you can work on that notebook. Any changes you make will be reflected in whichever other location that notebook is open.

When you start to work frequently with OneNote on your different devices, you might find that you do not need all your notebooks open all the time, on all devices. So, you have the option of closing a notebook.

Let's look at how to close a notebook next.

Closing a notebook

When you close a notebook, you are not deleting that notebook, you are simply choosing not to look at that notebook on your device.

Perhaps you are using OneNote for work and personal information. In the beginning, you may have both kinds of notebooks open on your smartphone. Over time, you may decide that you only need to see personal notebooks on your smartphone. If that is the case, then you can close all the work-related notebooks on your smartphone.

Here are the steps to close a notebook:

1. Click on the arrow beside your current notebook, so that you can see the full list of notebooks available to you on that device.

2. Right-click on the notebook you want to close. Refer to the following figure for the notebook's right-click menu:

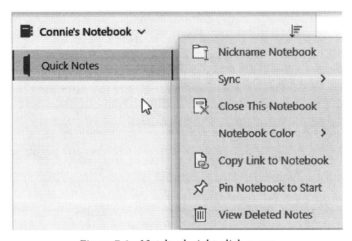

Figure 7.6 – Notebook right-click menu

3. Choose the **Close This Notebook** option from the right-click menu.

You will no longer see that notebook name in your notebook list. If you had that notebook open previously, you will be moved down in the notebook list and see the next notebook open now.

If you change your mind about having that notebook closed, you can always open the notebook again using the instructions from the *Opening a notebook on another device* section.

Now that you have learned how to open and close notebooks, let's look at your options for password protection.

Password protection

Password protection works only on sections within a notebook. You cannot password-protect an entire notebook or page. So, if you are sharing a notebook with others, you could password-protect a section of a notebook. Then, you could share the password with a limited number of people that share the notebook. This way you are creating a private area for sensitive information.

> **Important Note**
> Note that there is no way to recover a section if you forget the password.
> There is no *forgot password* functionality, so ensure you note the password
> in a secure place.

The instructions for password-protecting a section are as follows:

1. Right-click on the section that you wish to password-protect.

2. Choose **Password Protection** from the menu that appears. See the following figure for an example of how to password-protect the **Performance Management** section of the **HR** notebook:

Figure 7.7 – Password protection for a section of your notebook

3. Once you have the section password-protected, you will see a lock beside the section name. After you type in the password, the lock icon will show as unlocked. See the following figure for an example of the **Performance Management** section unlocked:

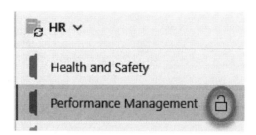

Figure 7.8 – Section unlocked

This section will remain unlocked until you close OneNote, or after a while if you are not viewing the section. If you want to lock this section while you are still in OneNote, then right-click again on the section, choose **Password Protection**, then choose **Lock Section**. See the example in the following figure for the **Password Protection** submenu:

Figure 7.9 – Use the Password Protection submenu to lock a section again

Notice in *Figure 7.9* that you have more options under **Password Protection**. You can change the password or remove the password from a section. **Lock All Protected Sections** is also a good shortcut if you opened more than one locked section in your notebook(s).

In addition to all these changes that we can do to our notebooks, sections, and pages, we have options for coloring! Let's look at how colorful your notebooks can be, next.

Working with colors and sorting within OneNote notebooks, sections, and pages

There are many opportunities to add color to your notebooks in OneNote. This color-coding can help in organizing and accessing your information faster. For instance, you could color a few of your notebooks different shades of green or the same green color so that you know they are all related. This same idea can work for coloring sections as well.

Another way to get to your information faster is sorting. Learn how you can sort your notebooks, your sections, and your pages. You will discover the automatic sorting options that are available to you, as well as the manual sorting that you can do.

Let's start with colors, then we'll move on to sorting.

Colors within OneNote

Within OneNote, colored icons are automatically attached to your notebooks and sections. When you first create a notebook, you can choose a color for the notebook icon. If you change your mind on that color, you can change the color. When you create a new section, a color is assigned for that section. This section's color can also be changed.

Let's start by changing the color of the icon beside one of your notebook names.

From a computer, the steps to change the color of the notebook icon are as follows:

1. Click on the arrow beside your current notebook, so that you can see the full list of notebooks available to you on that device.

2. Right-click on the notebook that you want to color.

3. Choose **Notebook Color** from the menu. Select a color that you like from the color palette.

This change of color will not only show on your computer but on any device that lists this notebook.

The next icon to change colors is the section tab icon that is beside the section name of your notebook.

When you create a section, the section tab is colored. This section tab color may not be what you prefer so you can go ahead and change it.

From a computer, the steps for changing the color of the section tab are as follows:

1. Right-click on the section that you want to change the tab color for.

2. Choose **Section Colour** from the menu. Select a color from the color palette. See the following figure for an example of section colors available when changing a section tab color:

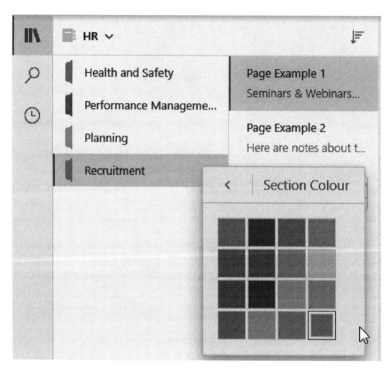

Figure 7.10 – Section color choices available for a section tab

There are 16 colors available to you, so if you run out of colors, don't be afraid to use the same color twice. In fact, using the same color more than once could help you highlight similar sections.

Editing your colors and location of notebooks on a smartphone or tablet

While using your smartphone or tablet, you may choose to change the color of a notebook or section. The steps for doing this are a bit different from those steps you followed on the computer.

Let's look at coloring while on a smartphone or tablet. And let's go even further and see our options for sorting or rearranging notebooks, sections, and pages.

The steps for editing your notebook color or location on your smartphone or tablet are as follows:

1. Hold down on any notebook name to activate editing for a notebook of your choice in the list. The following figure shows what your notebook list will look like once you have activated this editing:

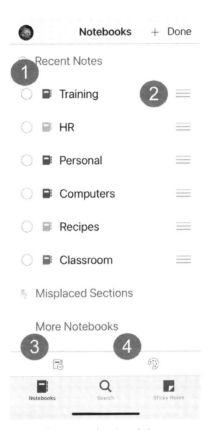

Figure 7.11 – Editing notebooks while on a smartphone

Referring to the preceding figure, there are several options available to you. The options are as follows:

1. Select any of the notebooks by selecting the radio button beside the notebook name. Once you select a notebook, items **2** to **4** are your choices.

2. With the three horizontal lines on the right side, if you select, hold, and move these lines, this will let you move the notebook somewhere else in the list. If you move the notebook on your smartphone, this will not affect the order of the notebooks on any other device you use that notebook on.

3. The icon at the bottom with the notebook and a *minus* sign is your way of closing a notebook. If you no longer want to have a notebook open on your smartphone or tablet, use this icon to close that notebook.

4. This is the color palette available for your notebook color. Choose this color palette to change the color of your notebook icon.

In addition to coloring your notebooks, you can color the sections of your notebooks while using your smartphone or tablet.

Editing the color of your notebook sections from your smartphone or tablet

If you want to change the color of your section tabs while you are on your smartphone or tablet, simply follow these steps:

1. Hold down on the section name.

2. Look at the bottom of that column and notice the pencil. Once you choose the pencil, you will have two options, **Rename** or **Change Section Color**. Choose **Change Section Color** and pick from the color palette available.

3. Choose **Done** in the top right (above the pages column) when you are done editing the sections of your notebook.

Just as colors can help you personalize your notebooks and sections, sorting can be a huge advantage to you as well. Let's look at sorting next.

Sorting sections and pages

As you accumulate notebooks, sections, and pages, you will see the need to sort them. When you add a new notebook, section, or page, each of these things goes to the bottom of the list. Unfortunately, there is no automatic sorting happening (within the notebook or section list), but you can use this to your advantage. You can sort based on priority or simply arrange your information in an order that is logical for you. Sort in any way you choose; it is up to you. Now, that is an advantage.

So, let's start with how to manually sort.

Manual sorting in OneNote on a computer

While using OneNote on your computer, you can simply click and drag to sort your information. For instance, you can click and drag your notebooks in whichever order you choose, you can click and drag your sections into an order of your choice, and lastly, you can click and drag your pages into any order that makes sense to you.

Do this sorting as often as you need to. As your notebooks grow and evolve, keep making them better and keep them in order with your sorting.

This sorting is just slightly different on a smartphone or tablet.

Manual sorting in OneNote on a smartphone or tablet

You can sort your notebooks, sections, or pages from a smartphone or tablet. Follow these steps to do manual sorting:

1. Select any notebook, section, or page by pressing down on the name of that notebook, section, or page.
2. Notice the three horizontal lines on the right side of your selection. Hold and move these lines; this will let you move the notebook, section, or page (whichever you choose) somewhere else in the list.

Rather than manual sorting, you can use a menu for sorting on some of your devices. Let's look at this menu next.

Sorting from the menu

Rather than manually sorting every page of a notebook section, you could use a menu to sort them quickly. The menu offers an alphabetical sort order and a date sort order. This menu is only available for sorting pages; there is no sorting menu for sections or notebooks.

This sorting menu is available to you while you are on your computer, or a smartphone or tablet. Let's start by looking at the menu options on Microsoft Surface.

While you are in one of the sections of your notebook, notice above the page list there is an arrow with lines, as shown in the following figure:

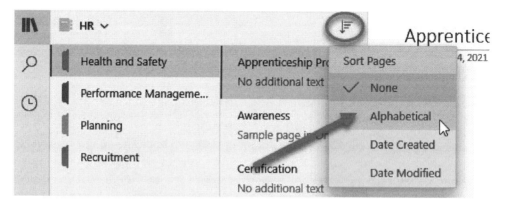

Figure 7.12 – Menu for sorting your notebook sections

This arrow icon is what you can choose to sort your pages. You have three choices for sort order that are displayed in *Figure 7.12*.

You can also sort pages in OneNote from your smartphone or tablet, using the three-lined menu above your pages list to access the sorting option.

Now that you have what you need to get your notebooks, sections, and pages in order, let's go on to a great shortcut that lets you access them instantly.

Getting to a page, section, or notebook without opening OneNote first

If you want to save time getting into your favorite notebook, section, or page, you can simply pin it to your **Windows Start** menu. So, rather than opening up OneNote and then maneuvering to that notebook, section, or page, you click on that notebook, section, or page from the **Start** menu.

See *Figure 7.13* for an example of three different notebooks pinned to the **Start** menu. Each of these notebooks shows up as a separate tile in your **Start** menu. You can click on the tile for the **Classroom** notebook, the **Marketing** notebook, or the **Personal** notebook, and then instantly access that notebook as shown here:

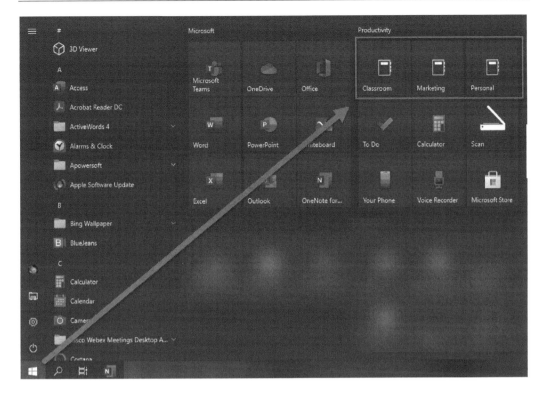

Figure 7.13 – Start menu with tiles for different notebooks in OneNote

Although the tiles shown in the preceding figure are for notebooks, you could also have tiles that instantly take you to a section or page in one of your notebooks.

To pin a notebook, a section, or a page to the Windows **Start** menu, do the following steps:

1. Right-click on the notebook that you want to see in your **Start** menu.

2. Then, from the menu, choose **Pin to Start**.

If you want to pin a section, then follow the same steps by right-clicking on the section you want to pin. And if you want to see a page in your **Start** menu, follow the same steps by right-clicking on the page you want to pin.

Your Windows **Start** menu has lots of room for tiles, so don't be shy about pinning as many notebooks, sections, or pages as you need. This way, you can get started right away within your favorite location of OneNote.

Summary

In this chapter, you learned how to make some significant changes to your notebooks, the sections in those notebooks, and even the pages within the sections. You now know that you can move a page to a different section, or even a different notebook altogether if you want to. You know how to move an entire section, which means you are moving lots of pages at once (that belong to that section). If you need to copy information, you learned how to copy a single page or an entire section so that you can save some typing and create some consistency within your notebooks. You learned how easy it is to rename a notebook, a section, or a page. Things change, and being able to reflect those changes with proper naming or color-coding is important. Sometimes things change and you no longer need a page or section, so you can delete it.

You discovered how to open your notebooks on other devices so that you could access the same information in multiple places (such as your smartphone or tablet). You also saw that closing a notebook is an option that may be necessary if you do not need to see it in the list on a particular device anymore.

We also explored color and you saw how you could use color for your notebook icons and your section tabs. Be creative, and use this color to help you group things or to give extra meaning to information.

And finally, you learned a great shortcut with your Windows **Start** menu so that you can open a page, section, or notebook without even having OneNote open first.

Now that you are more comfortable with editing your notebooks, sections, and pages, let's move on to add more exciting information to those pages. In the next chapter, you will be learning all about adding shapes, videos, web pages, and more to your notes.

Section 3:
Inserting Information and Links into Your Notebooks

Microsoft OneNote is a program like no other. It can house so much information. There is almost no limit to what you can store in your OneNote notebooks. Just as your paper notebook can get full with a lot of extra pages clipped in or sticky notes sticking out of it, so too can your OneNote notebook. A big difference with OneNote, though, is it will not look messy.

In this section, we'll learn how to do math, easily create shapes, and add media to our notebook pages. We'll discover the built-in highlighter pens and the camera, which you can use to add a picture to a page.

We'll also learn how to cross-reference any information from any notebook with the help of links. You'll also find out how to attach or link documents in your notebooks.

We'll then see how easily you can send an email or appointment from Outlook to OneNote.

This section comprises the following chapters:

- *Chapter 8, Adding Shapes, Videos, Web Pages, and More to Your Notes*
- *Chapter 9, Inserting Links and Attachments into Your Notebooks*
- *Chapter 10, Outlook and OneNote Belong Together*

8

Adding Shapes, Videos, Web Pages, and More to Your Notes

What makes OneNote so special is all of the information that you can add to your notebook pages. Your pages will come alive with shapes, colors, images, and more.

In a traditional paper notebook, it is normal to draw within your notebook pages, so you circle important information or draw arrows to stuff. This drawing feature is available in OneNote along with all kinds of other media choices that we can insert onto our pages.

In this chapter, we will cover the following topics:

- Using the Draw menu to create shapes, do math, and highlight
- Inserting tables into your notebooks
- Inserting pictures, videos, or audio clips into your notebooks

- Dictating is much better than typing!

- Referencing a website with a touch of a button

Let's get started by adding drawings onto our notebook pages.

Using the Draw menu to create shapes, do math, and highlight

The **Draw** menu has a lot of choices for us. In *Chapter 4, Entering Information into Your Notebook*, you learned how to draw freehand with fancy-colored pens. Now, we will use those same pens to help us with creating shapes, doing math, and highlighting.

Let's start by learning how to create shapes.

Creating shapes

Creating shapes in OneNote is almost instant when you use the **Draw** toolbar, as shown in the following screenshot:

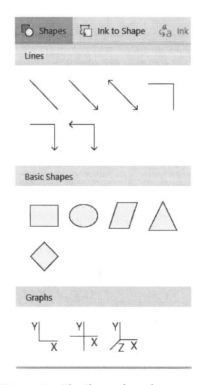

Figure 8.1 – The Shapes drop-down menu

When you choose **Shapes** from the **Draw** toolbar, you can pick one of the following:

- **Lines**
- **Basic Shapes**
- **Graphs**

Lines and basic shapes can be inserted onto your page anywhere. They can exist on their own, or they can be used with text or other information that is on the page. Let's look at the exact steps for adding a shape to your page. Our first shape example will be for adding a line.

Adding a line to a page

To add a line to a page, follow these steps:

1. Click on the **Draw** menu.
2. Choose the **Shapes** icon from the menu.
3. Choose the shape you want; for example, let's select a straight line.
4. Click once anywhere on your page. This will draw a line that is a default length, and the color will be based on whatever color pen or highlighter was used last. Please refer to the following example:

Figure 8.2 – An example of a line drawn on a page

5. While the shape is still selected, resize the shape. Move to the circular handle at either end of the line, and when you see the black plus (+) sign, as shown next, click and drag:

Figure 8.3 – An example of where to select the line for resizing

Alternatively, when drawing the line, you could have clicked and dragged the line to your desired length rather than clicking once, as indicated in *Step 4*.

> **Hint**
>
> If you are trying to draw a perfectly straight line, go to the **View** menu and choose **Rule Lines**, so you have lines on the page to use as a guide.

6. Click somewhere outside of the line to unselect the line.

Now you have a colored line on your page. Click anywhere over, under, or beside that line and add more information such as text or other shapes.

This line will remain a separate object on the page that can be moved or sized or even deleted if you choose.

Now, let's try a different choice from the **Shapes** drop-down menu. Let's add a **basic shape** to the page next.

Adding a basic shape to a page

When adding a basic shape to a page, the steps are the same as listed in the *Adding a line to a page* section. Here, the only difference is that the size of the shape you add could be based on any previous sizing you already used for that shape (somewhere else on the page or in your notebook). Let's understand this further with the following points:

- The very first time you add a basic shape, such as an oval, it has a default size when you click on that shape in the **Shapes** drop-down menu, and then you click on the page once to insert the shape.

- Then, if you change the size of that oval to be twice as large, for example, the next time you place that shape onto a page, it will be that new size. This is by using the click-once-on-the-page method.

- In essence, there is no default size for the basic shape that is saved and available in your notebooks. Your last sizing becomes the new default.

If you need to make more changes to your shape, then you will need to select the shape first. Let's discuss our options when selecting a shape.

Selecting a shape on a page

Once you have a shape on a page, you might still want to change that shape or even get rid of it altogether.

When you select a shape, you can do any of the following:

- Resize the shape.
- Change the color of the shape.
- Move the shape.
- Copy the shape.
- Delete the shape.

To select a shape, click on the shape itself. When choosing a line, this means that you are clicking directly on the line somewhere. However, with other basic shapes, you need to click on the actual border of the shape. For instance, if you have a **Rectangle** shape, do not click inside the rectangle because that will not select that shape. For the rectangle, click on any border or edge of that rectangle.

For our selection example, let's select a basic shape and change the color of that shape.

To change the color of a basic shape, follow these steps:

1. Click on one of the edges of that shape.
2. From the **Draw** toolbar, click on a colored pen.

The shape will change to that new color.

Additionally, you can change the color of a shape before inserting it on the page. To do this, simply choose a color from the pens shown on the **Draw** toolbar before inserting your shape onto the page. Be careful though, because if you choose a pen first, then draw your shape, every click you make will be creating a mark on your page from that colored pen once your shape has been drawn. So, to stop this marking, you can undo them after they occur, or simply click on the **Select Objects or Type Text** icon, as shown here:

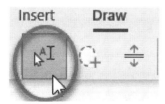

Figure 8.4 – The Select Objects or Type Text icon

One of the reasons you might create a shape on a page is because you want it to go around something that you already have on that page. However, there can be times when you create the shape first and then add the text second. Let's look at an example of typing text inside a basic shape, as follows:

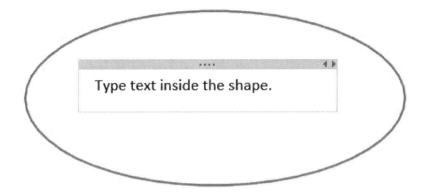

Figure 8.5 – Typing text inside a basic shape

Note that these are two different elements on your page. The text is in a container, which is one element. The basic shape, here an oval, is an object, which is another element. The reason that this is important is to show that one element is not connected to the other element. If you move or resize one of these elements, it will not move or resize the other element automatically. This might not be very convenient, so let's learn how to work with these two elements as one.

Working with multiple elements

If you want to move, copy, delete, or resize a basic shape and the contents of that shape, such as the text shown in *Figure 8.5*, then select those multiple elements first.

To select multiple items on your page, perform the following steps:

1. With your mouse, click starting from above the top edge of one corner of the shape or text. Drag your mouse to the opposite corner. Try to give yourself extra room above, below, on the left-hand side, and on the right-hand side of all the elements so that you can get everything selected. Refer to the following screenshot as an example of the selection:

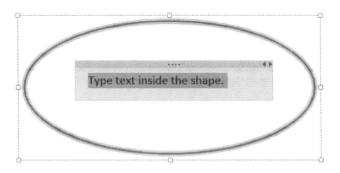

Figure 8.6 – Selecting the basic shape and text

2. In the preceding screenshot, notice that the shape is surrounded by a dashed line with handles and that the container with the text is also selected. Otherwise, you might only have the shape being selected or the text container being selected. With both selected, you can move, copy, delete or resize all elements at the same time.

In addition to drawing with **Basic Shapes** in the **Shapes** drop-down menu, you can draw freehand. And while drawing freehand, you can have OneNote fix it to one of the shapes available in the drop-down menu. Next, let's look at the **Ink to Shape** option in the menu to achieve this.

Ink to shape

Sometimes, you might prefer to draw with your pen on your tablet or straight onto your touchscreen. When doing these freehand drawings, you have the advantage of OneNote improving on those basic shapes. To do this, you will have to select **Ink to Shape** from the **Draw** menu. Let's review the steps here:

1. From the **Draw** menu, select **Ink to Shape**. It will appear as a darker gray color when selected.

2. Select one of the colored pens from the **Draw** toolbar.

3. Using your mouse, pen, or touch (on a touchscreen), draw the basic shape. As long as it resembles a basic shape, it will be converted into one of the basic shapes in the **Shapes** drop-down menu. Refer to the following diagram for examples of drawings:

Figure 8.7 – Ink to Shape examples

Notice in the preceding diagram, the freehand drawings of the oval and rectangle are not perfect; yet, they are converted into the basic shapes as shown.

Remember to turn off the **Ink to Shape** option if you want to do a drawing that is not to be converted or corrected into a basic shape. To turn off this **Ink to Shape** option, click on **Ink to Shape** from the **Draw** menu.

Moving down the **Draw** toolbar, we see the **Math** button. Let's explore this feature next.

Doing math in OneNote

A popular place for using OneNote is in schools and secondary education institutions. This group in particular can benefit from the **Math** options that are provided.

This feature is referred to as **Math Assistant**, and it can help you solve math equations. Let's look at the steps to perform math in OneNote:

1. Type in or handwrite your math equation. Refer to the following for an example of an equation:

$$1 + 3/x = 2$$

Figure 8.8 – A math equation example

2. Use the **Lasso** tool on the **Draw** toolbar to select the entire equation.

3. Click on the **Math** button from the **Draw** toolbar. Notice a math pane is placed on the right-hand side of your page:

   i. Choose **Fix it** if a number or the symbol of x is not interpreted correctly. You will then have a chance to fix it, so it reads correctly in the math equation.

   ii. Choose **Ink to Math** if you want to change your handwritten equation into a typed equation.

4. From the **Select an Action** drop-down menu, you have many choices based on your equation. This list, provided when solving for x, is different from the list provided when doing a basic math equation. The drop-down choices when solving for x include the following:

   • **Solve for x**

   • **Graph Both Sides in 2D**

   • **Graph in 2D**

5. Choose **Solve for x**. Then, the answer for *x* is shown, along with the **Show steps** option.

You also have a **Generate a practice quiz** option. Refer to the following screenshot to see what this can look like:

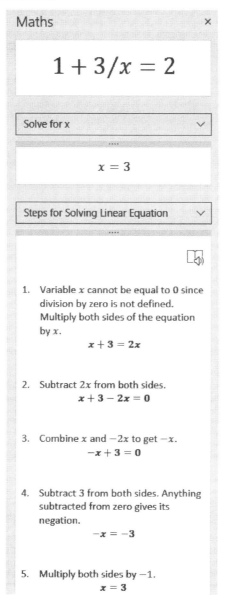

Figure 8.9 – Math Assistant with steps for solving linear equations

6. If you choose either of the graph options, OneNote will draw a graph that represents the equation, and you will have an **Insert on Page** option.

Aside from solving for x math equations, OneNote can evaluate, verify, expand, or factor applicable mathematical expressions. Additionally, matrices can be inserted into your pages. To specify the equation as a matrix, write the equation with square or round brackets.

You don't have to give OneNote just the hard math work, you can also create simple math equations on your pages. These simple equations are like a math shortcut for you to use at work or home.

Simple math shortcuts

A built-in math shortcut can be used as an instant calculator. Type in any math equation, and when you hit the equals key (=) and press *Enter*, you will get the answer. Follow these easy steps:

1. Type `10/2=`.
2. Hit *Enter* or the *Spacebar* key from your keyboard.
3. OneNote will add in the answer, 5, and show this after the equals sign (=) of your equation.

Now that we are done with math, let's move on to getting more color into your notebooks using the highlighter.

Highlighting with the highlighter pens

On the **Draw** toolbar, you have several colored pens to choose from, including a highlighter that you can use just as you would on paper. Highlight anything on your notebook page. Change the highlight color and the thickness of the highlighter pen.

To highlight something on your notebook page, follow these steps:

1. From the **Draw** menu, select the **Highlighter** button.
2. From the drop-down menu, choose the thickness of the highlighter pen. You can use the minus (-) to reduce the size and the plus (+) to increase the marker size.
3. There are 16 colors to choose from in the drop-down menu. If you choose **More Colours**, you will have a wide spectrum of colors to choose from.

If you choose **Delete** from the **Highlighter** drop-down menu, you will remove that icon from the **Draw** toolbar. If you do this accidentally, you can add a highlighter pen back onto the toolbar by clicking on the plus sign (+) that appears on the right-hand side of all the pens that are listed.

4. With the color and highlighter size chosen, you can now use your mouse, pen, or touchscreen to highlight whatever you wish. Just click on **Draw with mouse or touch** first.

5. When you are done highlighting, you can click on the **Select Objects or Type Text** button, as shown in *Figure 8.4*. This will allow you to return to adding and editing your notebook page.

Note that this highlighter pen on the **Draw** toolbar is different from the highlight option on the **Home** toolbar. Let's look at these differences:

- The **Highlighter** button on the **Draw** toolbar lets you highlight freehand. The highlight will go wherever you move the pen, and you can be as neat or messy as you want—OneNote will not correct you. You can highlight words, shapes, math, or anything that is on the page.

- From the **Home** toolbar, **Highlight** will only highlight text. This highlight feature will be perfectly straight behind the text—there is no freehand here. Additionally, you can use the keyboard shortcut of *Ctrl + Shift + H* for highlighting text. If you have clicked anywhere on a word, this shortcut will highlight the entire word. If you select the text first, then using the keyboard shortcut of *Ctrl + Shift + H*, you can highlight all of the text in your selection. Highlighting text in this way ensures the text remains highlighted even if you make edits, making it a preferred method when working with text.

Now that we have added some shapes, done some math, and highlighted information on our notebook page, we are ready to check out tables.

Inserting tables into your notebooks

Tables are a great way to organize information and keep everything lined up. When you first create a table, you have lines that separate your columns and rows.

There are two ways to create a table in OneNote:

- Using the **Insert** menu
- Using the *Tab* key

Let's look at each of these methods. We'll start with the **Insert** menu and the **Table** button.

Creating a table using the Insert toolbar

When you create a table by using the **Table** button available on the **Insert** toolbar, you can easily specify how many rows and columns you need. To create a table from the **Insert** toolbar, perform the following steps:

1. Select the **Insert** menu.
2. Click on the **Table** button.
3. Move your mouse to select the number of rows and columns you wish for the table.
4. With the mouse, click to select the size of your table and place it on your notebook page.

   Notice, in the following screenshot, that the size of the table marked in the red circle is also indicated at the top of this table, as a **2 x 3 Table** selection:

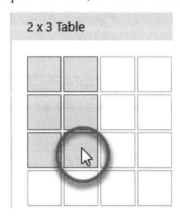

Figure 8.10 – An example of a table created from the Insert toolbar

Once you have this table on the page you can size it further by adding more rows or columns or removing rows and columns.

Now, let's look at how to create a table with the *Tab* key from our keyboard.

Creating a table using the Tab key

Another way to create a table in OneNote is to simply press the *Tab* key when you are finished typing some text. To create a table using the *Tab* key, follow these steps:

1. Type some text onto your page.
2. Hit the *Tab* key on your keyboard.

Note that each time you hit the *Tab* key, you are creating a new column.

3. You can type more text, then hit the *Tab* key again for another column for the table.

4. When you hit the *Enter* key on your keyboard, you will be creating a new row.

   You can hit the *Enter* key as much as you want to create blank rows, or you can type in the information then hit *Enter*; it's your choice.

Now that you have created a table in OneNote, you can use this table just as you would a table in Microsoft Word. There are a lot of possibilities for changing the table, and some of those changes are easy to make by using the **Table** toolbar.

Using the Table toolbar

Once you have a table on your page and you have clicked inside that table, notice that you have a new toolbar, the **Table** toolbar, as shown in the following screenshot:

Figure 8.11 – The Table toolbar

Some of the features on this toolbar are also available to you when you right-click while you are in your table.

With the **Table** toolbar, you can do the following:

- Select the entire table or any part of it.

- Insert or delete columns or rows.

- To insert a row in the middle of the table, hit *Enter* at the end of any row.

- Use *Shift + Alt + Up Arrow* or *Down Arrow* to quickly move a row.

- Shade the table cells, that is, add color to the table. You can select any part of the table and add color to just that column, row, or cell.

- Hide the borders of the table. When you choose this, you are hiding the borders or lines of the entire table. There is no way to select only a portion of the table lines to hide. If you hide the lines and want them back again, simply choose **Hide Borders** from the menu again.

- Sort the information in the table. You can sort any column in the table. When you sort the column, the accompanying text also gets sorted.

Tables can house any information neatly, including images, videos, and audio clips. Let's learn about these next so that you understand how to insert them into your notebooks.

Inserting pictures, videos, or audio clips into your notebooks

Going beyond text, basic shapes, and drawings, it is exciting to think of all the possibilities for your notebooks. This means including pictures, videos, and audio clips in your notebooks. You can have all of these things together on one page, or you can add them anywhere in any of your pages, as you see fit.

Let's start with looking at how to insert pictures into our notebook pages.

Inserting pictures

You have three choices in terms of the kinds of pictures that you can insert:

- **From File**: This allows you to choose a file that you have saved on your computer or in OneDrive or SharePoint.
- **From Camera**: This will use the camera on your device, which could include a webcam if you have it attached.
- **From Online**: This will open up a search pane on the right-hand side of your screen and let you search for a picture through **Bing**.

Once you place a picture on your page, you can size it or move it. Bear in mind the placement of that picture inside or outside of an existing container, as discussed in *Chapter 4, Entering Information into Your Notebook*.

Aside from using your computer or tablet to insert pictures, a far more popular picture-taking device is the smartphone. Let's look at this and see how to create pictures in OneNote with your smartphone next.

Creating pictures from the camera on your smartphone

What makes OneNote special is the camera that is available to you so that pictures can be taken and stored in your notebook instead of in the photo library of your smartphone, tablet, or computer. So, if you need to take a picture for work or a personal project, or need it to be in OneNote on the relevant page, then take the picture using the camera built into OneNote. This way, your picture is stored with the information that describes it, and you don't have to mix up those pictures with other personal pictures on your devices.

Let's look at how easy it is to take a picture on your smartphone while in OneNote. *Figure 8.12* is an example of a page that is open in OneNote on your smartphone. While you are on this page, note that there is an icon for a camera that you can use:

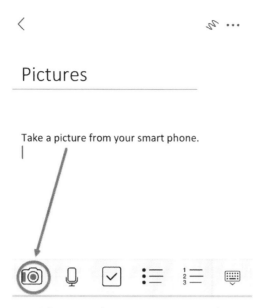

Figure 8.12 – The camera button in OneNote on the smartphone

So, rather than taking countless pictures on your phone, having to upload them to your computer, and then inserting them into a note, save yourself time and create the note first (for the pictures to go into). Then, use the camera in OneNote for picture taking, not the camera application on your phone.

Adding a picture to your notebook page is great, but what about a video? Let's look at how to add videos next.

Inserting videos

Videos are a great way to teach or share information. So, it's only natural that if we have a video regarding a topic in our notebook, we include it on the appropriate notebook page. Let's look at the steps for how to insert a video onto our page.

Steps for inserting a video on the page

The steps for inserting a video on the notebook page are as follows:

1. Select the **Insert** menu.
2. Click on the **Online Video** icon.
3. Type in or copy and paste the URL of the video that you wish to insert. You can find this video URL on YouTube, Vimeo, or any other video hosting platform.

When you add or insert a video into your notebook page, two things happen:

- A link to the actual video is created. If you click on this link, you will be taken out of OneNote and into the platform where the video is being hosted. For example, you could be taken to **YouTube** or **Vimeo** to watch that video.

- That video is embedded into your notebook page. You will see the video on your page using the play button so that you can watch it in your notebook.

If you do not want both the link and the embedded video on your page, you can delete either one of them from the notebook page and still have access to the video.

If the original video that you inserted onto your notebook page is moved or deleted, then the link and video that is embedded in OneNote will not work. When you insert a video into OneNote, you are creating a type of shortcut to the original video. You are not creating a separate copy of the video.

Video and pictures are a great addition to any notebook, but media choices would not be complete without including audio. Next, let's look at how to insert an audio clip into your notebook.

Inserting audio

OneNote has another great option available to you so that you can have a built-in voice recorder. From the **Insert** menu on your computer or tablet, you can choose the **Audio** icon to record your audio. Note that if you are trying to record audio on your computer, you, of course, need to have the correct equipment attached or built into your computer, such as a mic.

The following screenshot shows an example of what you will see after you record audio in OneNote with your computer or tablet:

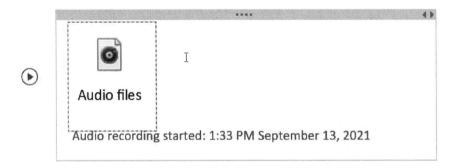

Figure 8.13 – An audio file clip on a notebook page

Once you have created a recording using the **Audio** icon, you will notice that you have a new toolbar for the audio. From this toolbar, you can playback, rewind, or fast-forward your audio recordings.

To playback an audio recording, follow these steps:

1. Click on the audio file's icon that appears on your page, or click anywhere next to that icon. You will notice a play arrow on the left-hand side of the audio file, as shown in *Figure 8.13*.

2. You can click on the play arrow, or you can choose the **Play** button in the **Audio** toolbar at the top of your screen.

If you encounter issues with recording from your computer, in the Windows Control Panel screen, be sure to verify that you have the right microphone and speakers set up by default.

Aside from the computers or tablets, let's look at how to work with audio in OneNote from your smartphone next.

Inserting audio using your smartphone

An easier and possibly more convenient way to record audio is to use OneNote on your smartphone to record audio rather than using your computer.

The steps for inserting an audio file onto the notebook page are as follows:

1. While on OneNote on your phone, open up a new or existing page.

2. Choose the **microphone** option, which is at the bottom of the page area, to start the recording.

To play the recording back, simply select the audio clip on the page and choose **Play** from the pop-up menu that appears.

OneNote is now the new voice recorder on your smartphone!

But let's face it, even better than a voice recorder is a voice dictation machine, and that is what we will explore next.

Dictating is much better than typing!

You might have noticed within your Microsoft suite of products that there is a dictation option available to you. This is usually displayed as a microphone on the **Home** ribbon. OneNote is no different; you can dictate rather than type and use your microphone for this purpose instead of saving audio files.

To activate dictation mode in OneNote, follow these steps:

1. Go to the **Home** menu.
2. Choose **Dictate**.
3. Now as you speak, OneNote will type for you.
4. To stop the dictation, you can select the **Dictate** icon (the microphone) from the **Home** toolbar.

To add in common punctuation, you can say the following while dictating:

*   Period
*   Comma
*   Question mark
*   Exclamation mark

Test out these words for punctuation, and notice that OneNote will give you the word period in a sentence rather than the punctuation for a period if it makes sense to do so.

This feature might take some practice—remember that nothing is guaranteed here. It is a good idea to double-check your work after dictating.

Getting the computer to do your typing seems like a real efficiency gain, doesn't it? But what if you didn't have to type anything at all, because it was already typed and available to you on the web? When you copy and paste anything from a website page, OneNote will also include the link to that source page. However, instead of copying and pasting, we can take advantage of a OneNote extension.

In the next section, let's look at the OneNote extension that helps you to document information that you reference on a website.

Referencing a website with a touch of a button

When referencing websites, rather than bookmarking a page, you can simply link to that page from OneNote. Or, better yet, you can capture a part of that website page and have it visible on your OneNote page. This is possible by installing an extension on your browser. At the time of writing, the compatible browsers are Google Chrome, Microsoft Edge, and Safari. Let's look at how to install this extension next.

Installing the Clip to OneNote extension

Rather than copying and pasting information from websites, use the **Clip to OneNote** extension to make a cleaner and quicker reference for yourself. First, you need to install this extension. Then, you can clip any part of a website page. This extension on Chrome or Edge makes it so easy!

Here are the steps to install and use the **Clip to OneNote** extension:

1. Do a web search for the words `clip to OneNote`. The words `web clipper for OneNote` also work as a search.

2. Choose the **OneNote Web Clipper installation from onenote.com** option if you are using **Chrome**. If you are using an older version of **Edge** as your browser, you will notice that there is a separate download link to choose from. Mac also has a separate download link for Safari. Be sure to pick the right download link for the matching browser that you have, and follow the prompts to complete the installation for this.

3. Once installed, notice that there is a OneNote icon in your **Extensions** bar at the top of your Chrome, Edge, or Safari browser screen.

4. Go to a website that you wish to capture as a reference for your OneNote notebook. Click on the **Clip to OneNote** button to select that website page information.

    You will be prompted to sign in to your **Microsoft** account the first time you use this button.

5. The clip button will give you several choices, as shown in *Figure 8.14* (**1**). These choices are as follows:

    • **Full Page**: This allows you to capture everything on that web page, including menus, ads, and anything you see on the screen while viewing that web page.

    • **Region**: This will give you the choice as to what area you wish to capture. You will need to click and drag around the area that you want to insert into your notebook page. Make sure the area you want to capture is visible on your screen before choosing this option.

    • **Article**: This is a very handy option as it will capture the article on that website page and exclude any menus, ads, or other extraneous information.

    • **Bookmark**: This inserts a bookmark for you on your notebook page, complete with a thumbnail image of the web page that you clipped.

    The following screenshot outlines these options along with other features that are available in the **Clip to OneNote** extension from your browser:

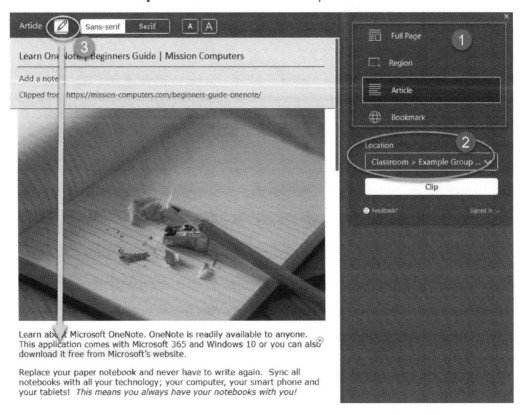

Figure 8.14 – The Clip to OneNote extension in action

6. Before you clip the web page to your OneNote, you can mark it up with the highlighter provided, as shown in *Figure 8.14* (**3**). Additionally, you have options regarding the font style, which can be changed before you clip the web page.

7. After you have highlighted information or changed the font style, you are ready to send this information to OneNote. Now you will need to decide the location for this information in OneNote. Decide which notebook and section you wish to add this web page reference to. Refer to *Figure 8.14* (**2**), which shows **Location**. This web page clip will be added as a new page to the section and notebook that you choose from the **Location** dropdown. You will most likely need to rename this notebook page once you are back in OneNote. This is because it will show the name of the web page or the name that shows on the browser tab for that web page. Either way, this name could be too long or not accurate enough for your page name.

8. Once the web page has been clipped successfully, you will be prompted with the **View in OneNote** option. You can click on the button to open the new notebook page on OneNote web. Alternatively, you can go to your desktop OneNote application and find this web clip at the bottom of the page list. If you don't see the new page immediately, wait, because sometimes it can take a moment for the page to sync to your computer. If you want to see these notes faster, force a sync by right-clicking on the notebook name and choosing **sync this notebook**.

9. Once this web page clipping is in your notebook, you will notice that, at the top of the clipping, there is a link to the source web page. All the text from this web page clip is available to you for editing if you wish. Any pictures can also be moved, sized, or deleted from your notebook page.

So, there you have it: OneNote making your life easier, once again. Just imagine how much quicker you can be when referring to information that you have already researched because it is already part of your OneNote notebook. Instead of trying to find that website again, you can simply recall a keyword and search your notebooks if, for some reason, you can't spot it easily. You are becoming so much more resourceful.

Summary

In this chapter, you learned how to insert shapes, tables, pictures, videos, audio files, and web page clippings. Additionally, you discovered how OneNote can help you with your math equations and even do your typing for you with the dictate feature.

By now, you should be seeing OneNote as a huge opportunity to change the way you do your work so that you can have all kinds of information together, available to you faster and in a more organized manner. You are in control here. You create what your notebook contains. There is lots of room for you to have what you need at your fingertips.

But wait! We are not done showing you what you can add to your notebooks. In the next chapter, we will teach you how to insert links and attachments so that you have more reach with your information and a way in which to make things interlinked.

9
Inserting Links and Attachments into Your Notebooks

In this chapter, we will learn how to create built-in shortcuts for your notebooks so that you can get to other information fast! You will learn how to create links within your notebooks so that you can quickly jump from one notebook, section, or page to another. This will help you to cross-reference your information so that there is less retyping and no redundant information. You can also create links to important documents so that you can instantly access them from your notes.

In this chapter, we will cover the following topics:

- Creating paragraph links in your notebooks
- Creating section and page links in your notebooks
- Editing your links and best practices for linking successfully
- Inserting documents or spreadsheets

Just as with a website, your notebook can be full of relevant information plus links to further reference information, other examples, definitions, or whatever will help the reader of those notes to work efficiently.

When you start gathering notes in OneNote, you may find that you need to reference something that already exists in one of your notebooks. The best way to reference this information is to create a link—don't copy and paste it. By creating a link to the original information, you create more dynamic notes that update together.

Let's start by creating links to paragraphs within your notebook pages.

Creating paragraph links in your notebooks

Within your notebooks, you may want to reference something that you wrote in a previous paragraph, so to do this, we create a link to that paragraph.

A **paragraph link** will always link the entire paragraph, whether you select the full paragraph or not. A paragraph ends when you hit the *Enter* key. Your paragraph could be on a single line or could take up multiple lines—it all depends on where that *Enter* key was used.

Creating paragraph links takes up no space and helps you give more meaning to your information without being repetitive. Think of this link as a means of cross-referencing information already provided somewhere else.

A paragraph link can be copied to any page, within the current or any other notebook. Let's look at how to copy this paragraph link.

How to copy links from a paragraph

If you have a paragraph that you want to reference somewhere else, then you need to copy the links from that paragraph. In the following steps, we will assume you want to copy a paragraph link to another page of the current section of your notebook.

Here are the steps to copy a link for a paragraph to another page:

1. Choose the paragraph that you want to reference with the link.
2. Click anywhere on that paragraph. You do not need to select the paragraph.

3. Right-click on the paragraph. From the menu, choose **Copy Link to Paragraph**, as illustrated in the following screenshot:

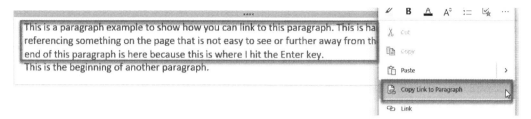

Figure 9.1 – Copy Link to Paragraph using right-click menu

4. Go to a new page where you want to view the link. Click anywhere on that page that is the best place for the link to appear.

5. Right-click, and from the menu, choose **Paste**.

6. You will now see an underlined word or phrase. The words you see are the first words in the paragraph that you copied the link from, as illustrated here:

This is a paragraph example to show how you can

Figure 9.2 – Example of how the paragraph link will look on a new page

7. Click on the link to test it. This link should move you to the original paragraph that was selected.

Note that the name of this link may not be the best, so you can edit the link to describe it better. We will look at this procedure later in this chapter, under the *Editing your links and best practices for linking successfully* section.

For now, let's continue and create another type of link. When linking to a paragraph is not enough, you have the option of linking to a page or a section of your notebook.

Creating section and page links in your notebooks

Linking to an entire page or section can help you or others remember where to find that important related information. This can truly make your notebooks easier to use because you are creating shortcuts so that you or others can find related information faster. You might even decide to use these links to create a table of contents or a table of reference so that everyone can quickly move to the pertinent sections and pages of your notebooks.

Let's start by looking at section links.

Just as with paragraphs, you can copy links from one section to a page in either of the following:

- A different section
- A different notebook

Let's look at the steps for creating a section link.

How to copy a link from a section

Let's say that within our **HR** notebook, we need to reference the **Emergency Procedures** section of another notebook, the **Health Safety** notebook. The following screenshot gives us an example of what that looks like:

Figure 9.3 – Copying link to Emergency Procedures section

Let's step through how we can make the example in the preceding screenshot work.

The steps to create a link to the **Emergency Procedures** section of the **Health Safety** notebook are provided here:

1. Right-click on the section name—for example, **Emergency Procedures**.

2. Choose **Copy Link to Section**. The following example has been copied from the **Emergency Procedures** section tab of the **Health Safety** notebook:

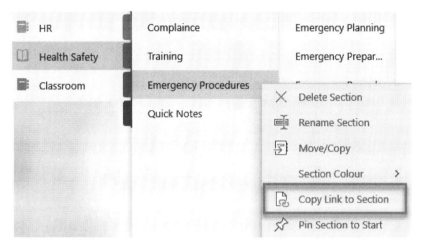

Figure 9.4 – Copy Link to Section | Emergency Procedures

3. Go to the page that you want to place this link in. For our example, we will go to the **HR** notebook, choose the **Planning** section, and add this link to the **Planning for new hires** page. See *Figure 9.3* for this example.

4. Right-click, and from the menu, choose **Paste**.

5. You will now see **Emergency Procedures** underlined, and if you click on this link, you will be taken to that section of the **Health Safety** notebook.

So, you can see that copying a reference to an entire section can help steer you or others in the right direction for what to do.

If you don't need to reference an entire section, you have the option of referencing or linking to a page instead. Let's look at how to do this next.

How to copy a link from a page

Sticking with the **HR** notebook, let's create another example of a link. Let's say that within our **HR** notebook, we need to reference the **Hazard Identification** page of the **Health Safety** notebook. The following screenshot gives us an example of what that looks like:

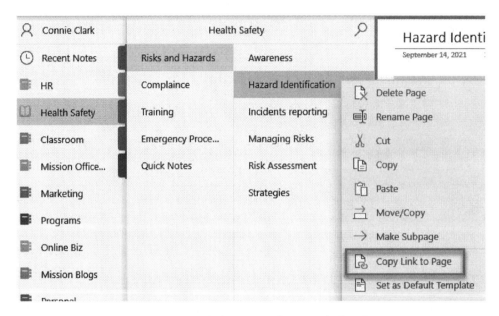

Figure 9.5 – Copying link to a page for Hazard Identification

Let's step through how we can make the example in the preceding screenshot work.

The steps to create a link to the **Hazard Identification** page of the **Health Safety** notebook are provided here:

1. Right-click on the page name—for example, **Hazard Identification**.

2. Choose **Copy Link to Page**. Our example, shown in *Figure 9.5*, has been copied from the **Hazard Identification** page of the **Risks and Hazards** section of the **Health Safety** notebook.

3. Go to the page that you want to place this link in. For our example, we will go to the **HR** notebook, choose the **Planning** section, and add this link to the **Planning for new hires** page.

4. Right-click, and from the menu, choose **Paste**.

As shown in the following screenshot, **Hazard Identification** is underlined on the **Planning for new hires** page:

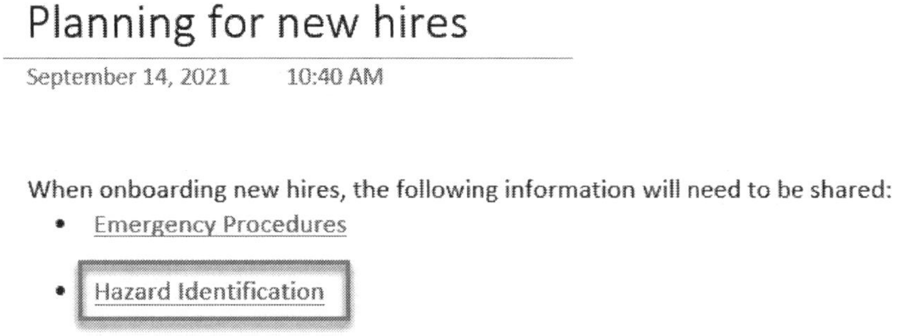

Planning for new hires

September 14, 2021   10:40 AM

When onboarding new hires, the following information will need to be shared:
- Emergency Procedures

- Hazard Identification

Figure 9.6 – Copying link to a page: as it shows when complete

5. If you click on this link, you will be taken to that page of the **Health Safety** notebook.

Another way to quickly link to an existing page in a notebook is to type `[[pagename]]`. This will automatically create a link to the page titled `pagename`. If *pagename* is not found in the current notebook, a new page will get created in the current section. This can be useful when you create new content and think of related topics you want to add as new pages later.

The links for the sections and pages seem to display well on the new page that they are pasted into. However, the words or phrases for these links may not always effectively explain why someone should click on the link. So, we will look at how best to edit your links and provide other tips for successful linking.

Editing your links and best practices for linking successfully

Once you create a link, there are some things you can do to edit that link. Also, if you are using links in your notebooks, let's talk about best practices so that these links work well in the long term.

Let's start by editing a link.

Editing link names

Whenever you create a link in your notebook, you can edit the name of that link so that it is a more suitable descriptor for the information it represents.

When you right-click on a link and choose the **Link** option, you have the following choices:

- **Open Link**: This is the same as just clicking directly on the link.
- **Edit Link**: With this, we can change the name or address of the link.
- **Copy Link**: Through this, we can copy the link another time and paste it somewhere else in our notebook.
- **Remove Link**: This option is to get rid of link references altogether.

Remember the paragraph link that we created in the *Creating paragraph links in your notebooks* section? These links copy the first words of the paragraph, which may not be adequate for a link name. Let's take that as our example here for renaming a link.

Here are the steps:

1. Right-click on the linked item.
2. Choose **Link** from the menu, then **Edit Link**.
3. Type new text into the **Text to display** box. See the following screenshot for an example of our paragraph link:

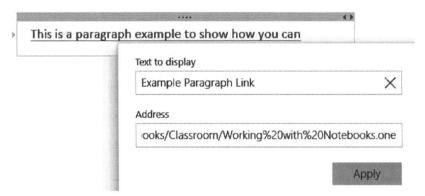

Figure 9.7 – Renaming a link

You also have the option to change what you linked, by using the **Address** box. Only do this if it is absolutely necessary. For example, if the page where the paragraph is in *Figure 9.7* were moved to a different notebook, you could change that notebook name by changing the word Classroom in this example to a different word that reflects the new notebook name.

4. Click on **Apply** to save the new link information.

    Similarly, you can use the *Ctrl + K* shortcut keys for creating or editing a link.

In addition to editing a link, we need to be aware of the best practices for a link so that the link is helpful. Let's look at some best practices next.

Best practices for creating links

When you create a link in your notebook, that link should be helpful and save time for the reader or writer of those notes.

Here is a list of best practices to keep in mind while creating links in your notebooks:

*   Create links for paragraphs, pages, or sections of notebooks as long as you are fairly certain that the location of those paragraphs' links is not going to move off the page they are linked from.

*   Page links can move to another section or another notebook and still be found. If you link a page from one notebook to another, ensure that everyone has access to both notebooks.

*   When creating a link, be sure to edit the link to a name that properly describes it. You may even want to add a sentence before or after the link so that the reader of this information knows why they should click on the link.

After you visit a link, you may want to go back to the page you were on, so let's look at this option next.

Going back to a previous page

To get back to the page you were just on, you can click on the *back arrow* button at the top-left side of the OneNote screen. This is a button you will have probably used before if you searched the web and went back to a previous website page.

The following screenshot shows an example of how the *back arrow* button is displayed in OneNote on a computer:

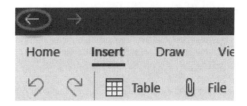

Figure 9.8 – Back button in OneNote

Instead of the *back arrow* button, you can go to **Recent Notes**—as described previously in *Chapter 6, Searching Notes and Finding Your Most Recent Notes Fast*—to return to the previous page.

The shortcut keys for navigating back and forth between pages are *Alt + left arrow* and *Alt + right arrow*.

Aside from linking within our notebooks, we can link to outside documents that we want to refer to in our notes. Let's look at how to insert file links next.

Inserting documents or spreadsheets

Another great advantage of using OneNote for your notes is that you can link or insert your files into those notes, as needed. What a great time-saver it would be to be able to reference a file in your notes and then actually open that file from within OneNote.

You can link files or insert files—let's explore this in the following subsections.

Inserting a file from your computer

If you have a file on your computer that should be included in your notebook page, you can use the **Insert** menu to add that file onto the page.

Let's go over the steps for inserting a file from your computer, as follows:

1. Click on the notebook page where you want the file to be placed. Be sure to give yourself enough room or white space for this file on the page.

2. Click on the **Insert** menu.

3. Choose **File**.

4. You will then be taken to the files on your computer so that you can browse to find the file that you want to add to the notebook page. Once you find the file, click on the file, then click on the **Open** button.

5. A dialog box with a **How do you want to insert this file?** prompt message will appear, as shown next:

Figure 9.9 – Insert file menu of options

Let's understand what these three options from the preceding screenshot mean.

Upload to OneDrive and insert link

When you choose this option, you are creating a copy of that file, which will be saved on your OneDrive. Then, this file is linked from OneDrive back to your OneNote page. If you choose this option, you will see a link and a preview of the file on your page, as shown here:

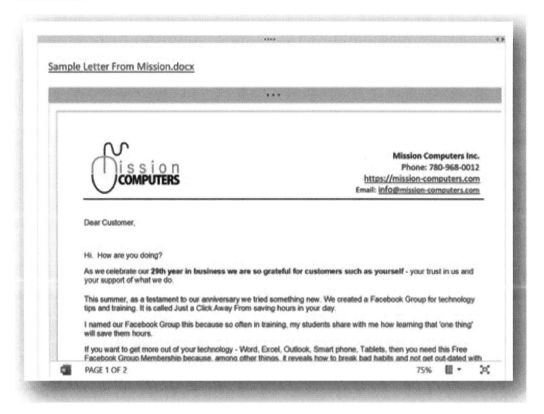

Figure 9.10 – Upload to OneDrive and insert link example

You have the flexibility to change the size of the preview or delete the preview entirely if you wish.

A link shows up on the page as the name of the file. You can edit this link by following the steps outlined in the *Editing link names* section of this chapter.

To access a file that is shown as a link, click once on the link, and the file will open. Adding the file to OneDrive will offer a better experience while editing this file in the future. As an example, if you insert a link to an Excel spreadsheet, multiple users will be able to edit the file at the same time.

Insert as attachment

With the **Insert as attachment** option, you will see that it works the same way as attaching a file in an email. The file is attached to the notebook page and this file is a copy of the original file. You can see an example of this here:

Figure 9.11 – Insert as attachment example

Because you now have two copies of the same file, decide which copy of the file you will be updating. If you want to make all changes to this file in the notebook, then you can delete the original file. This attachment sits on your notebook page, just like any other object. You can move this attachment around on the page if you desire.

To open a file that is shown in an attachment, double-click on the attachment. To delete this attachment from your page, you can click on the attachment once and then press *Delete* on your keyboard.

The main advantage of inserting an attachment is that the file can be available when you are offline. However, you will not be able to simultaneously edit the content of that file as you would if it were stored on OneDrive.

Insert as printout

Inserting a file as a printout is literally doing just that. The file will be printed on your notebook page. Along with the printout of the file, you will have two attachments: one attachment for the original file type and one attachment that has converted the file into a **Portable Document Format** (**PDF**) file. These printouts and attachments are copies of the original document.

You cannot edit this printout, but you can type over the top of it or mark it up with pens from the **Draw** toolbar.

Note that you can select each page of a printout. You may want to select a page(s) of the printout so that you can resize that page(s), move it, or delete it.

You can choose **File** from the **Insert** toolbar, or you can choose **Link** from this same toolbar so that you can link to files that reside on Microsoft SharePoint, OneDrive, or Teams.

Linking to SharePoint files

If you have files in SharePoint that you want to reference on your notebook page, use the **Link** option from the **Insert** toolbar. Let's look at how to get the file information from SharePoint first.

Creating a link from a file on a SharePoint site

We'll use the following steps to create a link from a file:

1. Go to the SharePoint site where the file exists.
2. Find the **Documents** area.
3. Click on the *three-dot menu* beside the document you want to link.
4. Choose **Copy link** from the menu.
5. Click on a page within OneNote where you want to place this file link.
6. Choose the **Link** button from the **Insert** toolbar.
7. Type in the **Text to display** box whatever text you want to show on the notebook page for the file link.
8. Paste the link from SharePoint (with *Ctrl + V* or right-click and paste) into the **Address** box given.

Let's move from linking to files in SharePoint to linking to files in Teams.

Linking to files in Microsoft Teams

You can also add to your notebook page links from files that are located in Microsoft Teams, as follows:

1. Within Microsoft Teams, go to the **Files** section of the appropriate team, channel, or chat.
2. Find the file you want to link to a OneNote notebook page.
3. Right-click on the *three-dot menu* beside the file.

4. Choose **Copy link**, as shown in the following screenshot:

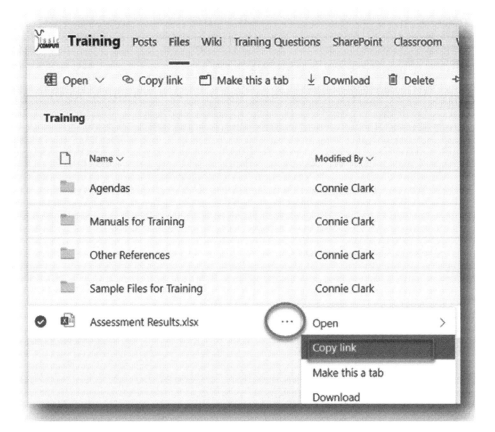

Figure 9.12 – Copying link from a file in Microsoft Teams to add to OneNote page

You can choose between getting that file from Microsoft Teams or SharePoint. This means that when you open that file in OneNote, the file will open in either Microsoft Teams or SharePoint. Choose based on where you spend the most time (in Teams or SharePoint). If you do not use Teams or SharePoint, that's OK because the link will open up in a web browser.

5. Click on **Microsoft Teams** at the top of the next screen for **Get link**.

6. Click on the **Copy** button to finish the copying process.

7. Click on a page within OneNote where you want to place this file link.

8. Choose the **Link** button from the **Insert** toolbar.

9. Type in the **Text to display** box whatever text you want to show on the notebook page for the file link.

10. Paste the link from Teams (with *Ctrl + V* or right-click and paste) into the **Address** box given. This link is usually very long and hard to read, so it is good that we rename the link.

Keep in mind that when you are linking to files in other locations, the permissions of those files from those locations will prevail. This means that if you have a notebook shared with five people but the file you are linking is not shared with those same five people, they will see the link, but they will be unable to open the file.

Summary

In this chapter, you have learned how to virtually link anything to your notebook pages. We started by linking to information inside our notebooks, such as other paragraphs, sections, or pages. You learned how to edit your links so that they were meaningful and relevant.

With these links, you saw how easy it was to jump back and forth between the information in your notebooks. You then discovered that you could link or insert files, documents, spreadsheets, or PDFs into your notebooks as well—no need to leave OneNote to find a file when you can access that file directly from inside your notebook pages.

And finally, you learned how to create links from Microsoft SharePoint and Teams so that you can connect to those files in OneNote.

In the next chapter, we go on to look at another Microsoft product that works well with OneNote—**Outlook**. You'll find out why you should move Outlook emails into OneNote, as well as how to get them there, plus will see the possibilities for connecting appointments into OneNote.

10
Outlook and OneNote Belong Together

How many emails do you have in your inbox that refer to a project you have notes on? Probably many! OneNote has become the one place to store everything around a topic or project, so naturally, OneNote supports attaching emails to your notes. The big benefit you get is less clutter in your inbox and more organization for your notes. You can also take a page of the notes that you are working on within OneNote and email it to a colleague.

When you're booking a meeting in Outlook, you can access that same meeting to record notes in your OneNote notebook. You will find out how in this chapter.

In this chapter, we will cover the following topics:

- Sending emails from Outlook to OneNote
- Using me@onenote.com to create a new note using email
- Sending a copy of a OneNote page via email
- Connecting Outlook appointments to OneNote

By the end of this chapter, you will know how to send an email from Outlook to OneNote, and why that is helpful. You will learn how to set up an email address that sends emails directly to a OneNote notebook and how to email a page from OneNote to anyone. You will also learn how to record meeting notes in OneNote while in an Outlook appointment.

Let's start by learning how to send an email from Microsoft Outlook to our notebook in Microsoft OneNote.

Sending emails from Outlook to OneNote

Now that you have OneNote storing information for your projects, meetings, or anything worth referencing, it is time to add emails to OneNote. A lot of emails you receive will be about a certain project or meeting, so they belong in the OneNote notebook alongside your other notes.

The other thing about email is that we tend to hold onto emails that are good reference information. This means that we don't want to lose that information because we may need to reference it in the future. It is these emails that belong in OneNote. Why? Because OneNote is the perfect program for referencing any kind of information. With OneNote, you can type your notes, store your emails, import your pictures or videos, and have a complete reference in one location. This will be faster for you to access than having to go into Outlook and other apps or websites to find that information that fits together so nicely in a notebook.

From Outlook, you can drag an email into your notebook page, or you can use a button on the **Home** toolbar. Let's look at this button first – the **Send to OneNote** button.

Using the Send to OneNote button

Follow these steps to copy an email from Outlook to OneNote:

1. In Outlook, click on the email that you want to copy to your notebook page in OneNote.

2. From the **Home** toolbar in Outlook, click on the **Send to OneNote** button.

3. You will see a **OneNote** panel open on the right-hand side of the screen. Here, you can choose the notebook and section that you want the email to go to, as shown in the following screenshot:

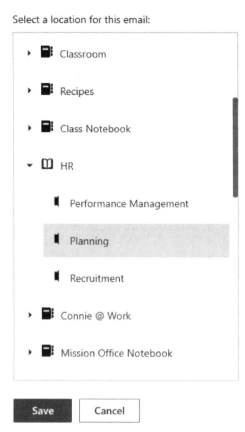

Figure 10.1 – OneNote side panel in Outlook

4. In this side panel, you have the following choices:

    I.   At the top of the list is **Recent Sections**. You can click on any of these if that is where you want to copy the email.

    II. Alternatively, you can click on the arrow beside any notebook's name in the list. Then, you can click on the section where you want the email to be copied.

5. Click the **Save** button at the bottom of the panel.

6. The button will now say **Saved** and you will see an **Open in OneNote** button. You can click this button to go directly to the saved email. This will open OneNote in your browser.

7.   If you didn't use the **Open in OneNote** button in Outlook, then go to your OneNote application and open the notebook and section where you saved the email.

Unless the page list is sorted in some way, the email will be listed as a page at the bottom of the page's list. The page's name will be the same as the subject line of the email.

8.   You can move this page and rename it if you wish.

To move the page, drag it wherever you wish on the list of pages. To rename the page, right-click on the page and rename or simply change the title of the page.

Notice that the email was saved as a complete message and printed out on the notebook page. This is great because you have all the details of the email, including the sender, date, time, subject, and body of the email. What this also means is that all of this is can be searched for in OneNote, so you can find this email quickly in the future by typing in any of this information. If there was an attachment in the email, the attachment will now be on your OneNote page.

There are a few things that you need to consider when copying emails to OneNote:

- The original copy of the email is in Outlook. You can decide whether you need to keep this copy in Outlook. This is a great time to reduce your number of emails.

- You can copy more than one email into the same OneNote page.

- Only one email can be copied into OneNote at a time, by using the **Send to OneNote** button.

> **Important Note**
>
> Note that this button will only be visible when you're looking at emails that belong to the same address that is associated with your OneNote account – in other words, the email address that is attached to your Microsoft account. If you have other email addresses, then you may not notice that this button is available in Outlook while you are viewing those emails. Don't worry – there are other methods for getting emails into OneNote.

If this button isn't available or if you prefer to not use it, there is another option. Let's take a look.

Dragging an email into OneNote

Clicking and dragging information around on your computer is commonplace these days. In this section, we'll explore the steps for taking an email from Outlook into OneNote.

To start, let's get Outlook and OneNote side by side.

Have both Outlook and OneNote open on your screen so that dragging will be easy. If you only have one screen, a quick trick to getting both of these programs side by side in Windows is to do the following:

1. Make sure that both Outlook and OneNote are open on your computer screen.

2. Click on Outlook. Hit the *Windows* key and the *left arrow* key so that Outlook is now on the left-hand side of your screen.

3. On the right, you should see all the other windows you currently have open, including OneNote. Click on OneNote. It should now be taking up the right-hand side of the screen.

4. In OneNote, go to the page that you want to drag an email into.

    Now, we are ready to start dragging emails.

5. Find the email in Outlook that you want to copy to OneNote.

6. Click and drag the email from the Outlook window to the OneNote page that is open in the OneNote window.

7. OneNote will then provide you with two choices, as shown in the following screenshot:

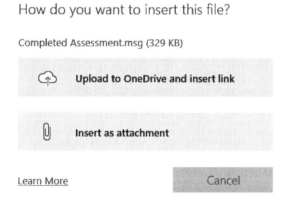

Figure 10.2 – Prompt when inserting an email into OneNote on Windows 10

8. Click on one of the two choices provided, as shown in the preceding screenshot:

    I.   If you choose **Upload to OneDrive and insert link**, you will see a hyperlink for the email on your notebook page. You will not see the contents of this email. The hyperlink will contain the same words as the email's subject line. The actual email will now be in your OneDrive folders and be linked back to your notebook page. The advantage of this choice is that this email will take up no space in your notebook.

    II. If you choose the **Insert as attachment** option, you will see an attachment for the email on your notebook page. To see the contents of this email, double-click on the attachment. On your notebook page, the subject line of the email will appear under the attachment.

With this method of inserting an email into OneNote, the original email is still in Outlook. You will have created a second copy of the email in OneNote or OneDrive, depending on what choice you made.

With the attachment email or hyperlink email, it may be a good idea to add more information to your OneNote page so that you can describe what these emails contain. You can type the text above, below, or beside this attachment or hyperlink.

As described in *Chapter 9, Inserting Links and Attachments into Your Notebooks*, you can edit the name of the link to the email that you've placed on your page.

If you are not using Outlook or do not like the methods we've described so far for inserting emails into OneNote, you have one more option. Let's look at setting up an email address for your OneNote account.

Using me@onenote.com to create a new note using email

You may not use Outlook for all your emails or perhaps you have other email addresses that are not attached to your Microsoft account. No problem – you can also associate your email address with your OneNote account so that you can send or forward any email to your OneNote notebooks.

To connect your email address to your OneNote account, you need to visit a website where you can set up this feature. Follow these steps:

1. Go to `https://www.onenote.com/emailtoonenote`.

2. Click the **Set up email to OneNote** button.

3. Sign in to your Microsoft account and click the **Next** button.

4. Choose a location for these emails to go to by choosing the notebook and section where the emails will be saved. There may be a suggestion in the **Choose Location** drop-down box, as shown in the following screenshot. You can use this location or pick another notebook and section from the drop-down list:

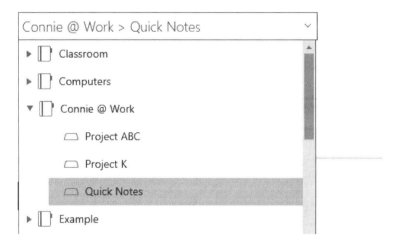

Figure 10.3 – Drop-down menu to choose a location for the email to be saved to

5. Click the **Save** button.

6. Now, you can use the me@onenote.com email address to send an email to OneNote.

When you send an email using the me@onenote.com address, the entire email will be visible as a new notebook page in the chosen section of your notebook. The subject line will be the page's name. If there are any attachments in the email, they will appear on the page as well.

Apart from choosing the location for the email to go to in your OneNote account, you can also modify the section of the notebook you've chosen by typing the section's name in the subject line of the email. Simply type the *at* (@) symbol in front of the section's name in the subject line, as shown here:

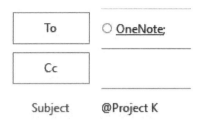

Figure 10.4 – Subject line filled in with a different section name

Also, keep in mind that you can move this page to a different section or different notebook. Refer to *Chapter 7, Organizing and Easily Working with Pages, Sections, and Notebooks*, for more details on moving pages.

Now that we know all the ways to move an email from Outlook or other platforms into OneNote, let's look at going in the opposite direction. Next, we will show you how to email a page from OneNote.

Sending a copy of a OneNote page via email

Sending a single page of any notebook can be done in OneNote for **Windows 10** but at the time of writing this book, this functionality is very limited. If you are emailing one notebook page, all you can send is the text from that page; none of the images will be included.

If you wish to just email the text from a notebook page, follow these steps:

1. Click the **Share** button at the top-right corner of the OneNote app.

2. Choose **Send Copy of Page** from the bottom of the dialog box.

3. Click on the Mail program icon. If you have more than one email addressed attached to your Microsoft Mail app, then you will be prompted to pick an email address that the email should be sent from.

4. Type the recipient's email address into the **To** box.

5.   The page's text will appear in the email message. You can add or edit this message, as well as edit the subject line.

6.   Once you've finished editing, click on the **Send** button at the top-right corner of the dialog box.

At this point, a better solution would be to print your page as a PDF and attach it to your email message. You can also use copy and paste to copy any information on a notebook page and paste it into an email message.

Sometimes, you may not want to just print off one page of your notebook; instead, you may wish to share all the pages in a notebook. Let's look at the **Share link** option.

Sharing a notebook link via email

Rather than just sending a single page from your notebook, you can share a link to the entire notebook, via email. To do this, simply click the **Share** button at the top right-hand side of your OneNote app screen. The share feature for OneNote (Win32) can be found behind the **File** menu.

The following screenshot shows an example of the **Send link** dialog box that appears when you choose **Share**:

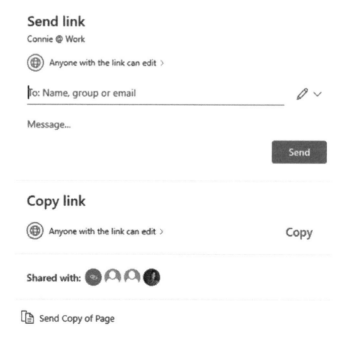

Figure 10.5 – The Send link dialog box when you choose Share in OneNote for Windows 10

Before you share like this, you must understand the available settings. When you click the first option in this dialog box, **Anyone with this link can edit**, you will see the following settings:

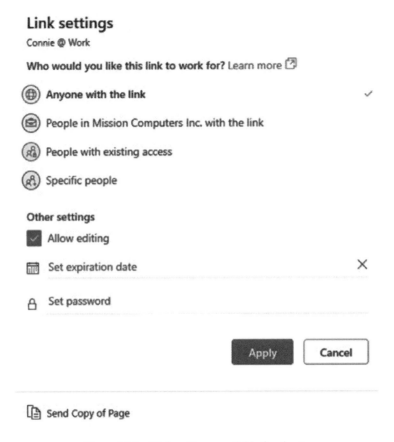

Figure 10.6 – Link settings available for sharing

The settings you can pick from, as shown in the preceding screenshot, are as follows:

- Who do you want to share the notebook with? Who do you want to have real-time group collaboration with? Decide whether they are within your organization or specific people; they can be inside or outside the organization. If you choose **Anyone with the link**, you will have all the setting options available to you.

- Are you allowing them to edit any page of your notebook? Check the **Allow editing** box if you are OK with them editing pages in the notebook.

- Do you want an expiration date for this share? With an expiration date, the share expires on a certain date, and the shared access to that person is removed from the notebook.

- A password is needed to open the notebook. This could provide another layer of security for your notebook.

> **Important Note**
> These settings are only visible to users who are using OneNote in an enterprise environment with a work or school account.

Once you have given shared access to a notebook, you may change your mind and want to edit or remove that access. We'll look at this next.

Editing or removing shared access

Changes can still be made once you have shared access to your notebook with someone. You can edit that access or remove that person from the share.

Follow these steps to edit or remove user access from a shared notebook:

1. Click on **Share** at the top-right corner of the notebook and notice the shared access, as shown here:

Figure 10.7 – Seeing who your shared notebook has been shared with

2. With your mouse, hover over any of the user icons in the **Shared with** area, as shown in the preceding screenshot. Then, once you find the user you want to edit access for, click on the icon.

3. The **Manage access** area will appear. Here, you can make changes to the share. The following screenshot shows an example of the **Manage access** dialog box:

Figure 10.8 – The Manage access options for sharing

4. Click on the three dots to the right of the links and copy boxes. Each of these three-dot menus will provide a separate prompt:

    I. One prompt for **Set expiration date**

    II. Another prompt to view or edit access

5. Under the links in the **Manage access** dialog box, you have access to the user for the share. As shown in the preceding screenshot, the username shows as **Connie @ Mi...** and has an **x** beside the username. If you click on this **x**, you will remove this user from sharing the notebook. If you do not see a username in this box, look for the user icon and click on the down arrow beside it.

Just like email and Outlook can work with OneNote, there is also potential for the calendar in Outlook to work with OneNote. Let's explore this.

Connecting Outlook appointments to OneNote

OneNote can be an amazing place for your meeting agendas, notes, and all related meeting information, so why not add the appointment itself to OneNote? You can have a notebook recording all your meetings in the year.

So, if you are invited to a meeting and that meeting is in Outlook, you can take all that meeting information and keep it in OneNote so that this historical information is together.

When you bring the meeting information from Outlook to OneNote, the following will be included in your notebook page (for that meeting):

- The meeting's subject
- All attendees, plus the sender of the meeting request
- Meeting date and location
- Any attachments and notes

To copy the meeting from Outlook into OneNote, follow these steps:

1. In **Outlook**, go to the calendar and open the meeting you want to be saved into OneNote.

2. From the **Appointment** toolbar in the Outlook calendar, click on the **Meeting Notes** button.

3. You will see a **OneNote** panel open on the right-hand side of the screen. Here, you can choose the notebook and section that you want the email to go to; see *Figure 10.1*.

   At the top of the list is **Recent Sections**. You can click on any of these if that is where you want the meeting's information to be copied.

   Alternatively, you can click on the arrow beside any notebook's name in the list. Then, click on the section where you want to copy the meeting.

4. Click the **Save** button at the bottom of the panel.

Now, all your meeting information will be copied to a page in OneNote, into the notebook and section you chose. This meeting will be on a separate page at the bottom of the page list and will have the same name as the meeting's subject.

You do not have to copy every meeting from Outlook into OneNote; instead, you can capture those important notes from meetings that you will need to refer to in the future. Create a good reference notebook for yourself, of all the meeting details you need.

Summary

In this chapter, you learned how to copy information from Outlook emails into OneNote. There are a few methods to choose from for copying those emails over to OneNote. Now, you have a better place to reference information you receive via email – there's no need to clutter up your inbox or folders in Outlook.

You also learned how to email a page from OneNote and the possibility of sending links to your notebooks.

Finally, you discovered a quick way to grab meeting information from your Outlook calendar and copy it into your notebook in OneNote.

In the next chapter, you will explore more Microsoft connections as you see how wonderfully OneNote plays with OneDrive, SharePoint, and Teams.

Section 4: Integrating OneNote with Other Microsoft 365 Apps

Microsoft OneNote is a vital part of the Office 365 suite of programs. This notebook app is a powerful means of collaboration and sharing information. With our world's shift to working more remotely, OneNote is an amazing application that can assist in connecting others. In this section, you will learn how OneNote seamlessly integrates with Teams, SharePoint, and OneDrive, as well as Outlook appointments.

You'll learn how to view or rename your notebooks that are created in OneDrive, SharePoint, or Teams. You'll also find out how to create a notebook in SharePoint and connect a notebook to an existing Teams channel.

We'll then discover printing from OneNote. We'll learn how to share information with OneNote as well as how to share a OneNote notebook with others.

This section comprises the following chapters:

- *Chapter 11, Using OneNote Online with OneDrive, SharePoint, or Teams*
- *Chapter 12, Printing and Sharing with OneNote*

11

Using OneNote Online with OneDrive, SharePoint, or Teams

For many of us, our OneNote notebooks would reside on **OneDrive** or **SharePoint**. In this chapter, we will look at working with them further by accessing them through OneDrive, SharePoint, or **Teams**.

One of the best things about working within Teams is creating a central OneNote notebook. You will find out how easy it is to add a notebook to your Teams channels and realize how valuable this is for team collaboration.

Through this chapter, you will learn about the following topics:

- Working with your notebook on OneDrive

- Working with your notebook on SharePoint

- Adding a notebook to Microsoft Teams

- Working with your notebook in Teams

By the end of this chapter, you will know how to access, rename, move, or delete a notebook within OneDrive, SharePoint, and Teams. You will also discover how collaborative you can be with others when using these applications.

Let's start with storing notebooks in OneDrive.

Working with your notebook on OneDrive

Microsoft has created a fantastic online world for you. With one username, you are connected to all Microsoft applications. In the case of OneDrive, you have a convenient place for your personal files as well as OneNote notebooks.

When you use the OneNote application on any of your devices, any notebook you create is stored in OneDrive.

If you create a notebook from your smartphone or tablet, you will be prompted to select a location for storing that notebook. The location choices consist of the following:

- **OneDrive - Personal**
- **OneDrive - for school or work** (it will display your work or school name)

If you create a notebook from your computer, then that notebook will be saved onto the OneDrive account that is noted in your computer settings, under **Accounts**, as described in *Chapter 1, OneNote - How and Where to Use it?*. In other words, that notebook is saved to the same location as the files that you save onto OneDrive.

It is possible for you to have more than one Microsoft account. You could have one or more personal accounts as well as a work or school account. If this is the case and you have listed all of these accounts on your computer, then you will see these locations pop up as options for where you can save your notebook. This can be a source of confusion for many of us. When we have too many accounts, then we do not know where we have saved our notebooks. Try to limit yourself to one personal account and one work or school account.

Viewing your notebook file on OneDrive

Each OneNote notebook is saved as a single file that you can view and open directly from OneDrive. To view your OneNote notebook files from OneDrive, do the following:

1. Log in to your Microsoft account and choose **OneDrive** from the waffle menu on the top left.

2. Your OneNote notebooks will show under the folder listing within your **OneDrive** area, as shown in the following screenshot:

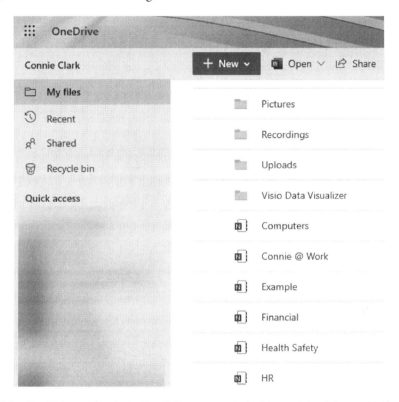

Figure 11.1 – OneNote notebooks in OneDrive represented with a notebook icon with the letter N

3. If you click on one of the notebooks listed, it will open up that notebook in OneNote on the web application.

If you wish to change the name of that notebook, it is best to have a proper strategy for this renaming.

Renaming your notebook

After creating your notebook, you may change your mind and want to rename it. There are a couple of solutions for this renaming. Let's look at the first option, which is nicknaming your notebook.

Renaming your notebook with a nickname

On the computer, you can nickname any notebook in your list. The reason you would nickname your notebook is that you want a better description of that notebook for yourself.

When first creating a notebook, you decide on a notebook name, but over time as the notebook evolves, you may find that the name is no longer as descriptive as you wish, so a nickname for that notebook could help you. Or, perhaps the notebook was created by someone else, and you do not like that name, so to describe it better, you want to create your own name for that notebook—a nickname can do that for you.

With a right-click, you can choose **Nickname Notebook** and then type in that new notebook name that you wish to see. This will not change the name of the notebook anywhere else. So, the original notebook name will continue to show in OneDrive and from any other devices that you use OneNote on.

The nicknaming a notebook feature is not currently available in the OneNote application on your smartphone or tablet.

Let's look at another solution for renaming your notebook.

Renaming your notebook filename

If your notebook name is not well suited to what your notebook is about, then a better solution is to rename the actual notebook file on OneDrive rather than nicknaming it. When you rename the filename for that notebook, that filename is changed and available from any device that you use OneNote on.

Here are the steps to rename your notebook filename:

1. Log in to your Microsoft account on the web and choose the OneDrive application.
2. From the OneDrive list of files, find the notebook that you want to rename. Right-click on this notebook or click the three vertical dots beside the notebook name and choose **Rename**.

3. Once you have renamed that notebook file, click on that file in OneDrive so that it activates and opens the notebook. This step is not mandatory, but it just helps to refresh the new name faster.

The new notebook name should show up on all of your devices. Here is how you can access that new notebook name:

- If you have the notebook open already on a device, the name will change. You may have to wait until it refreshes. You could close OneNote and open it up again to see the new notebook name in your list, or you could right-click on the notebook and choose **Sync this Notebook** to force the change to show.

- If the notebook was never opened before, then when you go to **More Notebooks**, you will see the changed notebook name when you browse. Searching is also an option from the **More Notebooks** area, so you can type in the new name of your notebook in the search box.

Remember to be patient when referring to a new notebook name on a different device, as it takes time for everything in the cloud to get updated.

> **Important Note**
>
> If you have already nicknamed a notebook, then when you rename the notebook file, the new notebook name will not show. You will have to nickname the notebook again to that new notebook name if you want it to be the same as your filename and the notebook names on your other devices.

Once you have settled on a final name for your notebook, then you may want to consider sharing the contents of that notebook. Let's look at sharing notebooks next.

Sharing your notebook

Just as you can share a file through your OneDrive application, you can also share a notebook from OneDrive. This sharing can take place while in OneDrive on the web or while in your OneNote application, as outlined here:

- From within OneDrive on the web, you can click on any notebook and choose **Share** from the right-click menu or the toolbar at the top of the screen.

- Alternatively, from within OneNote on the web or in the desktop application, open a notebook and choose **Share** from the top-right corner of the screen.

By default, you can share your notebook with anyone, and this sharing will give that person the ability to edit within the notebook. Here are the steps for sharing a notebook:

1. Type in one or more email addresses on the **To** line.

2. If you prefer not to share editing rights, then you can click on the pencil at the end of the line and change the option to **Can view**, as shown here:

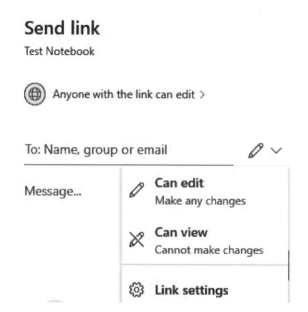

Figure 11.2 – Changing edit permissions when sharing a notebook with others

After the shared notebook is received and opened by the recipient(s), they can add information to that notebook.

When one person adds new information to the notebook, everyone else will notice that notebook name in bold. Within the notebook, the section and page are also shown in bold so that you can easily identify where changes or additions have been made by others. The author's initials can be seen beside additions or changes—the following screenshot provides an example of this:

Figure 11.3 – Section and page are shown in bold when changes are made by someone else

Now, if you change your mind on who you want to share access with or what you want to share, then you will have to do this with the shared **Manage Access** feature.

You can edit or remove shared access by following the same steps as outlined in the *Editing or removing shared access* section of *Chapter 10, Outlook and OneNote Belong Together*. If you decide that you no longer want to access that notebook, then you also have the option to delete a notebook. Let's look at that next.

Deleting your notebook

When you delete a notebook in OneNote, you are deleting all sections and all pages in that notebook.

You cannot delete a notebook from within OneNote. However, you can close a notebook within OneNote, and you should definitely do this before deleting that notebook. Refer to *Chapter 7, Organizing and Easily Working with Pages, Sections, and Notebooks* for more details on how to close a notebook.

Once you have closed the notebook on all your devices, follow these steps to delete that notebook:

1. Log in to your Microsoft account on the web and choose the OneDrive application.
2. From the OneDrive list of files, find the notebook that you want to delete. Right-click on this notebook or click the three vertical dots beside the notebook name and choose **Delete**. Alternatively, you can also choose **Delete** from the menu at the top.

    You will be asked whether you are sure that you want to send this item to the **Recycle bin**—click the **Delete** button to confirm that you are sure.

Once you have deleted that notebook file, you have 30 days to recover it from the **Recycle bin** if this OneDrive notebook is accessed with a personal Microsoft account; otherwise, you have 93 days if you are using a work or school Microsoft account.

If you have left that notebook open on any of your devices, you will notice a *triangular warning symbol* on the notebook icon, and if you try to add to or edit that notebook in any way, it will show that the notebook is offline. If you have shared this notebook with anyone, they will have the same experience. Close this notebook and advise others to do the same.

If you want to get that deleted notebook back, let's look at the steps for restoring it from OneDrive.

Restoring your deleted notebook from OneDrive

Deleting a notebook that resides in OneDrive means that you have the possibility of retrieving that deleted notebook from the **Recycle bin** (of OneDrive).

The following screenshot shows an example of how to go about restoring your notebook file from your OneDrive's **Recycle bin**:

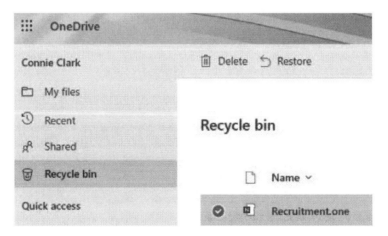

Figure 11.4 – Restoring a deleted notebook from OneDrive

Here are the steps to restore a deleted notebook:

1. Log in to your OneDrive account on the web.
2. Choose **Recycle bin** from the menu list on the left side of the screen.
3. Find your deleted notebook and click on this file to select it.
4. Click on **Restore** from the top of the **Recycle bin** area.

Now, your notebook is back, and you can open this notebook again and use it whenever you wish.

Instead of deleting a notebook, you can consider moving it.

Moving your notebook

Sometimes, archiving information is better than deleting it. For this reason, consider moving the notebook file somewhere else on your OneDrive account.

Maybe you need to reorganize your OneDrive so that all notebooks are in the appropriate folder(s). Moving a notebook file on the same OneDrive where it was created does not affect this notebook at all in OneNote. In other words, you can do your housekeeping in OneDrive and OneNote will follow the file, without any interruption.

Storing your notebooks on OneDrive provides accessibility to those notebooks from every device and gives you the luxury of sharing notebooks. However, if the notebook you are using is completely meant to be shared among a group of people, then SharePoint may be a better choice for that notebook file.

Let's look at working with your notebook on SharePoint next.

Working with your notebook on SharePoint

SharePoint is an application that Microsoft has created for you so that you can share information easily. The name says it all—SharePoint is for sharing. So, provided you have access and permissions to SharePoint with your Microsoft account login, let's look at how to create a notebook here. The other assumption we have to make here is that you have SharePoint sites set up and available to you.

Creating a notebook in SharePoint

You can create a notebook in one of your existing SharePoint sites, and then everyone who is a member of that SharePoint site will have access to that notebook.

The steps for creating a notebook in SharePoint are listed here:

1. Navigate to the appropriate SharePoint site so that you have that site open.
2. Click on **Site Contents** from the top menu on a communication site or from the side menu of a team site.
3. Click on **Site Assets** from the list.
4. Click on the **New** button on the top left and choose **OneNote notebook** from the drop-down menu.
5. Enter a name for your shared notebook.

The notebook will show on the SharePoint site under **Site Contents** and **Site Assets**. Each member of this site can also follow the steps to open up the notebook on any device that they use for OneNote. Steps for opening up a notebook are detailed in *Chapter 7*, *Organizing and Easily Working with Pages, Sections, and Notebooks*.

If you want to rename, move, or delete this notebook, you can follow the same instructions as provided in the *Working with your notebook in OneDrive* section. The SharePoint notebook behaves the same way as the OneDrive notebook in these instances.

Instead of logging in to SharePoint, you can work with Teams to create a shared notebook. Let's look at how easy it is to add a notebook within Microsoft Teams.

Adding a notebook to Microsoft Teams

Microsoft Teams is all about sharing and collaboration with team members, and OneNote provides a perfect way to do this.

For this section, we will assume that you have teams set up in Microsoft Teams and that you have the proper permissions to add to these teams.

The steps for creating a notebook in a team are listed here:

1. Open the **Microsoft Teams** application.

2. Click on the team's name and choose a channel you want to add the notebook to.

3. Click on the plus sign (+) at the top of the **Posts** area, as shown in the following screenshot:

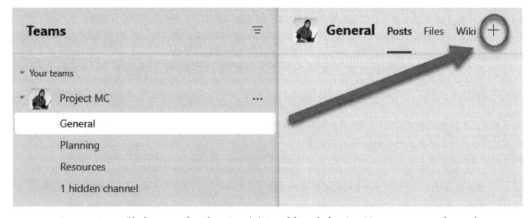

Figure 11.5 – Clicking on the plus sign (+) to add a tab for OneNote to a team channel

4. You should see OneNote listed as an application. Click on the OneNote icon.

5. You are prompted to select a location for your new tab. You can create a new notebook or use the default notebook created for your existing team, as shown next:

Figure 11.6 – Choices for creating your OneNote notebook in Teams

Using the default notebook is a good idea and will make it easier to keep everything consistent.

6. After making your choice, click on the **Save** button at the bottom right. This notebook will display in the **Posts** section of the channel, as illustrated in the following screenshot, unless you turn off this option:

Figure 11.7 – Notebook showing as a tab in the team channel

If the notebook name is too long, as shown in the preceding screenshot, then you can rename that notebook.

Renaming a notebook in Teams

You can rename a notebook easily as it shows in the tab at the top of the team channel. Right-click on this tab name and choose **Rename**. This will change this tab in the team channel on any device that you access the team from. This acts as a nickname for the notebook, but it will not rename the notebook filename.

Let's understand where this notebook file within Microsoft Teams really resides.

Understanding where your notebook in Teams is saved

When you create a team in Microsoft Teams, you are actually creating a Teams site in SharePoint. The files and notebooks saved in your team, within your channels, are actually saved in SharePoint. Follow the steps as shown in the *Working with your notebook on SharePoint* section to rename the notebook filename.

To find this notebook file from Microsoft Teams in SharePoint, follow these steps:

1. Navigate to the SharePoint site that has the same name as your team in Microsoft Teams.
2. Click on **Site Contents** from the side menu.
3. Click on **Site Assets** from the list. Your OneNote notebook will show in this list. You can rename this notebook here if you wish. Make sure you have a good reason to rename a notebook, as this name is referenced in the team and shared with all team members.

When working in Microsoft Teams, we have some unique options for our notebooks, so let's look at this next.

Working with your notebook in Teams

Just as a notebook has sections, a team has channels, and it is this division within Microsoft Teams that we can use to our advantage.

If we revisit our example from *Figure 11.7*, **Project MC Notebook** is connected to the **General** channel of the **Project MC** team. This means that from within the **General** channel, team members can access any section and page of **Project MC Notebook**.

Rather than connecting the entire notebook to one channel of the team or creating multiple notebooks for your team and the related channels, let's consider this strategy:

- Use the default notebook that comes with the team. It has the same name as the team's name.
- Create sections in this notebook that match the channels of your team.
- Connect the channels to the appropriate notebook sections.

Let's look at how to connect these sections to channels.

Connecting sections of a notebook to a team channel

Let's organize your team to have access to just the right information in your notebook. We can easily do this by connecting the team channel to the appropriate notebook section rather than the entire notebook.

The steps for connecting a section of a notebook to a channel within your team are listed here:

1. Click on the team's name and choose a channel you want to add the notebook to.

2. Click on + at the top of the **Posts** area.

3. Click on the OneNote icon from the listed applications.

4. When prompted to select a location for your new tab, choose the default notebook created for your existing team. Click on the arrow to the left side of the notebook name, and this will show you the sections in the notebook or allow you to create new sections.

5. Either pick an existing section that matches the channel name or create a new section with the same name as the channel. Note that in the following screenshot, the **Resources** section will be chosen to connect to the **Resources** channel within **Project MC Notebook**:

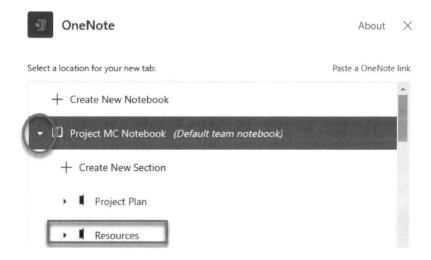

Figure 11.8 – Connecting a section of a notebook to your team channel

6. After that section is selected, click on **Save** to add this tab to the channel of your team.

This method helps keep everything consistent and easy to follow, but unfortunately, this will not stop people from clicking around and possibly getting into other sections of that same notebook. Pay attention to where you are in your notebooks so that what you add has meaning. Share this message with your teammates so that everyone is on the same page (literally).

When working with a shared notebook in Microsoft Teams, it would also be handy to know who is updating that notebook. To do this, you need to ensure you have the right view settings. Let's do this next.

Showing changes by changing the view in your notebook

While in OneNote within Teams, it would be nice to know who is changing or adding what to your notebook pages. Let's change the view settings in OneNote for this to happen.

The steps to track who is making changes are listed here:

1. Click on your **OneNote** tab within an existing team channel. In the following screenshot, **Resources** is the notebook section name:

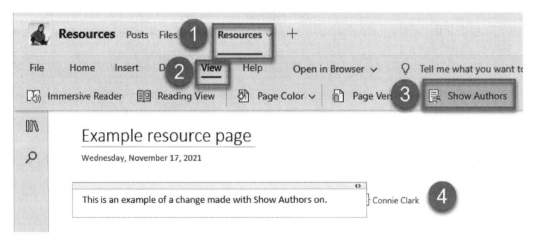

Figure 11.9 – Steps for viewing authors in OneNote within Teams

2. From the **OneNote** toolbar at the top of your screen, under the **Teams** toolbar, choose the **View** menu.

3. From the **View** menu, click on **Show Authors**.

4. You can now see who is making changes.

Another indicator that something has been updated will be that the channel name will be shown in bold.

Summary

In this chapter, you learned how to work within the different locations where your OneNote notebook is saved. You have seen how Microsoft easily stores all your notebook data either on OneDrive or SharePoint, and you have found out how to create, rename, move, or delete these notebooks.

You also discovered that OneDrive is your default location for personal notebooks, while Microsoft Teams or SharePoint makes it super easy to create a shared notebook.

And lastly, you learned some tips to help you work better with your team in a shared notebook environment.

In the next chapter, we will explore more about sharing and discovering options for printing our notebook pages.

12
Printing and Sharing with OneNote

It is hard to compare OneNote to your other Microsoft applications, such as **Word** or **Excel**, because OneNote behaves so differently when it comes to sharing and printing. In most cases, there is no need to print from OneNote, since you can access your notes from anywhere, but on rare occasions, it is nice to know that printing is an option.

Additionally, sharing notes is a huge advantage, not to mention a time-saver for everyone. Plus, it cuts down on the need to email back and forth.

In this chapter, we will learn about the following topics:

- Printing your notebooks is a different experience

- Printing any document to OneNote

- Sending information to OneNote from your smartphone

- Understanding the sharing of notebooks stored in Teams, SharePoint, or OneDrive

By the end of this chapter, you will be equipped to print and share notes. Let's start by learning about your printing options.

Printing your notebooks is a different experience

Microsoft programs have taught us to expect great options for printing our work. In OneNote, you have print options, but they are a bit limited when compared to other programs, such as Word or Excel. Don't worry too much about these limitations as you will benefit so much more by using OneNote as it is, digitally. However, if you need to print from time to time, here are the steps to do so:

1. Go to the notebook page that you wish to print.

2. Click on the three-dots menu at the top right of your screen, as the following screenshot shows:

Figure 12.1 – Menu to access Print

3. Choose **Print** from this menu.

4. Within the **Print** dialog box, you have several options, as shown in the following screenshot:

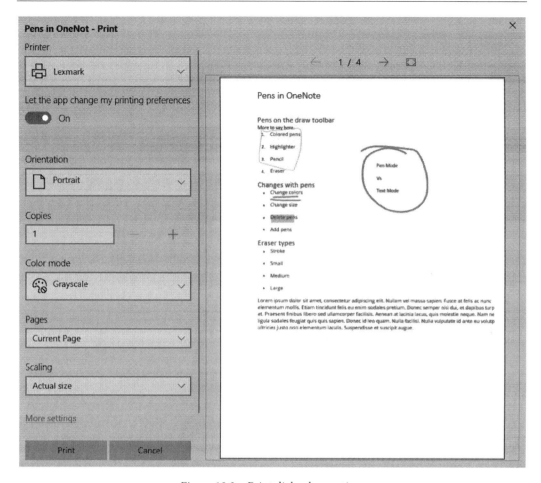

Figure 12.2 – Print dialog box options

The options worth noting are listed here:

- **Pages**: This option lets you choose from the following: **Current Page**, **Current Section**, **Current Section Group**, or **Current Notebook**. Be sure to pay attention to how many pages it predicts for printing. In *Figure 12.2*, the predicted pages are listed above the preview as **1 / 4**, a total of four pages in this example. **Current Page** is the default option provided when you choose to print.

- **Scaling**: This option lets you choose between **Actual size** and **Fit to page**. Try out this option if you suspect that your page doesn't fit as easily as it should. In *Figure 12.2*, the **Scaling** option is set to **Actual size**, but this is not a good setting as it is cutting off the paragraph shown at the bottom of the preview screen. **Fit to page** is a better option for this notebook page and, when chosen in this example, it reduces the pages from four pages to two pages. The **Scaling** option changes allow the width of the page to fit on the printed page. **Fit to page** is the default option provided when you choose to print.

5. Click on the **Print** button at the bottom when you have explored the options and are happy with the preview results.

> **Important Note**
>
> If you go into the **Print** menu and see by the print preview that your information is not quite fitting nicely on the page, you do also have the option of changing that container width. See *Chapter 4, Entering Information into Your Notebook*, for further details on sizing containers.

In addition to printing information from OneNote, we can print any information or document to OneNote. That's right—we can use OneNote as our printer. Let's see how next.

Printing any document to OneNote

Because OneNote is such an ideal place for holding information of any kind, we have this extra option of being able to print to OneNote. You don't need to copy and paste information from another program into OneNote when you can print to OneNote. **Windows 10** sets up OneNote as a printer for us. So, in any program where you can choose to print, all you must do is change the printer to OneNote.

This will create a copy of that information in your notebook. The **Printout** option from the **Insert** toolbar menu provides the same feature, but the method I am sharing with you here is convenient when you are inside the program and want to have that information copied to your notebook.

Let's look at the steps to achieve this printing, as follows:

1. Within your program of choice, choose to print your file. For our example here, let's say we are in an Excel spreadsheet.

2. From the **Print** menu, change your printer to **OneNote for Windows 10**.

3. Change any of the printer settings to make your printout look better. For instance, in my spreadsheet, I chose **Fit All Columns on One Page** so that the width of my spreadsheet would not get broken up across pages.

4. Then, click on the **Print** button to print.

5. A dialog box from OneNote will pop up so that you can specify where this printout should go in your notebooks. See the following screenshot for an example of that dialog box:

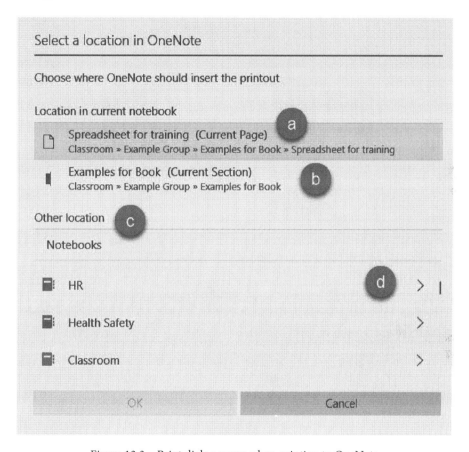

Figure 12.3 – Print dialog menu when printing to OneNote

6. This print dialog lets you choose from your current notebook location or any other notebook location that is available. With the example from *Figure 12.3*, we are currently on a page called **Spreadsheet for training**, in a section called **Examples for Book**. Here are the choices we have within this menu:

   A. If we choose **Current Page**, then our new printout will go to the bottom of the current page that we are on in OneNote—**Spreadsheet for training**.

   B. If we choose **Current Section**, then our new printout will go to a new page within the current section that we are in within OneNote—**Examples for Book**.

   C. **Other location** will let us pick a different notebook and section to place this printout in.

7. Click on the notebook of your choice. Choose a section within that notebook for your printout. Then, click on **OK**.

When you add the printout to a new page, the page is always called **Printout**, so you will want to change this page name or title to describe the page contents better.

After you are done printing to OneNote, remember to change your printer back to what it should be for the program you printed from. That program will reset to your default printer as long as you have closed the program and then reopened it.

Now that we have looked at printing options from OneNote on our computer, let's move on to what we can do from our smartphones.

Sending information to OneNote from your smartphone

You can send any picture or screenshot from your smartphone or tablet to OneNote. When you select that picture, choose the **Share** button at the bottom of the device. Then, you will see OneNote as an available destination.

Let's start with sharing a picture or website page from an iPhone or iPad.

Sharing with OneNote from an iPhone or iPad

Here are some instructions on sharing a picture or website page from an iPhone or iPad:

1. Navigate to select the picture or go to the website that you wish to share with OneNote.

2. Choose the **Share** icon at the bottom of your screen.

You will see several choices for what to do with that picture. On the application line, you may need to scroll to the left to find and choose the **OneNote** icon, as shown in the following screenshot:

Figure 12.4 – Sharing a picture with OneNote from your iPhone

3. You are now prompted with a few details for this note, as follows:

    A. On the **Location** line, choose which notebook and section this picture should go into.

    B. As shown in the following screenshot, **Photo: IMG_4095** is the name of the notebook page based on the name of the picture. You can change this by removing the name altogether and creating a new page name or by editing the existing name:

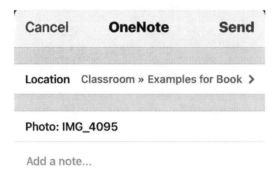

Figure 12.5 – Choosing a location and page name for a picture in OneNote

    C. **Add a note...** is where you can start typing to add a note to the page right away. You can, of course, add notes later at any time as well.

4. Click on **Send** when you are ready to share that picture with OneNote.

Sharing from a website on your iPhone or iPad works in exactly the same way and will add the website URL to the **OneNote** page.

> **Important Note**
>
> Note that the instructions here are from **iOS 15**, and other versions of iOS may differ slightly in the preceding steps.

So, this is the iPhone and iPad sharing and sending to OneNote. Let's look at Android devices now.

Sharing a picture or web page with OneNote from Android devices

Sharing a picture from an Android device is slightly different from sharing a web page, so let's start by looking at the steps for sharing a picture with OneNote.

Sharing a picture from your Android device

Here are some instructions on sharing a picture or website page from an Android device:

1. Navigate to select the picture or go to the website that you wish to share with OneNote.

2. Choose the **Share** icon at the bottom of your screen. You will see several choices for what to do with that picture. From the applications listed, choose the **OneNote** icon.

3. To choose a notebook and section for this picture, you will need to select the OneNote badge that is floating at the top right of your screen.

4. Once you select this OneNote badge, you will see the following choices:

Figure 12.6 – Choosing a location and page name for a picture in OneNote

5. When you choose **Untitled page**, you will have several options available, as shown in the following screenshot:

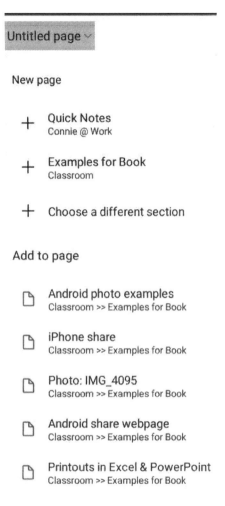

Figure 12.7 – Menu of choices for location and page in OneNote

The options for **Untitled page** are listed here:

- **Quick Notes** is where the picture will be shared by default. You will learn more about quick notes in *Chapter 14, Customizing OneNote Settings*.

- **Examples for Book** is the most recent section I visited, so it is listed next in the dropdown.

- **Choose a different section** will let you choose a notebook and section that you want the picture to go to.

- **Add to page** will let you add a picture to an existing page. This list shows the most recent pages you visited in OneNote.

6. Once you've made your choice on the destination, you can then visit that page in your OneNote to see this picture.

You now know how to share any picture from your Android device to OneNote. Let's look at a tiny difference that occurs when sharing a web page from your Android device to OneNote.

Sharing a web page from your Android device

On Android, when you choose to send information from a web page to OneNote, you have two options, as follows:

- Choose the hamburger menu at the top-right side of the screen. Then, choose **Share** and follow *step 3* to *step 6* from the previous section.

- Choose the OneNote badge partially displayed as a OneNote icon at the top right of the web page. When prompted for the location of the notebook, follow the steps as indicated previously.

See the following screenshot for these two options:

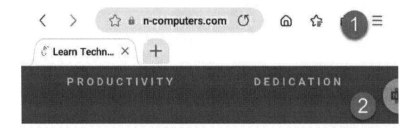

Figure 12.8 – Two ways to share a web page from your Android device to OneNote

You are not limited to just sharing pictures, screenshots, or websites from your smartphone or tablet. Any time you see these *share* buttons, you can share other things with OneNote. Other examples include maps and files.

> **Important Note**
>
> Note that the steps could differ depending on the software version or brand of smartphone or tablet. The preceding Android instructions refer to **Android version 10**.

Another sharing feature we will look at is the sharing of notebooks that are stored in Teams, SharePoint, or OneDrive.

Understanding the sharing of notebooks stored in Teams, SharePoint, or OneDrive

When considering which information to add to your notebooks, it is helpful to remember who you are sharing that notebook with. Which information is of benefit to the group? From time to time, the group could change. You have members to remove or members to add. This could be because the membership of your department, project, or committee has changed, and they are the ones accessing the notebooks.

Let's start with sharing in Teams.

Sharing notebooks in Teams

If the shared notebook is in Teams, then the default membership is that team's membership. There are exceptions to this that could affect your notebook membership. If you have a private channel in your team and the notebook resides in that channel, then membership is restricted to a smaller group that is assigned to that private channel. Other sharing exceptions are possible through editing the permissions within the SharePoint site that are connected to the team. Let's look at SharePoint next, to understand this further.

Sharing notebooks in SharePoint

A SharePoint site has a lot of complexity and opportunity when it comes to sharing information. Usually, the management of a SharePoint site is left up to **Information Technology** (**IT**) experts, but it doesn't hurt you to understand the opportunities available.

In SharePoint, your notebook can be shared within the main documents area of a site or within a separate document library. Within SharePoint, there is a lot of flexibility with permissions so that you can give the right group of people the right access to your information.

These permissions can allow members different levels of access. You may need some people with the right to create and edit, while others can only read, and others still may have no access.

Different permissions in SharePoint can be given to any of the following areas where your notebook could reside:

- The entire SharePoint site
- The files area of the SharePoint site
- A separate document library in the SharePoint site

Alternatively, you can create special sharing permissions for just the notebook file itself.

Within a SharePoint site, there are several places to create a notebook. Let's start by looking at an example of a notebook that has been created on your SharePoint site because you have that notebook within a team.

If your notebook is created on your Teams site, then within SharePoint, this notebook will show up as part of **Site contents**. Work with your IT experts to place the right permissions on your notebooks, and store those notebooks in the best place possible within your existing SharePoint sites.

For details on sharing notebooks in OneDrive, refer to *Chapter 10, Outlook and OneNote Belong Together*.

Summary

In this chapter, you learned how to print and share successfully from OneNote. You saw the genius feature that allows you to print from any application into OneNote notebooks—how convenient!

When printing your notes from OneNote, you learned how to make things fit better on your printed page and how to include more than one page of notes on that printout. In fact, you can print out just a section or your entire notebook when choosing to print.

Also, when you are in other programs such as Word or Excel, you can simply print your pages to OneNote directly so that you have the benefit of that information in your notebooks.

And lastly, you gained more understanding of the implications of sharing notebooks and how that can be changed in Teams or SharePoint.

You are all set, and now, we will move on to an important chapter that will help make using OneNote a regular habit.

Section 5: Making Lasting Changes with OneNote

Microsoft OneNote is one of my favorite programs and after teaching it for years, the best (and most common) feedback I get is, "*OneNote has changed my life!*"

I can't promise that you will feel the same after finishing this book but I do know that if you wholeheartedly commit to this program, anything's possible. In this section, you will learn how to make OneNote a good habit, find out how to share and customize the settings more (to suit you), and see some real-life examples of how to use it best.

We'll find out how to truly make the switch to OneNote and have it last. We'll replace current note-taking habits with the new habit of OneNote.

We'll also discover the settings in OneNote on a computer or smartphone that help you customize your experience further. We'll also learn about the Class Notebook and Sticky Notes.

We'll then see OneNote in action with real-life examples of notebooks for your work or personal life. You should be inspired by these examples to make your own.

This section comprises the following chapters:

- *Chapter 13, Making OneNote a Habit*
- *Chapter 14, Customizing OneNote Settings*
- *Chapter 15, Real-Life Examples of OneNote Notebooks*

13
Making OneNote a Habit

Now that you have learned all the ins and outs of using OneNote, I would really like to take some time to encourage you to use it.

Just as breaking a bad habit is tough, it's equally hard to embrace and take on a new one. I recommend making OneNote a habit because, with full buy-in, it is a powerful tool. Using OneNote should be a regular part of your routine. Using it sporadically or applying it sometimes makes it another place to look for things, which could in fact add to your problems. Consistency is key to making anything a habit, and using OneNote for everything will ensure you reap the benefits.

In this chapter, we will cover the following topics:

- Making OneNote a habit
- Replacing other methods
- Moving to unconscious competence

Through this chapter, our goal is to help you create habits and the necessary momentum to make OneNote work smarter for you.

Making OneNote a habit

If you don't develop the right habits with your technology, you may find yourself frustrated or giving up on new systems too soon. Understand that it takes time and energy to make anything a habit, so if you are committed to working smarter with OneNote, then you will need to commit to the habit of using it effectively.

Let me share with you my experiences of making OneNote a habit.

When I am working with a client and in consulting mode, I take endless amounts of notes. In fact, I admit I am an avid notetaker. So, before developing the habit of using OneNote effectively, I would carry around my laptop and a spiral notebook to all my client consulting sessions. I tried to use OneNote on my laptop, but I found myself reverting to the paper notebook too often, just because of convenience.

One day, I decided that this wasn't working. I had to make a drastic change, and I made a commitment. For the next appointment, I did not carry any paper and informed my client that I was going to take my notes on the laptop. All went well, a little clunky at first, but within weeks I had a system set up and had transitioned to OneNote. I later switched to using my tablet for notetaking, so I had the benefit of handwriting and typing on that tablet. One of the many advantages of this was I could share those notes with my client immediately, rather than having the chore of typing them up and sending them days later.

The habit took hold. Later that same year, I took my mom to an appointment with an eye specialist, and when they asked about her medication list, I realized I had forgotten to bring it. Then, I thought: *Why not create a notebook for my mom and dad and have information such as medication included?* That was the beginning of the next phase of my habit-forming. Any time I was out and about and needed to access some personal information for myself or my family, I discovered examples of a notebook, section, or page, as follows:

- My daughters' school information
- Destination research for family vacations
- Vaccine records for the dogs

These are some examples of what has evolved.

Here's a step that can help you—anytime you find yourself reaching for a piece of paper or opening up notes on your smartphone, decide whether this is something you will need beyond this moment in time and if it is part of a bigger topic. Searching for it later or collecting information over time becomes a reason for creating a note in OneNote, so take that step.

The thing about forming a habit is that in the beginning, it seems like an extra chore, such as taking the dogs' vaccine records and scanning them into your notebook, as opposed to filing them away somewhere (that you may or may not find later). With vaccine records in OneNote, you have all the records you need without having to remember them when you take your pet to that next vet appointment.

Build the momentum. Consider what else belongs here in this notebook. Start with one piece, such as a vaccine record for the dog, but grow it to include much more. This can include other websites or papers, or information stored in your head that you could easily include in this notebook. Challenge yourself to go further to use OneNote the way it is intended, keeping all your information together, and you can benefit from the fast and easy access it offers.

Normally, when teaching a group of students about any Microsoft product, I provide a learning manual as a reference guide. Now, the manual is a OneNote notebook. After all, a manual is simply a collection of notes—how great it is to have those notes organized in a digital notebook and all linked to each other.

Your imagination is your only limit for creating your notebooks.

Now, let's talk about how to get everyone else on board with OneNote as a habit.

Getting others on board with OneNote as a habit

Even if you adopt the habit of using OneNote and sharing a notebook with others, you want to encourage them to get on board too so that as a team or group you can be as effective as possible.

A **shared notebook** is a resource for everyone, providing one place to look for information, which reduces the number of emails and other communications back and forth. *So, how do you get everyone on board?* Be the example! Take the initiative and create a notebook that has the shared information everyone on the team or committee needs, such as emails, notes, or documents. Start a notebook that benefits everyone and encourage them to use it. Implement the notebook and follow through with a vision of collaboration and team efficiencies. If you get an email from someone who didn't remember to use the notebook, go ahead, and put that email in OneNote. Keep going—don't give up if you don't see instant buy-in.

Create a clear vision of what this notebook is going to do for everyone and how it can be used. Communicate the purpose to everyone. Get their feedback, good and bad, and tweak as necessary.

New systems take time and cooperation from others. Many people enjoy their comfort zone and tend to resist change. If you are going to be a champion for OneNote, you will need to be patient, stay true to your vision, and keep the enthusiasm for OneNote going.

As inspiration for you and a case to have others join in the OneNote habit, let's look at all the things that OneNote can replace.

Replacing other methods

Part of your success in applying the habit of using OneNote is going to be replacing other methods of notetaking or information storage that you currently use.

I can still see the face of my student who declared *I'm not giving up my paper notebook* as he walked into the training session on OneNote. I smiled and assured him that he did not have to, although I was hoping he would change his mind, and he did. By the end of the training session, he said it was time to retire that notebook. OneNote was just so much more effective for his work.

While this habit has to be created, another likely needs to be broken. You may need to give up something that you have done or used for a long time, to gain the true advantages of OneNote. However, let's be careful about our methods for doing this, especially if it affects others. We do not want to tell people that they have to give up something—we want them to figure it out for themselves. One of the best ways for doing this is to show the possibilities of a digital notebook and to look for real-life situations that can be applied to it.

A OneNote notebook could replace the following:

- Meeting notes that are saved in Word documents and emailed to all meeting participants.

- A company policy book. There could be various OneNote notebooks for different types of policies, such as an Office Policy notebook, a Health and Safety Policy notebook, and any others that you currently have in a file or binder.

- Emails sent back and forth on a particular subject or project. Rather than sending emails, create a section or a notebook on that topic or for that project.

- Word documents created just to record reference information that you (or others) need to access. Have that information in a notebook that relates to the reference topic.

- Bookmarks in your web browser. These website references could easily be part of a notebook and could give more than just the **Uniform Resource Locator** (**URL**); we could include the article or even a thumbnail of that web page in your notebook.

- Notes on your smartphone. You may have a lot of different types of notes, so here's your chance to organize all of them into a meaningful notebook or two.

- Photos in your smartphone gallery that do not belong in a photo album. Maybe we took a photo of an item that we wanted to purchase for ourselves or someone else. You can create a notebook that includes that photo and other details of your wish list or someone else's wish list. Or, perhaps that photo was to document something for work. Create a notebook page or section that has that photo, along with the date and other useful details.

- Vacation research papers, website URLs, and notes. Have all this vacation information together in your vacation notebook. Clear the kitchen table and include brochures received from travel agents. You can also include notes from conversations with others about that destination, and the vacation itinerary.

- Paper notebooks that could include anything we've already listed here. Think hard here. What else do you track in your paper notebook? Ideas, plans, thoughts, or maybe even memories. I used to keep a notebook when my girls were young so that I could write down cute things they did or said. Now, I keep track of the cute things and amazing memories that my elderly parents share.

Everything has its place—paper and emails alike. However, ask yourself if you will need to find that information in a week, month, or year from now. It will be much easier to find it if you can search through your digital notebook. If you are thinking that you can search emails easily and sort those emails into folders, I would still encourage you to picture the benefit of seeing that email along with all other emails or related information on your notebook page of OneNote.

When you fully replace one of the ways you used to store notes with OneNote, you become more committed to implementing and applying this new technology. If you keep your paper notebook and use OneNote, then you are possibly allowing yourself a crutch. For example, if last month you used your paper notebook for meeting notes and today you use OneNote, you will not have everything you need in one place. If you forget about the paper notebook while in today's meeting, you may miss something. This disorganization could make you feel more frustrated and possibly less patient with a new system. As a result, you may decide to just use and trust your paper notes. The crutch is still there, and it holds you up (supports you), so you choose it because it is more convenient and familiar. You need to get rid of the crutch—dump the old habit.

Starting with one thing

After learning something new, it is always our goal to apply it, but we might want to put that application off until we have time. I see this too often with my students. If they don't take action right away, they forget about it, and all the excitement of what they have learned is lost.

Instead of thinking you need to change everything to get started, start with one small thing. What one thing can you do in OneNote? Maybe it is to record all your weekly meeting notes, or maybe it's to list all information on the kids' activities or medical records. Decide on one thing and convert all papers and other storage systems to this notebook. Use this notebook for this purpose, and once you have practiced with one example, you can expand further to other examples.

Make OneNote the familiar choice by making OneNote a habit. Let's look at what it means to move to unconscious competence, as this is where you want to go.

Moving to unconscious competence

When learning something new, there are different stages of competencies that we go through.

Martin M. Broadwell, the management trainer, described the different stages as *the four levels of teaching* in February 1969, in his paper *Teaching For Learning (XVI)* (`https://edbatista.typepad.com/files/teaching-for-learning-martin-broadwell-1969-conscious-competence-model.pdf`).

The first stage is not knowing what you do not know. This stage is called **unconscious incompetence**.

Unconscious incompetence

Before you hear about a program such as OneNote, you do not know anything about it. You have never heard of it or seen it in action, so how would you know?

Let's find out how the next stage starts when we get conscious of our incompetence.

Conscious incompetence

Then, someone introduces OneNote to you. Now, you are aware that an application named OneNote exists, but you do not know how to use it. This is the next stage—**conscious incompetence**.

The stage of conscious incompetence is sometimes a stage that we can get stuck in. If something feels too overwhelming or like too much work, then we could feel as though we do not know enough and that we are not competent. This stage can shake our confidence and make us want to give up.

This is the stage where we need to build ourselves up with all the reasons why this new program, OneNote, is worth it. We need to find out more about the possibilities and make a plan to learn how to use it.

The biggest thing I usually have to say to my students at this stage when I see the doubt or unease creeping in is to try it, practice it, and have fun with it. Don't take it so seriously. Pretend you are a teenager with a smartphone, and just go for it.

Having someone to learn from or talk to when you are learning new technology is very helpful at this stage too. Learn from an expert, not your loved ones (they may not have the patience you deserve).

So, how do you move from conscious incompetence to the next stage—**conscious competence**? Let's go there next.

Conscious competence

As you learn about this new program, OneNote, and as you try things and practice, you will soon feel more comfortable with the program and feel as though you know how to work with OneNote. This stage is called conscious competence.

You still have to think about how to do something, you may have to look up the instructions or follow along with a video, but you know you can do it. You are conscious of your competence in this program.

Keep trying new features, keep learning, and don't give up. Find more ways to apply this program to your work and everyday life.

The more you work on learning and applying OneNote, the sooner you will move to the next stage—**unconscious competence**. Let's look at that stage next.

Unconscious competence

When working with OneNote just seems natural and easy to do, you have probably reached unconscious competence.

You have worked with the program so much and have used it so well in your day-to-day activities that you don't even think about how to do things in OneNote anymore—you just do them. You may not even realize how much you know because it is unconscious now.

At this stage, it is easy for you to take the role of champion of OneNote, showing how at ease and natural you are with this program. This will inspire others and possibly motivate them to get on board too.

Even though you have reached the unconscious competence stage, remember that things change, and you should always stay curious and keep learning. There's always a new perspective or feature around the corner.

Summary

In this chapter, you learned about embracing OneNote as a system and creating a habit of using OneNote for your notes and information storage. You discovered the importance of keeping up the momentum and using your imagination.

You also found out about the many things that can be replaced with OneNote and the importance of getting rid of the crutch. We also shared ideas on how to get buy-in from your team when sharing notebooks.

Finally, you unlocked the secrets behind the learning curve we all face and how we can combat resistance toward new applications. With the help of this book, you should be able to easily go from unconscious incompetence to unconscious competence.

Now that you are equipped with the motivation and inspiration for building that OneNote habit, let's move to the next chapter, which will teach us all about the settings and other special features in OneNote.

14
Customizing OneNote Settings

Setting up OneNote to work for you on your computer, phone, or tablet is important. Some settings are crucial to your success with OneNote, while other settings are *nice to have*. In this chapter, we will learn how to access and change your settings to suit your needs. We will also discover the extra options available to you on OneNote for your computer and OneNote for your phone or tablet.

Specifically, we will cover the following topics:

- Settings for your notebooks on your computer and other devices
- Activating the Class Notebook
- Working with Sticky Notes and Quick Notes

We are in the final stages of making OneNote work amazingly for you. Take the time now to see whether you need to tweak any of your notebook settings or access any more features.

Let's start with the settings available in OneNote.

Settings for your notebooks on your computer and other devices

Within the settings of OneNote, you have options that you can change to improve your notebook experience. Some of these settings affect the appearance of your notebooks, while other settings will give you shortcuts you don't want to miss out on.

Let's start with the settings in the OneNote desktop application.

Settings in OneNote on the computer

To access the settings within OneNote for **Windows 10**, on your computer, follow these steps:

1. Click on the three-dots menu at the top-right corner of the screen.

2. Choose **Settings | Options**.

   You have a long list of options to choose from within your OneNote settings. These options include the following:

   - **Color**: This option is set to **Light** but you can change it to **Dark** or use the system setting.

   - **Sync notebooks automatically**: This option should be set to **On** so that your notebooks are synced automatically with every edit you do.

   - **Sync down all files and images**: This option can be set to **Off**. If you do not have a high-speed connection, you may not want to have pictures or files syncing in the background. Don't worry, because as soon as you go to a page that has a change within a picture or file, the sync will happen.

   - **Class Notebook tools**: This option is set to **Off** unless you need a teacher and student notebook system. This system was built with the classroom in mind, creating a space to share and collaborate. More details on this feature are in the next section, titled *Activating the Class Notebook*.

   - **Quick Notes**: This option allows you to choose a notebook for your Quick Notes to go to. Quick Notes becomes a section in that notebook. More details on this feature are in the section titled *Working with Sticky Notes*.

   - **Start Tile | Pin transparent tile to Start**: This option will pin a OneNote application tile to your Windows **Start** menu. It is a great idea to do this so that you have fast access to starting your OneNote application.

- **Start Tile | Pin new page tile to Start**: This option will allow you to create a new notebook page from your Windows **Start** menu. This tile opens the OneNote application and starts a new page in a notebook. This new page is the equivalent of a Quick Note, so it will be located in the notebook that you assigned to Quick Notes.

- **Navigation | Legacy navigation panes**: This option, when turned on, will allow you to see a separate column on the left side for your notebooks, as well as your sections, and your pages. Otherwise, you will only see the notebook you are currently viewing, and to access other notebooks, you will have to click on the current notebook name.

- **Navigation | Enable Page Previews**: This option shows the first line of your notes under the page name and can also show a preview image of the pages, as shown in the following figure:

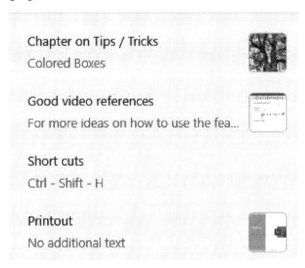

Figure 14.1 – Page Preview setting turned on

> **Important Note**
>
> If you turn on the **Legacy** navigation panes, you will not see the **Enable Page Previews** option. To see the Legacy navigation active, you will have to restart your OneNote application.

- **Navigation | Create new pages**: This option lets you select where new pages will appear in your list. Choose whether the new page goes at the top or the bottom of the list of pages. You also have a choice to place the new page, **Below the selected page**.

- **Default Font**: This option lets you select the default font style and size for all the text on your pages.

- **Proofing | Hide spelling errors**: This is a good option to set to **Off** so that you can see and correct any spelling mistakes.

- **AutoCorrect | Capitalize the first letter of sentences**: A good option to have set to **On**.

- **Paste Options | Set the default paste option**: This option lets you decide what happens when you paste something into OneNote. You have three choices – **Keep Source Formatting**, **Merge Formatting**, and **Keep Text Only**.

- **Paste Options | Include link to source**: With this option turned on, when you copy and paste something from a website or cloud file location, you will always get a link to the source location. This makes it easy for you to go back to that source location to reference other information.

Within the **Settings** menu, you will also find **Help** online, as well as a place to give **Feedback** directly to Microsoft.

Next, we'll look at the settings on your smartphone and tablet.

Accessing the OneNote settings on your smartphone or tablet

While on your smartphone, you may also want to access settings for OneNote. The settings available on smartphones are a bit different than those found in OneNote on your computer.

To access the settings on your smartphone, please refer to the following figure:

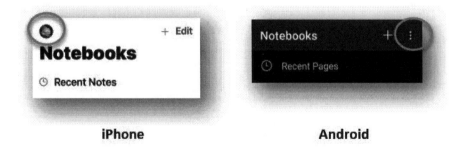

iPhone   Android

Figure 14.2 – Settings icon at the top corner of OneNote on your smartphone

The **Settings** menu on the iPhone is explained in *Chapter 2*, *Exploring Screen Layout and Toolbars*. The settings on the iPad are virtually the same as shown on the iPhone, with the exception of the option to **Enable Class Notebook**. We will discuss the Class Notebook feature in detail later in this chapter.

On Android devices, there are a few special setting options that we should explore further.

Exploring the OneNote settings on your Android device

Android smartphones and tablets have the same **Settings** menu available as shown here:

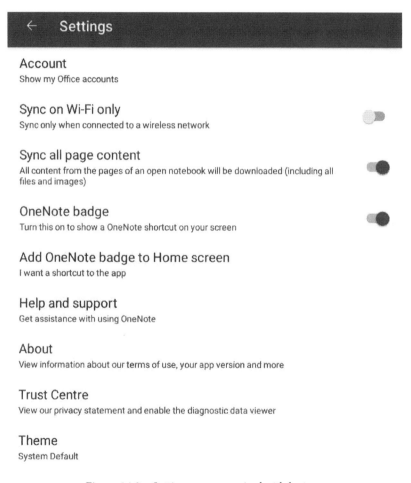

Figure 14.3 – Settings menu on Android devices

One of the first options worth considering is how you sync your notebooks. The two sync options listed include the following:

- **Sync on Wi-Fi only**: If you are on a shared notebook and you know there are a lot of updates happening, you may want to limit the synchronization of that content to your devices until you have Wi-Fi available.

- **Sync all page content**: If you turn off this option, then updates of images and file attachments on pages will not be synced until you click on that page. This means your OneNote application will not be slowed down when large amounts of data are being added to notebook pages that you don't need to visit.

Another unique option available on Android is the **OneNote badge**. Choosing the **Add OneNote badge to Home screen** option enables a floating OneNote icon to always be present on the screen, no matter what you are doing. Notice in the following figure how the OneNote badge is shown on the screen as partially cut off:

Figure 14.4 – OneNote badge floating on the screen

This badge will always stay on top of any application you open so that you can use it. Once you select this OneNote badge, you will see a dialog box of options, as shown in the following figure:

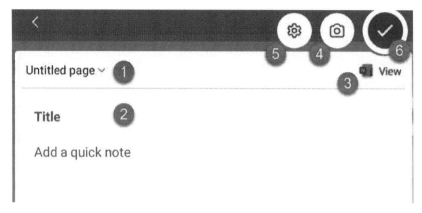

Figure 14.5 – Dialog box of options available when you select the OneNote badge

The OneNote badge provides you with many options, including the following:

1. If you select **Untitled page**, you can create a Quick Note, add a new page to a recently accessed notebook or section, or choose to add to any section or notebook you have available.

2. Enter the title of your page, and type in your notes.

3. If you choose **View**, you will be taken to your most recently viewed or edited page in OneNote. This opens the OneNote app, and you can then move to any other page, section, or notebook that you wish.

4. With the *camera* button, you can take a picture with your device and add that picture to the page. The picture does not have to be just a photo. You can also capture a document, whiteboard, or business card with the camera. Another option you have is to access the photos on your device and add any one of them to your page. Follow prompts on your screen as you navigate into pictures or use the camera. Once you indicate you are done, you will see the pictures or captured document on your page.

5. The *settings* icon will take you into the settings for OneNote on your Android device.

6. The *check mark* symbol is how you indicate you have completed your note. Select this to save and close out of the OneNote badge.

Take advantage of these options in the settings on your Android smartphone or tablet. The settings on the OneNote web application are a bit different; let's look at these next.

Accessing the settings in the OneNote web application

The settings available to you while in the web application of OneNote are similar to the settings in any of the Microsoft 365 products.

These settings include choosing your language and time zone, changing your password or contact preferences, as well as updating your accessibility preferences.

No matter what device you are on, there are several settings that you can configure to suit your needs. One setting that could open up a lot of possibilities for you is the Class Notebook option. Let's dive into this option a bit further.

Activating the Class Notebook

If you are an educator with students, then you could benefit from creating a Class Notebook in OneNote. This special type of notebook creates a system that you can use to share and collaborate with your students or other teachers.

Once this **Class Notebook** option is set to **On**, you will have the following types of notebooks available to you:

- **Student Notebooks** that you can assign to each student. As the teacher, you will be able to see these notebooks, but students cannot view each others' notebooks.

- **Content Library** for storing and sharing materials for the students. The teacher can edit this notebook, and the students view this notebook as read-only.

- **Collaboration spaces** where students and teachers can input ideas and share information.

You will see a new toolbar and menu option at the top of the OneNote screen for **Class Notebook**. The icons on this toolbar will help you create and manage notebooks, as well as allow you to distribute pages or sections to the students, and add or remove students or teachers.

After activating the **Class Notebook** option, you will need to create a notebook for your class. Follow these steps to create a Class Notebook:

1. From the **Class Notebook** toolbar, choose **Create Class Notebook**. This will take you to the OneNote web application, where you will be prompted to answer several questions about the Class Notebook.

2. Add teachers to share your notebook with, by simply typing in their email addresses in the prompt box provided.

3. Add each student as well, by typing in their email addresses when prompted for student names.

4. You can add more sections to the notebook when you are in the **Design Private Spaces** step, as shown in the following figure:

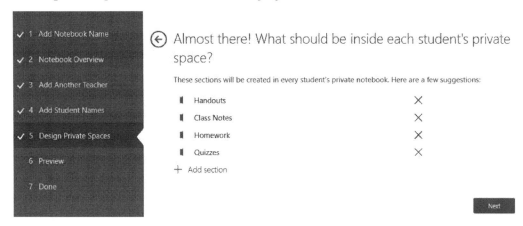

Figure 14.6 – Steps for creating a Class Notebook

5. In the **Preview** step, you will be able to preview the **Teacher's notebook** as well as the **Student's notebook**. If you need to make a change, use the *Back* button, otherwise, select **Create**.

6. If the next screen prompts you to **Download the Class Notebook Add-in**, skip this step with OneNote for **Windows 10** and **Mac** users.

7. From within the OneNote desktop application, go to the **Class Notebook** toolbar and choose **Manage Notebooks**.

8. From the OneNote web application, choose **Open Notebook**.

9. Choose **Open in Desktop App** from the top toolbar. Now, that Class Notebook will be listed with your other notebooks in your desktop application.

Populate this notebook as normal, keeping in mind that the section you are working in has different permissions as noted by the section name.

Other special tasks that can be done in this Class Notebook include the following:

- From the **Distribute Page** icon on the toolbar, you can distribute a page to all students at once by selecting the section of the student notebook for the page to go to. Alternatively, if you choose **Individual Distribution**, you can handpick which students get the page and into which of their sections that page goes.

- If you choose **Group Distribution** from the **Distribute Page** icon, you can create groups and distribute a page that way.

- Sometimes a page that you create could be useful in more than one of your Class Notebooks, so you have the option from the **Distribute Page** icon to do **Cross Notebook Distribution**.

- If you want to add more structure to your students' notebooks, then **Distribute New Section** or **Distribute New Section Group** could be useful. For instance, if you decide you need to have a separate place for projects within the student notebooks, you can use the icon to create that new section.

- After creating a page of content for your students to read or review, use the **Copy to Content Library** icon.

- Once assignments or quizzes have been handed out and completed, you can go to the **Review Student Work** icon to quickly go to the appropriate section and page of the students' notebooks.

This Class Notebook is an amazing addition to OneNote and an absolute must if you are a teacher. It has so many great extra features built in to make a teacher's life more efficient.

Let's move on to another feature that is meant for efficiency, **Sticky Notes**.

Working with Sticky Notes and Quick Notes

Most of us have grabbed a paper sticky note or two so that we could quickly jot down something we didn't want to forget. Sticky notes are not just on paper, they are found on most of our digital devices as well. So, it's nice that OneNote has included this type of feature and it integrates so seamlessly with other digital note applications.

Understanding Sticky Notes in OneNote

Let's use digital style sticky notes whenever we need to make a quick note. There are several places where you can find an application for notes on your devices. Here are a few examples:

- The Notes app on your smartphone or tablet (specifically referring to the Notes app on iPhone or Samsung smartphones).

- The Notes application within Outlook. This application fully integrates with OneNote. If you add **Quick Note** in OneNote, this note is visible in the **Notes** area within Outlook and vice versa.

- Windows 10 has a Sticky Note app that you can access from the **Start** menu. Or you can use the shortcut keys *Windows key + Alt + N* to create a Sticky Note anytime.

All these notes will integrate with, or be visible in, OneNote as a note. The only catch is that you need to use the same email account in all these applications.

So, let's look at where these notes show in OneNote and how you can create more within OneNote as well.

In OneNote, you can find **Sticky Notes** or any of the previously mentioned **Notes** in the following places:

- On the desktop OneNote application, look for the **Sticky Note** icon at the top-right corner toolbar. Click on this icon and it will show a **Feed** area of notes. This will include the Sticky Notes, notes from other applications, as well as any recent notes created in any notebook. See the following figure for an example of this **Feed** area:

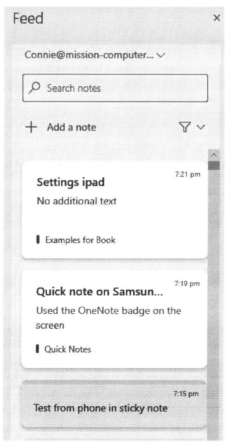

Figure 14.7 – Feed within OneNote on the computer

- From the top of the **Feed** area, there is an **Add a note** option; this will add a Sticky Note here, which will be visible in both Outlook and Windows as a note.

- When you open the OneNote application on a smartphone, the **Sticky Notes** icon is shown at the bottom of the screen. It is available for you to use if you need to make a quick note; you do not have to go into your notebooks.

- On Android devices, if you are using the OneNote badge, you are creating a Quick Note that shows up in the **Feed** area with all your other notes.

Understanding Quick Notes

On your smartphone, OneNote offers **Quick Notes** as an option for sending or sharing information from your phone to that Quick Notes area. The Quick Note is assigned to a notebook through the settings menu in OneNote on your phone. Choose a notebook for these Quick Notes to go to, and they will reside in a section called **Quick Notes**.

Summary

In this chapter, you learned about the settings that help you customize OneNote on any of your devices. You discovered options for background color, when to sync, and how to pin notebooks as shortcuts, just to name a few. Be sure to activate the OneNote badge if you have an Android device, as this provides an amazing shortcut.

You were also introduced to the Class Notebook and learned about how special this custom notebook is, and why it is a must for teachers, enabling collaboration between teachers and students alike.

Finally, you learned how to use Sticky Notes in OneNote on your phone, tablet, or desktop application. One of the neat things about Sticky Notes in OneNote is that they integrate so well with Notes applications on your phone, as well as within Windows and Outlook. Now, there is no excuse; if you have a quick note to make, OneNote is the place for it. Whether you choose to use a notebook page, Sticky Notes, or a Notes application, you have a fast method to capture your ideas or information in OneNote.

In the next and final chapter, we will help set you on your way to greatness in OneNote by sharing with you some examples of notebooks to create. I am very excited for you!

15

Real-Life Examples of OneNote Notebooks

Getting started on making notebooks with sections and pages can seem like an easy task once you understand the mechanics of it, but having a picture of how the whole thing can look will set you up for instant success.

In this chapter, we'll take a look at some real-life examples and copy or tweak them so that you can save time in your notebook-building process.

In this chapter, we will cover the following topics:

- Exploring examples of notebooks used at work
- Touring my personal notebook examples

You can use these examples for inspiration and ideas so that you can get started on the best notebooks for your work and/or personal life.

Exploring examples of notebooks used at work

Nowadays, the amount of information we must keep track of and remember at work is so vast that keeping it all in our heads is not an option. In a lot of cases, we must access that information often and quickly, so we need to have a good place for it. By now, you should be seeing OneNote as an amazing place for storing your information.

In this section, we'll look at some examples of notebooks that you could use at work.

Small business notebook

If you manage a small business, then you most likely have a lot of information to remember and details to handle. You may even find yourself wearing multiple hats as you try to keep track of everything.

Let's look at how you could divide up your information into a notebook. In the following screenshot, you can see an example of how to do this:

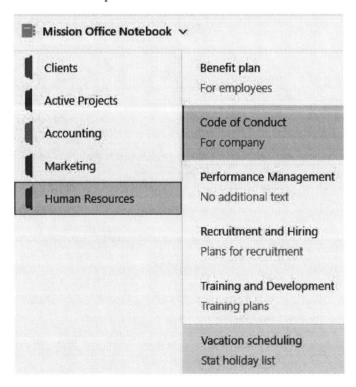

Figure 15.1 – Example of small business notebook sections and pages

In the preceding screenshot, we have a small business notebook divided into the following sections:

- **Clients**: This section could list information about each client on separate pages.

- **Active Projects**: This section could have a separate page for each active project that the company is working on.

- **Accounting**: This section could include pages for the budget, forecasts, communications with the accountant, and anything else related to the accounting of the business.

- **Marketing**: This section could include separate pages that detail the marketing plan, social media strategy, resources, targets, and other information that supports marketing the business.

- **Human Resources**: The example pages for this section are shown in the preceding screenshot. You have a page for details on **Benefit plan**, another page for **Code of Conduct**, and separate pages for **Performance Management**, **Recruitment and Hiring**, **Training and Development**, and—lastly—**Vacation scheduling**.

Do these sections and pages make sense to you? If not, adjust as you see fit. Your notebook should suit you and your purposes. These are simply ideas for you to get started with so that the creative juices start flowing.

This notebook could be shared with others, and certain sections could be password-protected if necessary. This notebook could also be housed in a team within **Microsoft Teams**.

Let's look at another example notebook. If you are a project manager within your organization, you may want to have your own notebook specifically for that project.

Project notebook

If you are working on a project with a group, then a perfect place to share information is within a notebook. This notebook could be part of a team within Microsoft Teams, or it could just stand on its own as a shared notebook—your choice.

Let's look at how this project notebook can be organized. You can see an example of how to do this in the following screenshot:

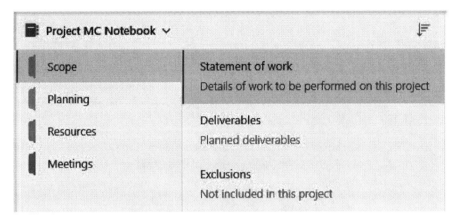

Figure 15.2 – Project notebook sections and pages

In the preceding screenshot, we see the pages that are part of the **Scope** section for the project notebook.

Let's look at the next section of this project notebook—the **Planning** section. You can see this in the following screenshot:

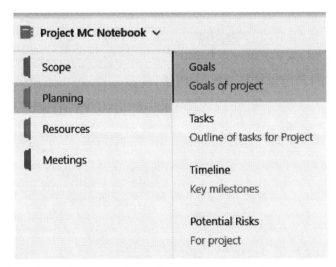

Figure 15.3 – Project notebook showing pages of the Planning section

Planning for a project can involve a lot of information, and the preceding screenshot shows a quick glimpse of a few planning pages that you can include.

Moving on to the next section of the project notebook, let's look at the pages in the **Resources** section, as follows:

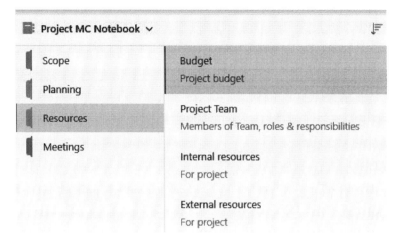

Figure 15.4 – Project notebook showing pages of the Resources section

Tracking all the resources needed for a project can be a big task and one that might be shared with many people on the project. This example of the **Resources** section can help give you and the rest of the project team the required information.

The last example shown in this project notebook is the **Meetings** section, as follows:

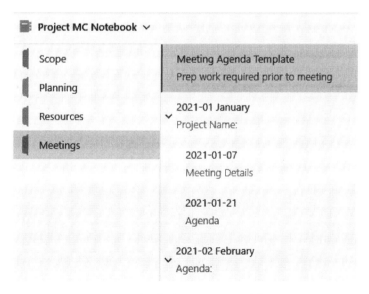

Figure 15.5 – Project notebook showing pages of the Meetings section

In this example of meeting pages, we start with a template so that you can reuse the same page template for your meeting agenda pages. Do this by simply copying and pasting the page. Then, rename the new page to the date of the meeting.

Here is an example of what this **Meeting Agenda Template** page could look like:

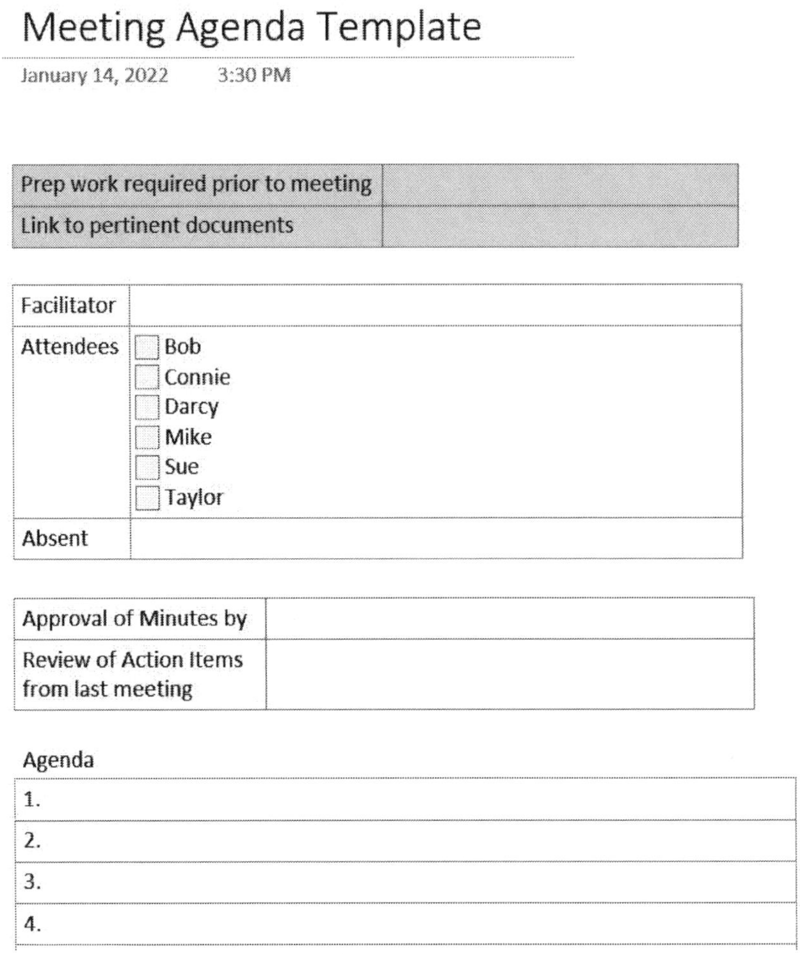

Meeting Agenda Template

January 14, 2022 3:30 PM

Prep work required prior to meeting	
Link to pertinent documents	

Facilitator	
Attendees	☐ Bob ☐ Connie ☐ Darcy ☐ Mike ☐ Sue ☐ Taylor
Absent	

Approval of Minutes by	
Review of Action Items from last meeting	

Agenda

1.
2.
3.
4.

Figure 15.6 – Meeting Agenda Template page that can be copied

In the preceding screenshot of the **Meeting Agenda Template** page, we have used the **table** feature and **to-do tags** so that information can be easily entered or checked off.

Figure 15.5 also shows a separate **Meeting Details** page, which could be the meeting minutes, and then another page, **Agenda**. Since agendas are usually sent prior to any meeting, we have shown those using separate pages so that they are easy to spot. Notice that the **Meeting Details** and **Agenda** pages are grouped with the meeting month. In this grouping, you might also want to include pages for supporting documents or other relevant resources pertinent to that meeting date.

This **Project MC Notebook** notebook is one example of how you can go about creating an organized notebook for your next project. Don't be afraid to be creative and add more sections or pages. Experiment with the grouping of sections and pages so that they can help you keep the right information together.

At work, there could be many reasons for utilizing OneNote. Another example of a notebook that I personally use is for professional development.

Professional Development notebook

Because you are reading this, I know you are someone that appreciates learning. When you take notes, remembering or applying what you just learned is easier.

You can use this **Professional Development** notebook to help you record lessons, ideas, and to-dos while you are learning from a book, video, blog, or seminar.

Here is an example of how I have divided up my **Professional Development** notebook:

Figure 15.7 – Professional Development notebook sections

Professional development can be different for everyone, so be sure to use section names that help you group the type of learning that you participate in. Within each section, you can then have a page for each book, video, or seminar you want to remember. How you organize your pages is up to you. You could have more than one book included in a single page because you want to organize by topic, not the book name.

Unlike the project notebook example, this **Professional Development** notebook can be for your eyes only. It's about what you have learned and want to retain. Although you may share some of your learning with others, you probably do not want to share everything. Keep in mind that you can share one page by emailing it to someone.

In *Figure 15.7*, the **Technical-Computer** section could capture all that you learn about applications, such as OneNote, and many other tips and shortcuts you discover about the technology that you use every day. Because this is all about my industry and the work that I do every day, I have another notebook I want to share with you—a notebook I call **Programs**.

Programs notebook

In order to capture all the research, ideas, and questions I have for teaching different software programs, I created a **Programs** notebook. Perhaps you could benefit from this as well. You can see a screenshot of this notebook here:

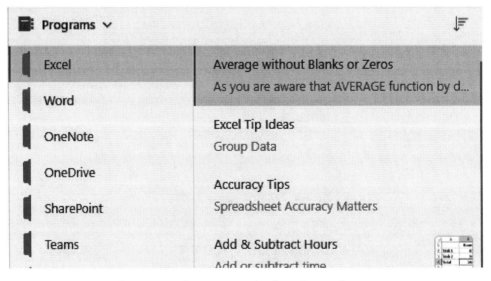

Figure 15.8 – Programs notebook sections and pages

This **Programs** notebook is divided into sections with the name of each software program that I support. The pages of this notebook contain research I have done or ideas and information I have written about a feature, tip, or shortcut within that program.

I think of this notebook as my resource or research notebook. *Which big topic do you need to research within your line of work? Is the amount of information that you can gather on this topic worthy of its own notebook?*

Does part of your work or personal life entail being part of a board? If so, you will like this next example.

Board Member notebook

As an active member of many different boards, I have found the amount of information shared hard to manage at times. Emails back and forth could be reduced (or maybe even eliminated) if, as a board, we shared a common notebook.

Here is an example of how that **Board Member** notebook could be organized:

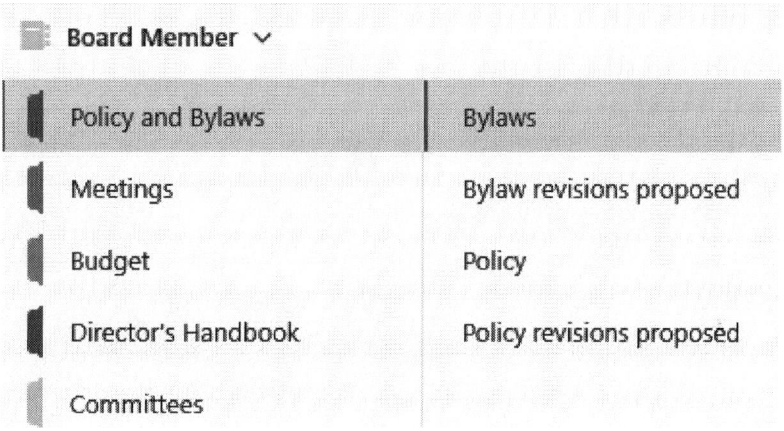

Figure 15.9 – Board Member notebook sections and pages

Rather than a large binder on my desk for the policies and bylaws of the organization, I would suggest a notebook section. The number of pages in this section should reflect the different areas of the policy and bylaws. The preceding screenshot may have simplified this too much.

Let's look at the next section of this notebook—the **Meetings** section. You can see an overview of this in the following screenshot:

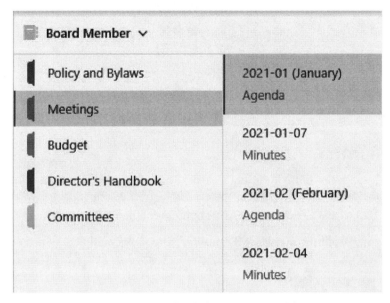

Figure 15.10 – Board Member notebook showing pages of the Meetings section

The **Meetings** section in the preceding screenshot shows pages with the date as the title and separate pages for **Agenda** and **Minutes**. This makes it very easy and fast for anyone on that board to go back to a previous meeting discussion.

The other sections shown in *Figure 15.10* can be organized into pages that are relevant and helpful to the board.

The naming of your sections and pages helps with easy navigation within your notebook. Another feature you have learned that can also improve navigation is the creation of links in your notebooks. We spoke about links in detail in *Chapter 9, Inserting Links and Attachments into your Notebooks*. Let's look at an example **table of contents** (**TOC**) that you can include in any one of your notebooks.

Making a TOC for your notebook

Using the **links** feature within OneNote, you can create a TOC in your notebook. This is especially useful in shared notebooks so that you can teach others where to find the right information.

The example TOC that I am using here is useful for me because it becomes my agenda while I teach OneNote and it helps me quickly move to the correct page of instruction:

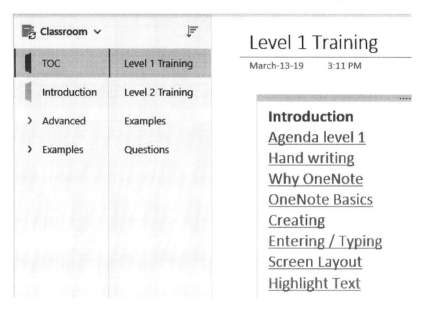

Figure 15.11 – An example TOC used for OneNote level 1 training

As you can see in the preceding screenshot, all items on the page are underlined. These underlined texts are links to other pages, sections, or paragraphs within OneNote.

Refer to *Chapter 9, Inserting Links and Attachments into your Notebooks,* for creating a TOC for yourself and using it as an agenda for a presentation or as a TOC that helps you remember where certain topics are within your notebooks.

Now that we have shown you a few examples of work notebooks and pages, let's move on to personal notebook examples.

Touring my personal notebook examples

Outside of work, when you return home, I am sure there is no shortage of information that you are trying to keep track of.

Here are some examples of notebooks that you could use personally.

Let's start with how you might divide up your **Personal** notebook into sections. You can see an example of this here:

Figure 15.12 – Example sections within the Personal notebook

Each section of your **Personal** notebook could contain a number of pages that relate to the topic. Let's look at the **Dogs** section further and see which pages could be included, as follows:

Figure 15.13 – Example pages within the Dogs section of the Personal notebook

We have two dogs, and remembering which vaccine they had last or which kennel is best for them is important. The **Vaccines** page has a copy of the vaccine paper included. When we adopted our first dog, the vet gave us a **Puppy first 15 months** brochure. I took a picture of both sides of that brochure and included it on its own page, as shown in the preceding screenshot.

Let's look at another section of this **Personal** notebook to see examples of pages we could include.

The **Gardening** notebook could have a lot of pages to help you organize your plans or information for your yard or garden, as illustrated in the following screenshot:

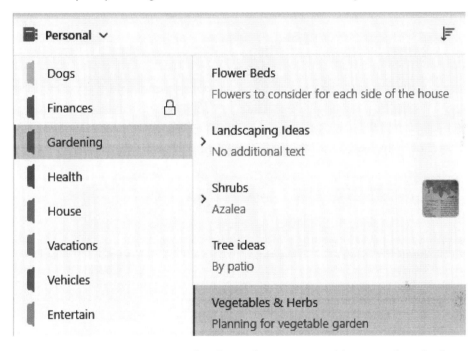

Figure 15.14 – Example pages within the Gardening section of the Personal notebook

When we first built our house on the acreage, it seemed like there was no end to how much planting and gardening we had to do. I acquired a lot of books on the topic, read lots of articles, watched videos, and received unending advice from friends and neighbors. The notebook became a great place for me to organize all that useful information. Once I had my ideas in the notebook, going to the gardening center was easy because I could reference the flower, shrub, or tree I wanted. In fact, I could share the picture with them because I just opened up this notebook on my phone to show them.

The sections of your personal notebook can be anything that you need. *How would you like to divide up the information you need to reference?* These could be your sections.

This personal notebook could be just for yourself, or you could share it with other family members. If you are sharing a notebook, that might influence which sections you create because you may want certain sections locked for yourself while others are shared. **Family** might be a better name for this notebook if sharing with others in the family is your intention.

In my **Family** notebook, I have a couple of main sections, as follows:

- **Girls** (for my two daughters)
- **Mom and Dad** (for my elderly parents)

The pages within the **Girls** section of my notebook include the following:

- The **Christmas wish list** page has a separate area for each girl, listing items they like, the stores the items are from, and even a hyperlink to the item picture in some cases.
- A **School trips** page with an itinerary and other details on school trips.
- A **Grade information** page for details on grades for each girl.
- Health history with notes on doctors' visits over the years.
- Funny stories capturing memories of times I don't want to forget.

The pages within the **Mom and Dad** section of my notebook include the following:

- A medication list that was captured by taking a picture of my mom's pill pack.
- Medical visits to doctors, recording information and advice shared by the doctor.
- A **Financials** page listing bank names and account numbers for my parents, as well as information on regular income and expenses they had.
- A **Sale of house** page is what I used to track all that I needed to help them sell their home.
- **Garage sale** was the page that listed the hundreds of items by category, along with the selling price.
- The **Personal care home** page had emails and various documents that helped me keep track of correspondence received and how everything worked at my parents' new home.

My dad passed away recently, but I still used my notebook to gather all the information I needed as the executor. This was a huge help in staying organized and focused during this difficult time.

Another personal notebook to create would be one that helps you with a major project around the home, such as a home improvement project.

Here is an example of how you might organize a **Home Improvement** notebook:

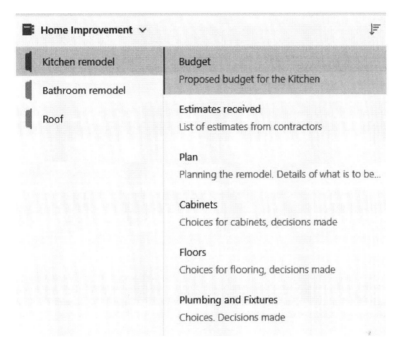

Figure 15.15 – Home Improvement notebook with sections and pages

Being married to a carpenter and having lived through many home improvement projects, I thought it was fitting to show you this example.

In *Figure 15.15*, we show the area to improve, as the section—for example, the **Kitchen remodel** section—has all the pages involving that part of the home improvement. We have a separate section for other improvements on the home and can have similar page titles.

Take a look here at the same notebook, whereby we reverse the section and page names:

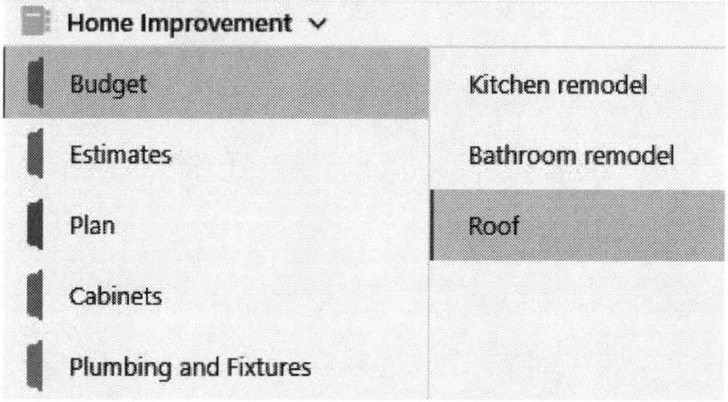

Figure 15.16 – Home Improvement notebook reorganized

If you compare Figure 15.15 with the preceding screenshot, which one works better? It all depends on your personal preference and how you like to group information.

When creating your own notebooks, you may change your mind about how you organize your pages or sections. That's no problem because you have learned how to move notebook pages and sections around (see *Chapter 7, Organizing and Easily Working with Pages, Sections, and Notebooks*).

Summary

In this chapter, you have seen examples of notebooks that you can create for work or for personal use. You've also explored the different ways these example notebooks could be organized with sections and pages.

I've taken you into my world and shared my stories of how some of my notebooks have come about, hopefully inspiring you to create your own world of notebooks that can help you.

Please visit my YouTube channel at `https://www.youtube.com/c/MissionComputers` for helpful videos on learning OneNote. You can contact me directly for support or training programs about OneNote—just email `info@mission-computers.com`.

Over time, your notebooks will grow and evolve, so embrace that. Enjoy the process and keep trying new things. As you use OneNote more, you will love it more. This is what I hear over and over again from my clients and friends that take my advice to create that first page in their first notebook.

You now have everything you need to get started and make something great. I am so excited for you! Good luck!

Index

Packt.com

Subscribe to our online digital library for full access to over 7,000 books and videos, as well as industry leading tools to help you plan your personal development and advance your career. For more information, please visit our website.

Why subscribe?

- Spend less time learning and more time coding with practical eBooks and Videos from over 4,000 industry professionals

- Improve your learning with Skill Plans built especially for you

- Get a free eBook or video every month

- Fully searchable for easy access to vital information

- Copy and paste, print, and bookmark content

Did you know that Packt offers eBook versions of every book published, with PDF and ePub files available? You can upgrade to the eBook version at packt.com and as a print book customer, you are entitled to a discount on the eBook copy. Get in touch with us at customercare@packtpub.com for more details.

At www.packt.com, you can also read a collection of free technical articles, sign up for a range of free newsletters, and receive exclusive discounts and offers on Packt books and eBooks.

Other Books You May Enjoy

If you enjoyed this book, you may be interested in these other books by Packt:

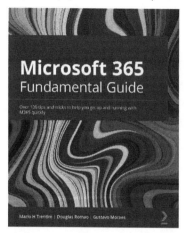

Microsoft 365 Fundamental Guide

Mario Trentim, Douglas Romao, Gustavo Moraes

ISBN: 978-1-80107-019-5

- Understand your Microsoft 365 apps better
- Apply best practices to boost your personal productivity
- Find out how to improve communications and collaboration within your teams
- Discover how to manage tasks and automate processes
- Get to know the features of M365 and how to implement them in your daily activities
- Build an integrated system for clear and effective communication

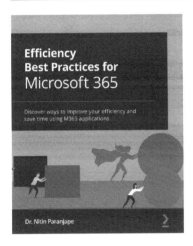

Efficiency Best Practices for Microsoft 365

Dr. Nitin Paranjape

ISBN: 978-1-80107-226-7

- Understand how different MS 365 tools, such as Office desktop, Teams, Power BI, Lists, and OneDrive, can increase work efficiency
- Identify time-consuming processes and understand how to work through them more efficiently
- Create professional documents quickly with minimal effort
- Work across multiple teams, meetings, and projects without email overload
- Automate mundane, repetitive, and time-consuming manual work
- Manage work, delegation, execution, and project management

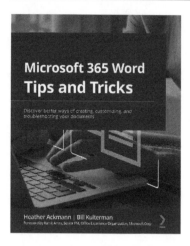

Microsoft 365 Word Tips and Tricks

Heather Ackmann, Bill Kulterman

ISBN: 978-1-80056-543-2

- Track a document's changes as well as comment on and review changes by others, both locally and remotely

- Use Word's navigation and view features to improve productivity

- Generate more consistently formatted documents with Styles

- Perform common tasks through simple formatting techniques, Quick Parts, customizing AutoCorrect/AutoFormat, and memorizing keyboard shortcuts

- Troubleshoot the most frustrating formatting problems experienced by Word users

- Create more universally accessible documents by adding Alt Text using the accessibility checker and other Word features

Packt is searching for authors like you

If you're interested in becoming an author for Packt, please visit `authors.packtpub.com` and apply today. We have worked with thousands of developers and tech professionals, just like you, to help them share their insight with the global tech community. You can make a general application, apply for a specific hot topic that we are recruiting an author for, or submit your own idea.

Share Your Thoughts

Now you've finished *Work Smarter with Microsoft OneNote*, we'd love to hear your thoughts! Scan the QR code below to go straight to the Amazon review page for this book and share your feedback or leave a review on the site that you purchased it from.

`https://packt.link/r/1-801-07566-2`

Your review is important to us and the tech community and will help us make sure we're delivering excellent quality content.

Made in the USA
Coppell, TX
25 October 2023